AI-Enhanced Solutions for Sustainable Cybersecurity

Mourade Azrour
Faculty of Sciences and Techniques, Moulay Ismail University of Meknes, Morocco

Jamal Mabrouki
Faculty of Science, Mohammed V University in Rabat, Morocco

Azidine Guezzaz
Cadi Ayyad University, Morocco

Abdulatif Alabdulatif
Qassim University, Saudia Arabia

IGI Global
Scientific Publishing
Publishing Tomorrow's Research Today

Vice President of Editorial Melissa Wagner
Director of Acquisitions Mikaela Felty
Director of Book Development Jocelynn Hessler
Production Manager Mike Brehm
Cover Design Phillip Shickler

Published in the United States of America by
IGI Global Scientific Publishing
701 East Chocolate Avenue
Hershey, PA, 17033, USA
Tel: 717-533-8845
Fax: 717-533-7115
Website: https://www.igi-global.com E-mail: cust@igi-global.com

Library of Congress Cataloging-in-Publication Data

Names: Azrour, Mourade, editor. | Mabrouki, Jamal, editor. | Guezzaz, Azidine, 1988- editor. | Alabdulatif, Abdulatif, editor.
Title: AI-enhanced solutions for sustainable cybersecurity / edited by Mourade Azrour, Jamal Mabrouki, Azidine Guezzaz, Abdulatif Alabdulatif.
Other titles: Artificial intelligence-enhanced solutions for sustainable cybersecurity
Description: Hershey, PA : IGI Global, [2025] | Includes bibliographical references and index. | Summary: "This book covers a variety of topics, including an overview of cybersecurity issues, and provides detailed analysis of each application's security challenges, taking into account the architecture and technologies employed"-- Provided by publisher.
Identifiers: LCCN 2024042855 (print) | LCCN 2024042856 (ebook) | ISBN 9798369363713 (hardcover) | ISBN 9798369363720 (paperback) | ISBN 9798369363737 (ebook)
Subjects: LCSH: Computer security--Technological innovations. | Artificial intelligence. | Computer networks--Security measures.
Classification: LCC QA76.9.A25 A4145 2025 (print) | LCC QA76.9.A25 (ebook) | DDC 006.3--dc23/eng/20241223
LC record available at https://lccn.loc.gov/2024042855
LC ebook record available at https://lccn.loc.gov/2024042856

British Cataloguing in Publication Data
A Cataloguing in Publication record for this book is available from the British Library.

Table of Contents

Preface xi

Chapter 1
Security and Privacy for Fog and Edge Computing 1
Rajeshwari Sissodia, Galgotias University, India
ManMohan Singh Rauthan, Hemwati Nandan Bhaguna Garhwal University, India
Varun Barthwal, Hemwati Nandan Bhaguna Garhwal University, India
Vinay Dwivedi, Galgotias University, India

Chapter 2
Deep Learning for Threat Detection and Analysis 27
Kiran Sree Pokkuluri, Shri Vishnu Engineering College for Women, India
S. S. S. N. Usha Devi N., University College of Engineering-Kakinada, Jawaharlal Nehru Technology, Kakinada, India
Alex Khang, Global Research Institute of Technology and Engineering, USA

Chapter 3
Experimenting With an AI-Based Sequential Generative Adversarial Network for Detecting Web Server Security Exploits 47
Chintha Reddy Sai Kiran, VIT Bhopal University, India
Nilamadhab Mishra, VIT Bhopal University, India
S. Hariharasitaraman, VIT Bhopal University, India
Narottam Das Patel, VIT Bhopal University, India
Saroja Kumar Rout, Vardhaman College of Engineering, Hyderabad, India

Chapter 4
How to Ensure Data Integrity in Water Monitoring Networks Using IoT and Blockchain Technology 77
Khadija El-Moustaqim, Faculty of Sciences, Ibn Tofail University, Kenitra, Morocco
Jamal Mabrouki, Faculty of Science, Mohammed V University, Rabat, Morocco
Driss Hmouni, Faculty of Sciences, Ibn Tofail University, Kenitra, Morocco

Chapter 5
Cutting Edge Building Safety: Harnessing the Power of Cloud Automation 97
Gyananjan Paul, School of Computer Engineering, KIIT University (Deemed), Bhubaneswar, India
A Vignesh Rao, School of Computer Engineering, KIIT University (Deemed), Bhubaneswar, India
Ashirwaad Dhir, School of Computer Engineering, KIIT University (Deemed), Bhubaneswar, India
Hitesh Mohapatra, School of Computer Engineering, KIIT University (Deemed), Bhubaneswar, India
Soumya Ranjan Mishra, School of Computer Engineering, KIIT University (Deemed), Bhubaneswar, India

Chapter 6
Challenges in Maritime Sector Cybersecurity 125
Driss Azdem, Faculty of Science, Mohammed V University in Rabat, Morocco
Jamal Mabrouki, Faculty of Science, Mohammed V University in Rabat, Morocco
Souad El Hajjaji, Faculty of Science, Mohammed V University in Rabat, Morocco

Chapter 7
Cyber Security in Cyber Physical Systems: Challenges and Opportunities 149
Muhammad Muzamil Aslam, Universiti Brunei Darussalam, Brunei
Sajid Ali, University of Education, Pakistan
Haji Gul, Universiti Brunei Darussalam, Brunei
Ali Tufail, Universiti Brunei Darussalam, Brunei

Chapter 8
Advanced Technologies for Precision Agriculture in Environmental and Meteorological Prediction 181
Mrutyunjay Padhiary, Assam University, Silchar, India
Raushan Kumar, Assam University, Silchar, India
Bhabashankar Sahu, Parala Maharaja Engineering College, India

Compilation of References 217

Related References 263

About The Contributors 295

Index 301

Detailed Table of Contents

Preface.. xi

Chapter 1
Security and Privacy for Fog and Edge Computing 1
Rajeshwari Sissodia, Galgotias University, India
ManMohan Singh Rauthan, Hemwati Nandan Bhaguna Garhwal University, India
Varun Barthwal, Hemwati Nandan Bhaguna Garhwal University, India
Vinay Dwivedi, Galgotias University, India

Fog and edge computing have emerged as critical paradigms for processing data closer to its source, facilitating real-time analytics and reducing latency. However, this decentralized approach introduces significant security and privacy challenges. This chapter provides a comprehensive overview of the security and privacy considerations inherent in fog and edge computing environments. It discusses the unique vulnerabilities associated with edge devices, emphasizing the importance of data encryption, robust authentication mechanisms, and effective intrusion detection systems. Additionally, it explores privacy concerns, regulatory compliance, and the role of emerging technologies such as artificial intelligence (AI) and blockchain in enhancing security measures. By addressing these challenges and implementing robust security protocols, organizations can leverage the full potential of fog and edge computing while safeguarding sensitive data and ensuring user privacy.

Chapter 2
Deep Learning for Threat Detection and Analysis 27
Kiran Sree Pokkuluri, Shri Vishnu Engineering College for Women, India
S. S. S. N. Usha Devi N., University College of Engineering-Kakinada, Jawaharlal Nehru Technology, Kakinada, India
Alex Khang, Global Research Institute of Technology and Engineering, USA

Deep Learning has revolutionary potential to improve cybersecurity threat identification and analysis. This system quickly and accurately analyses large datasets by using Deep Learning, spotting patterns and anomalies that more conventional approaches would miss. This ability is essential for identifying sophisticated cyberthreats that traditional rule-based systems find difficult to detect, such as advanced persistent threats (APTs) and zero-day assaults. Deep learning models are constantly adapting to the trends in cybersecurity threats since they are taught on a variety of dynamic data sets. This flexibility lowers operational costs and speeds up response times by preserving the efficacy of cybersecurity measures without the need for frequent manual updates. Deep learning is also used to improve overall system reliability by lowering false positives, a typical cybersecurity concern and improve overall system reliability by lowering false positives, a typical cybersecurity concern.

Chapter 3
Experimenting With an AI-Based Sequential Generative Adversarial Network for Detecting Web Server Security Exploits 47
Chintha Reddy Sai Kiran, VIT Bhopal University, India
Nilamadhab Mishra, VIT Bhopal University, India
S. Hariharasitaraman, VIT Bhopal University, India
Narottam Das Patel, VIT Bhopal University, India
Saroja Kumar Rout, Vardhaman College of Engineering, Hyderabad, India

In today's world, the internet and web applications have become extremely popular. In contrast, these applications offer many benefits to organizations, such as fame, profits, etc. They also pose some risks. Malicious attackers take advantage of vulnerabilities in web applications to steal sensitive information. One significant threat is web server log attacks, which can compromise the security of online systems. This paper introduces a new approach to address this challenge, using a Sequential Generative Adversarial Network with Long Short-Term Memory networks. This model combines the capabilities of generative adversarial networks to create realistic web server log entries. Additionally, it utilizes long short-term memory networks for sequence modeling, allowing it to distinguish between normal and malicious log entries effectively. The outcomes of the experiment demonstrate how successful the suggested method is. The accuracy of the proposed methodology is 95%.

Chapter 4
How to Ensure Data Integrity in Water Monitoring Networks Using IoT and Blockchain Technology 77
Khadija El-Moustaqim, Faculty of Sciences, Ibn Tofail University, Kenitra, Morocco
Jamal Mabrouki, Faculty of Science, Mohammed V University, Rabat, Morocco
Driss Hmouni, Faculty of Sciences, Ibn Tofail University, Kenitra, Morocco

Sustainable urban water management is crucial to address contamination, inefficient distribution, and water scarcity issues. Global problems include the allocation and management of water resources among users. It is imperative for the nation to keep an eye on how various users are utilizing seawater and to put clever strategies into place to minimize water loss. Among the technology that has gained popularity over the past several years is blockchain. The potential to use this architecture in many different industries while including innovative concepts such as crowdsensing, IoT, critical applications, and decision-making tools provides many options and methods for creating contemporary applications. This paper presents viewpoints on water management to support sustainable water management. It suggests a solution based on technology utilizing blockchain and Internet of Things sensors for accurate data reporting and effective water distribution.

Chapter 5
Cutting Edge Building Safety: Harnessing the Power of Cloud Automation...... 97
Gyananjan Paul, School of Computer Engineering, KIIT University (Deemed), Bhubaneswar, India
A Vignesh Rao, School of Computer Engineering, KIIT University (Deemed), Bhubaneswar, India
Ashirwaad Dhir, School of Computer Engineering, KIIT University (Deemed), Bhubaneswar, India
Hitesh Mohapatra, School of Computer Engineering, KIIT University (Deemed), Bhubaneswar, India
Soumya Ranjan Mishra, School of Computer Engineering, KIIT University (Deemed), Bhubaneswar, India

This study explores integrating cloud computing into smart building automation systems (BAS) to enhance building operations and safety. BAS, by amalgamating sensors, actuators, and control systems, aims to boost energy efficiency, occupant comfort, and operational effectiveness. However, conventional BAS face challenges in scalability, flexibility, and data processing. The focus here is on bolstering the security of BAS with cloud integration. It's shown that cloud technology significantly enhances BAS security, addressing potential vulnerabilities and fortifying against cyber threats better than previously thought. This integration not only improves physical security but also ensures data privacy and optimizes operational protocols. This holistic approach underscores the importance of using technology to create safer building environments. This research lays the groundwork for future developments, as cloud automation security systems represent a comprehensive approach to building safety, with features like centralized management, real-time monitoring, and cost-effectiveness.

Chapter 6
Challenges in Maritime Sector Cybersecurity 125
Driss Azdem, Faculty of Science, Mohammed V University in Rabat, Morocco
Jamal Mabrouki, Faculty of Science, Mohammed V University in Rabat, Morocco
Souad El Hajjaji, Faculty of Science, Mohammed V University in Rabat, Morocco

The surge in cyberattacks, despite the maritime industry's recent digitalization, has alarmed experts. Previously deemed secure due to limited internet access and remote ship locations, operational technology now faces significant cybersecurity threats. This article investigates this emerging issue by analyzing common vulnerabilities, reported incidents, and the impact of unauthorized access. It delves into onboard systems at risk and proposes proactive measures for mitigation. Finally, it identifies unresolved issues and suggests future research directions in marine cybersecurity.

Chapter 7
Cyber Security in Cyber Physical Systems: Challenges and Opportunities...... 149
Muhammad Muzamil Aslam, Universiti Brunei Darussalam, Brunei
Sajid Ali, University of Education, Pakistan
Haji Gul, Universiti Brunei Darussalam, Brunei
Ali Tufail, Universiti Brunei Darussalam, Brunei

This chapter provides a comprehensive exploration of the crucial topic of cyber security within the realm of cyber-physical systems (CPS). In the age of smart living, ensuring the validity of our data has become a formidable task. It's more convenient to live in smart cities and residences. Even with the use of difficult passwords, there is always a security risk due to the intricate network of the IoT and the Internet of Everything (IoE). First step in bolstering security against ever-changing threats. Next, the chapter delves into the specific challenges and unique characteristics of securing cyber-physical systems. To address these challenges, the chapter presents an overview of current cyber security techniques and practices employed in CPS. Furthermore, the chapter explores emerging trends and future directions in the field of cyber security for CPS. The chapter also highlights the importance of collaboration among stakeholders, including researchers, industry professionals, and policymakers, to address the evolving cyber security landscape of CPS.

Chapter 8
Advanced Technologies for Precision Agriculture in Environmental and Meteorological Prediction 181
Mrutyunjay Padhiary, Assam University, Silchar, India
Raushan Kumar, Assam University, Silchar, India
Bhabashankar Sahu, Parala Maharaja Engineering College, India

Precision agriculture, which combines modern technology with conventional farming techniques, has significantly transformed the efficient use of water, soil and farm resources. This chapter examines the dynamic relationship between technology and security within this particular industry, with a specific emphasis on emerging technologies such as IoT, IDS, authentication mechanisms, AI, and cyber security. The integration of IoT enables real-time environmental sensing, while Intrusion Detection Systems (IDS) provide protection for agricultural networks against cyber threats. Authentication mechanisms play a crucial role in safeguarding essential agricultural equipment and control systems. The purpose of this chapter is to provide guidance to researchers, practitioners, and policymakers regarding the complex connection between technology and security within the context of precision agriculture. The article adds to the ongoing dialogue surrounding the preservation of agricultural practices, presenting a vision of a sustainable future in which innovation and resilience are complementary.

Compilation of References 217

Related References 263

About The Contributors 295

Index 301

Preface

The rapid evolution of artificial intelligence (AI) has introduced new possibilities in virtually every domain of modern life. Among its most promising applications is the enhancement of cybersecurity measures, a field increasingly threatened by complex and evolving cyberattacks. As we witness unprecedented levels of connectivity and data exchange, ensuring the security of critical systems and infrastructures has become more important than ever. This edited volume, *AI-Enhanced Solutions for Sustainable Cybersecurity*, gathers the expertise of a diverse group of scholars and professionals from around the world to explore how AI can be integrated into cybersecurity frameworks to address these challenges effectively. The chapters within this book provide a detailed examination of how AI, combined with other advanced technologies, is reshaping the landscape of cybersecurity.

The contributions in this volume span a wide array of topics, from securing decentralized computing environments like fog and edge computing, to the deployment of deep learning algorithms for real-time threat detection. The rise of AI has opened up new opportunities for automating and optimizing security protocols, reducing human error, and enhancing the resilience of digital infrastructures. However, these technologies also present new challenges, particularly in areas such as data privacy, system reliability, and ethical considerations. Each chapter delves into these challenges, offering innovative solutions, case studies, and emerging research that highlights the potential for AI-driven cybersecurity to meet the demands of an increasingly digital world.

The editors have sought to include a comprehensive range of perspectives, ensuring that the volume not only covers theoretical insights but also offers practical approaches to tackling the real-world problems facing the cybersecurity industry today. By drawing from expertise in AI, blockchain, IoT, and more, this book serves as a critical resource for researchers, practitioners, and policymakers seeking to leverage AI for a more secure and sustainable digital future.

As we move forward into an age defined by smart cities, connected devices, and automated systems, the role of AI in cybersecurity will continue to expand. However, it is crucial that the solutions we implement today are scalable, adaptive, and sustainable, ensuring long-term security and resilience. This book emphasizes that the intersection of AI and cybersecurity is not just about defending against current threats but also preparing for future challenges. The editors hope that the ideas and solutions presented in this book will inspire future research, innovation, and collaboration in the pursuit of a more secure digital ecosystem for all.

Chapter 1: Security and Privacy for Fog and Edge Computing

Fog and edge computing represent the next frontier in decentralized data processing, where data is processed closer to the source to reduce latency and improve real-time analytics. However, this architecture introduces significant security and privacy concerns. This chapter provides an in-depth look at the unique vulnerabilities associated with edge devices, discussing the importance of data encryption, robust authentication, and intrusion detection mechanisms. The authors explore how emerging technologies like artificial intelligence (AI) and blockchain can enhance security measures in fog and edge computing systems. By addressing these challenges with comprehensive security protocols, organizations can leverage these technologies to fully realize their potential while ensuring sensitive data protection and user privacy.

Chapter 2: Deep Learning for Threat Detection and Analysis

Deep learning is revolutionizing the field of cybersecurity by enabling the rapid identification and analysis of potential threats in large datasets. Traditional cybersecurity measures often fall short in detecting sophisticated attacks like advanced persistent threats (APTs) and zero-day exploits. This chapter highlights how deep learning models are trained on dynamic datasets to identify emerging threats more accurately and efficiently. It explores the ability of deep learning to adapt to evolving cybersecurity challenges, reducing the need for frequent manual updates and enhancing system reliability by minimizing false positives. The authors also discuss how these models are used to optimize cybersecurity protocols, reducing operational costs and improving threat detection capabilities.

Chapter 3: Experimenting with an AI-Based Sequential Generative Adversarial Network for Detecting Web Server Security Exploits

The digital transformation has increased the use of web applications, but it also exposes organizations to new cybersecurity risks, particularly in the form of web server log attacks. This chapter introduces an innovative approach using a Sequential Generative Adversarial Network (SGAN) combined with Long Short-Term Memory (LSTM) networks to identify and mitigate security threats. The SGAN generates realistic web server log entries, while the LSTM model analyzes these sequences to differentiate between normal and malicious log activity. With an impressive accuracy rate of 95%, the proposed methodology offers a promising solution to detecting and preventing web server security exploits, providing a robust tool for web security professionals.

Chapter 4: Ensuring Data Integrity in Water Monitoring Networks Using IoT and Blockchain Technology

The need for sustainable water management is becoming more urgent as urbanization and climate change exacerbate water scarcity and pollution. This chapter discusses the potential of combining Internet of Things (IoT) sensors with blockchain technology to improve data accuracy and integrity in water monitoring systems. The integration of blockchain ensures transparent and tamper-proof data reporting, while IoT devices provide real-time environmental monitoring. The authors explore how this combined approach can help prevent water loss, ensure equitable distribution, and enhance decision-making in water management systems, offering a scalable and secure solution for the future of sustainable water resource management.

Chapter 5: Cutting Edge Building Safety: Harnessing the Power of Cloud Automation

This chapter investigates the integration of cloud computing into smart building automation systems (BAS) to enhance security and operational efficiency. Cloud-based BAS offer significant advantages over traditional systems, including scalability, flexibility, and improved data processing capabilities. The authors examine how cloud technology can bolster BAS security by addressing vulnerabilities, fortifying against cyber threats, and improving data privacy. By centralizing management, enabling real-time monitoring, and optimizing operational protocols, cloud automation systems offer a comprehensive approach to building safety. This research sets the stage for future developments in cloud-based building security, which can create safer, more efficient living and working environments.

Chapter 6: Challenges in Maritime Sector Cybersecurity

As the maritime industry embraces digital transformation, it has become increasingly vulnerable to cyberattacks. This chapter explores the cybersecurity challenges unique to the maritime sector, where operational technology was once considered secure due to the isolation of ships and limited internet access. The authors delve into the vulnerabilities of onboard systems and the risks associated with unauthorized access. The chapter provides a thorough analysis of past incidents and discusses proactive cybersecurity measures for mitigating threats. It also highlights the need for continued research and development to address the evolving cybersecurity landscape in the maritime industry, ensuring the protection of critical infrastructure.

Chapter 7: Cybersecurity in Cyber-Physical Systems: Challenges and Opportunities

Cyber-physical systems (CPS), which integrate physical processes with digital systems, are at the heart of modern infrastructure, from smart cities to industrial automation. This chapter addresses the unique cybersecurity challenges faced by CPS, where the interconnectedness of devices and systems creates complex security risks. The authors discuss current techniques for securing CPS, including encryption, authentication, and intrusion detection systems. Additionally, the chapter explores emerging trends in CPS cybersecurity, such as the role of AI and machine learning in threat detection. The authors emphasize the importance of collaboration between researchers, industry professionals, and policymakers to address the ever-evolving security challenges of CPS.

Chapter 8: Advanced Technologies for Precision Agriculture in Environmental and Meteorological Prediction

Precision agriculture is transforming the way farming operations manage resources, optimize yields, and ensure sustainability. This chapter focuses on the role of advanced technologies, including IoT, AI, and cyber-physical systems, in enhancing agricultural practices. The authors discuss how IoT devices enable real-time environmental monitoring and how cybersecurity measures, such as Intrusion Detection Systems (IDS), protect agricultural networks from cyber threats. They also emphasize the importance of authentication mechanisms to secure critical agricultural equipment and control systems. The chapter provides valuable insights into the intersection of technology and security in precision agriculture, offering a roadmap for sustainable farming practices in the future.

In conclusion, *AI-Enhanced Solutions for Sustainable Cybersecurity* reflects the urgent need for a multidisciplinary approach to tackling cybersecurity challenges in an era dominated by AI and emerging technologies. As we explore the various chapters within this volume, we gain valuable insights into how AI can be harnessed not only to detect and prevent cyberattacks but also to build more resilient systems that can withstand the ever-growing sophistication of cyber threats. Through this collaborative effort, we aim to contribute to the global conversation on creating safer, smarter, and more sustainable digital environments.

The book's scope is not limited to the theoretical aspects of AI in cybersecurity but extends to the practical implications, challenges, and opportunities that arise when implementing these solutions in diverse sectors. Whether it's protecting the infrastructure of smart cities or securing the data streams of precision agriculture, the contributions herein underscore the versatility of AI technologies. By addressing both the opportunities and the challenges posed by AI, the authors provide readers with a comprehensive understanding of the role these technologies play in shaping the future of cybersecurity.

Chapter 1
Security and Privacy for Fog and Edge Computing

Rajeshwari Sissodia
https://orcid.org/0000-0002-9978-0187
Galgotias University, India

ManMohan Singh Rauthan
Hemwati Nandan Bhaguna Garhwal University, India

Varun Barthwal
https://orcid.org/0000-0002-5289-9471
Hemwati Nandan Bhaguna Garhwal University, India

Vinay Dwivedi
https://orcid.org/0009-0007-7502-3222
Galgotias University, India

ABSTRACT

Fog and edge computing have emerged as critical paradigms for processing data closer to its source, facilitating real-time analytics and reducing latency. However, this decentralized approach introduces significant security and privacy challenges. This chapter provides a comprehensive overview

DOI: 10.4018/979-8-3693-6371-3.ch001

of the security and privacy considerations inherent in fog and edge computing environments. It discusses the unique vulnerabilities associated with edge devices, emphasizing the importance of data encryption, robust authentication mechanisms, and effective intrusion detection systems. Additionally, it explores privacy concerns, regulatory compliance, and the role of emerging technologies such as artificial intelligence (AI) and blockchain in enhancing security measures. By addressing these challenges and implementing robust security protocols, organizations can leverage the full potential of fog and edge computing while safeguarding sensitive data and ensuring user privacy.

1. INTRODUCTION

The rapid advancement of the Internet of Things (IoT) and the growing demand for real-time data processing have driven the evolution of new computing paradigms, leading to the emergence of fog and edge computing. These paradigms extend the capabilities of traditional cloud computing by decentralizing data processing, storage, and analytics closer to the data sources. This approach significantly reduces latency, enhances response times, and optimizes bandwidth usage, thereby meeting the requirements of applications that need immediate data handling and decision-making. However, while fog and edge computing bring numerous benefits, they also introduce a range of security and privacy challenges that must be addressed to ensure the safe and reliable operation of these distributed environments.

Fog computing, introduced by Cisco, serves as an intermediary layer between cloud computing and edge devices. It leverages a network of decentralized nodes—fog nodes—that perform substantial computational tasks closer to the data source. This architecture consists of three main layers: edge devices (such as sensors and IoT devices) that generate data and perform initial processing; fog nodes (like gateways and local servers) that handle more intensive processing and storage tasks; and the cloud, which provides advanced analytics and long-term storage. The key characteristics of fog computing include low latency, scalability, bandwidth efficiency, and enhanced security through local data processing. Fog computing is particularly beneficial in applications such as smart cities, industrial IoT, healthcare, and retail, where real-time data processing and decision-making are critical.

Edge computing, on the other hand, focuses on processing data directly at or near the data source. This paradigm deploys computational resources at the edge of the network, reducing the need to transmit large volumes of data to centralized cloud data centers. The architecture of edge computing includes edge devices that generate and process data, edge servers that perform more extensive data processing and storage tasks, and the cloud for additional resources and complex analytics. Edge computing improves response times, optimizes bandwidth, enhances resilience, and bolsters data privacy and security by minimizing data transmission over the network. Applications of edge computing range from autonomous vehicles and smart homes to agriculture and telecommunications, where real-time or near-real-time data processing is essential.

Despite their advantages, fog and edge computing introduce unique security and privacy challenges due to their decentralized nature. Unlike traditional cloud computing, where data is processed and stored in secure, centralized data centers, fog and edge environments involve numerous distributed nodes that can be potential targets for attacks. Key security challenges include ensuring the physical security of nodes deployed in less controlled environments, securing the communication between edge devices, fog nodes, and the cloud, maintaining the confidentiality, integrity, and availability of data processed and stored locally, and managing access control for a large number of distributed devices. Privacy concerns revolve around protecting data privacy during local processing, ensuring user anonymity, and adhering to legal and regulatory requirements for data privacy and security in a distributed setting.

Addressing these security and privacy challenges is crucial for the successful adoption of fog and edge computing. Developing robust security frameworks, employing advanced encryption techniques, and implementing comprehensive privacy policies are essential steps toward mitigating risks. This chapter will delve into these challenges, providing a detailed exploration of the current state of security and privacy in fog and edge computing and discussing potential solutions and best practices to safeguard these innovative computing environments.

2. LITERATURE REVIEW

Smith, J. (2019) This literature review provides an in-depth analysis of the security challenges faced by edge computing environments, including authentication, access control, data encryption, and intrusion detection.

Patel, S. et al. (2020) This review explores the privacy risks and concerns associated with data processing in fog and edge computing environments, discussing regulatory compliance, privacy-preserving techniques, and data anonymization methods.

Lee, H. et al. (2021) This literature review examines emerging trends in edge AI security, including federated learning, homomorphic encryption, and blockchain, highlighting their potential to enhance security and privacy in edge computing environments.

Wang, Q. et al. (2022) This review provides an overview of state-of-the-art intrusion detection and prevention systems tailored for edge computing environments, discussing design principles, deployment strategies, and real-time threat monitoring techniques.

Kim, Y. et al. (2023) This literature review evaluates secure communication protocols such as MQTT, CoAP, and HTTPS in fog and edge computing environments, comparing their security features, performance, and suitability for edge deployments.

Gupta, A. et al. (2024) This review explores advancements in data encryption techniques for ensuring confidentiality in edge computing, including homomorphic encryption, attribute-based encryption, and secure multi-party computation.

Li, W. et al. (2019 This literature review investigates the role of AI technologies such as machine learning, deep learning, and natural language processing in enhancing security and privacy in fog and edge computing environments.

Chen, L. et al. (2020) This review examines the challenges and opportunities of blockchain technology for enhancing security in edge computing environments, discussing use cases, scalability issues, and consensus mechanisms.

Zhang, H. et al. (2021) This literature review explores the application of federated learning techniques for enhancing security and privacy in edge computing environments, discussing privacy-preserving model training, federated aggregation, and model update mechanisms.

Liu, X. et al. (2022) This review investigates the integration of IoT and edge computing technologies for enhancing security in smart environments, discussing edge-based threat detection, anomaly detection, and real-time response mechanisms.

Tan, Z. et al. (2023) This literature review examines privacy-preserving techniques such as differential privacy, secure enclaves, and trusted execution environments for protecting sensitive data in edge computing environments.

Wang, Y. et al. (2019 This review evaluates scalable intrusion detection systems designed for edge computing environments, discussing lightweight detection algorithms, distributed detection architectures, and anomaly detection techniques.

Huang, Q. et al. (2020) This literature review examines security challenges specific to industrial edge computing environments, including industrial IoT security, operational technology (OT) security, and supply chain security.

Yang, J. et al. (2021) This review provides an overview of security threats and countermeasures in edge computing environments, discussing edge-based attacks, insider threats, and supply chain risks.

Park, S. et al. (2024) This literature review explores advancements in privacy-preserving analytics techniques for edge computing, including federated learning, secure aggregation, and homomorphic encryption, highlighting their applications and limitations.

3.1 Definition and Characteristics of Fog Computing

Fog computing, introduced by Cisco, is a decentralized computing architecture that extends cloud computing to the edge of the network. It aims to address the limitations of cloud computing, such as latency and bandwidth constraints, by bringing computational resources closer to where data is generated. In fog computing, data processing, storage, and analysis occur in a distributed manner across a network of nodes called fog nodes. These nodes can include various devices such as gateways, routers, and local servers positioned between the cloud and edge devices. Key characteristics of fog computing include low latency, as data is processed near its source, which is crucial for real-time applications (Smith, 2019). Fog computing also offers scalability by distributing resources across numerous nodes, allowing systems to grow and adapt to increasing data volumes and processing demands. Additionally, it enhances bandwidth efficiency by reducing the need to transmit large amounts of data to centralized cloud data centers, and improves security by processing sensitive data locally, thereby minimizing the risk of data breaches during transmission (Li et al., 2019).

3.2 Definition and Characteristics of Edge Computing

Edge computing is a distributed computing paradigm that focuses on processing data at or near the source of data generation. Unlike fog computing, which introduces an intermediate layer between the edge and the cloud, edge computing processes data directly on edge devices or nearby local servers. This approach significantly reduces the need to transmit large volumes of data to centralized cloud data centers, enhancing response times and reducing latency (Lee et al., 2021). Edge computing encompasses devices such as sensors, actuators, mobile phones, and IoT devices that generate and initially process data. Edge servers or local gateways handle more substantial data processing and storage tasks. Key characteristics of edge computing include improved response times due to local data processing, which is essential for applications requiring real-time or near-real-time operations. It also optimizes bandwidth usage by transmitting only critical data to the cloud, thereby minimizing data transfer costs (Wang, Y., et al., 2019). Edge computing enhances resilience and reliability, as local processing ensures continued operation even with intermittent or lost cloud connectivity. Additionally, it bolsters data privacy and security by limiting the exposure of sensitive information over the network (Tan et al., 2023).

3.3 Comparison of Fog, Edge, and Cloud Computing

Fog computing, edge computing, and cloud computing represent different approaches to data processing and resource management within a network. Cloud computing relies on centralized data centers that provide vast computational power, storage, and advanced analytics. It excels in handling large-scale data processing tasks but often suffers from latency and bandwidth limitations when dealing with data from geographically dispersed IoT devices (Li et al., 2019). In contrast, fog computing introduces a decentralized architecture that distributes resources across intermediate fog nodes, offering a balance between centralized cloud capabilities and localized edge processing (Gupta et al., 2024). Fog computing reduces latency and bandwidth usage by processing data closer to its source, making it suitable for applications requiring real-time or near-real-time responses (Huang et al., 2020). Edge computing takes this decentralization a step further by processing data directly on edge devices or nearby local servers, thereby achieving the lowest possible latency and optimal bandwidth efficiency. While cloud computing remains essential for large-scale data analytics and long-term storage, fog and edge computing complement it by addressing latency, bandwidth, and data privacy challenges inherent in IoT and real-time applications (Patel et al., 2020).

3.4 Use Cases and Applications

Fog and edge computing have a wide range of use cases and applications across various industries due to their ability to provide low-latency, real-time data processing, and improved bandwidth efficiency. In smart cities, fog computing is used for traffic management, smart street lighting, and surveillance systems, where real-time data processing is crucial for efficient and safe city operations (Lee et al., 2021). Industrial IoT applications benefit from fog and edge computing through real-time monitoring, predictive maintenance, and automation in manufacturing environments, leading to increased productivity and reduced downtime (Yang et al., 2021). In healthcare, remote patient monitoring, emergency response systems, and healthcare data management are enhanced by local data processing, providing timely interventions and improving patient outcomes (Wang,

Q., et al., 2022). The retail sector leverages fog and edge computing for real-time inventory management, personalized customer experiences, and smart checkout systems, enhancing operational efficiency and customer satisfaction (Kim et al., 2023). Autonomous vehicles rely on edge computing for real-time navigation, collision avoidance, and other safety features, processing data directly on the vehicle to ensure rapid responses (Li et al., 2019). Smart homes utilize edge computing for home automation, security monitoring, and energy management, enabling responsive and efficient smart home solutions (Tan et al., 2023). Agriculture benefits from precision farming, livestock monitoring, and environmental sensing, where real-time data processing improves productivity and resource management (Liu et al., 2022). In telecommunications, edge computing optimizes network performance and enhances content delivery by processing data closer to the user, reducing latency, and improving user experiences (Chen et al., 2020). These diverse applications demonstrate the critical role of fog and edge computing in modern technology landscapes, providing tailored solutions to meet the specific needs of various industries (Park et al., 2024).

4. SECURITY CHALLENGES IN FOG AND EDGE COMPUTING

4.1 Threat Landscape

4.1.1 Physical Threats

Physical threats in fog and edge computing environments are a significant concern due to the widespread and often less secure deployment of devices. Unlike centralized data centers, which benefit from robust physical security measures, edge devices and fog nodes are frequently placed in remote, exposed, or publicly accessible locations. This makes them vulnerable to physical tampering, theft, and destruction. Attackers can gain physical access to devices, potentially leading to data breaches, hardware manipulation, and the installation of malicious software. To mitigate these risks, physical security measures such as tamper-resistant hardware, secure enclosures, and surveillance systems must be implemented (Smith,

2019). Additionally, regular physical inspections and maintenance can help identify and address vulnerabilities in the deployment environment.

4.1.2 Network Threats

Network threats in fog and edge computing involve unauthorized access, data interception, and disruptions to communication channels. The distributed nature of these environments means that data frequently travels across various networks, making it susceptible to attacks such as eavesdropping, packet sniffing, and man-in-the-middle (MitM) attacks (Kim et al., 2023). These threats can lead to the exposure of sensitive data, unauthorized control of devices, and disruptions in service. Securing the network involves implementing strong encryption protocols for data in transit, using secure communication channels (e.g., VPNs), and ensuring robust authentication and authorization mechanisms (Gupta et al., 2024). Regular network monitoring and intrusion detection systems can help identify and respond to potential threats in real-time (Wang, Q., et al., 2022).

4.1.3 Data Threats

Data threats in fog and edge computing pertain to the risks associated with data integrity, confidentiality, and availability. Given that data is processed and stored at multiple decentralized locations, ensuring its security is more complex compared to centralized cloud environments. Threats include data breaches, unauthorized data access, data tampering, and loss of data due to hardware failures or malicious attacks (Patel et al., 2020). Protecting data involves employing strong encryption for both data at rest and data in transit, implementing access controls to restrict data access to authorized personnel, and ensuring regular backups to prevent data loss (Tan et al., 2023). Additionally, robust data integrity checks and audit trails can help detect and mitigate unauthorized data modifications (Gupta et al., 2024).

4.2 Attack Vectors

4.2.1 Man-in-the-Middle Attacks

Man-in-the-Middle (MitM) attacks are a significant threat in fog and edge computing environments, where attackers intercept and potentially alter communication between two parties without their knowledge. These attacks can compromise data integrity and confidentiality, leading to data breaches and unauthorized access (Kim et al., 2023). In fog and edge computing, where data often travels across various networks and devices, MitM attacks can occur at multiple points. Mitigating these attacks involves implementing strong encryption for all communications, using secure protocols such as HTTPS and TLS, and employing mutual authentication mechanisms to verify the identities of communicating parties (Li et al., 2019). Regular network monitoring and the use of intrusion detection systems can also help identify and prevent MitM attacks (Wang, Q., et al., 2022).

4.2.2 Denial of Service (DoS) Attacks

Denial of Service (DoS) and Distributed Denial of Service (DDoS) attacks aim to disrupt the availability of services by overwhelming the network, servers, or devices with excessive traffic or resource demands (Yang et al., 2021). In fog and edge computing environments, these attacks can target various components, including edge devices, fog nodes, and communication networks, leading to service outages and degraded performance. Protecting against DoS and DDoS attacks requires implementing robust network defenses such as firewalls, rate limiting, and traffic filtering (Smith, 2019). Additionally, leveraging cloud-based DDoS mitigation services can help absorb and mitigate large-scale attacks. Regular monitoring and anomaly detection can also identify and respond to potential DoS attacks before they impact services.

4.2.3 Malware and Ransomware

Malware and ransomware pose significant threats to fog and edge computing environments. These malicious software attacks can compromise devices, steal sensitive data, and disrupt services (Lee et al., 2021). Ransomware, in particular, encrypts data and demands payment for its release, posing a severe risk to data availability and integrity. The decentralized nature of fog and edge environments increases the attack surface, making it easier for malware to spread across devices. Protecting against these threats involves implementing robust endpoint security measures, such as antivirus software, intrusion detection systems, and regular software updates to patch vulnerabilities (Zhang et al., 2021). Additionally, user education and awareness programs can help prevent the introduction of malware through phishing and other social engineering attacks (Chen et al., 2020).

4.3 Vulnerabilities in Fog and Edge Infrastructure

4.3.1 Hardware Vulnerabilities

Hardware vulnerabilities in fog and edge computing environments can arise from weaknesses in the physical components of devices. These vulnerabilities may be due to design flaws, manufacturing defects, or the use of insecure hardware components. Attackers can exploit these weaknesses to gain unauthorized access, execute malicious code, or cause hardware failures. Mitigating hardware vulnerabilities involves selecting hardware from reputable manufacturers, ensuring devices undergo rigorous security testing, and implementing tamper-resistant designs (Smith, 2019). Additionally, regular firmware updates and patches are crucial to address newly discovered vulnerabilities and maintain the security of hardware components (Gupta et al., 2024).

4.3.2 Software Vulnerabilities

Software vulnerabilities in fog and edge computing environments stem from flaws or bugs in the software running on devices. These vulnerabilities can be exploited by attackers to gain unauthorized access, execute arbitrary code, or disrupt services. Given the diverse range of software used in fog and edge environments, including operating systems, applications, and middleware, ensuring software security is a complex task (Wang, Y., et al., 2019). Mitigating software vulnerabilities involves regular software updates and patch management, conducting security audits and code reviews, and employing secure coding practices during software development (Lee et al., 2021). Additionally, using security frameworks and tools to detect and respond to software vulnerabilities can enhance the overall security posture (Zhang et al., 2021).

4.3.3 Network Vulnerabilities

Network vulnerabilities in fog and edge computing environments arise from weaknesses in the communication infrastructure that connects devices, fog nodes, and cloud services. These vulnerabilities can be exploited to intercept data, disrupt communications, or launch attacks such as MitM or DoS (Kim et al., 2023). Securing the network involves implementing strong encryption for data in transit, using secure communication protocols, and ensuring robust network segmentation to isolate critical systems (Yang et al., 2021). Regular network monitoring and the deployment of intrusion detection and prevention systems can help identify and mitigate potential network vulnerabilities (Wang, Q., et al., 2022). Additionally, employing redundancy and failover mechanisms can enhance network resilience and ensure continuous operation despite attacks or failures (Chen et al., 2020).

5. PRIVACY CONCERNS IN FOG AND EDGE COMPUTING

5.1 Data Privacy Issues

In fog and edge computing environments, data privacy issues are paramount due to the decentralized nature of data processing and storage. Unlike centralized cloud computing, where data is stored and processed in highly secure data centers, fog and edge computing involve numerous distributed nodes that are often situated in less secure environments. This distribution increases the risk of unauthorized data access and breaches (Patel et al., 2020). Sensitive data processed at the edge, such as personal information, health records, and financial transactions, can be exposed if adequate security measures are not in place. To address data privacy issues, it is essential to implement robust encryption techniques for data at rest and in transit, ensuring that even if data is intercepted, it remains unintelligible to unauthorized users (Gupta et al., 2024). Additionally, access controls and authentication mechanisms must be rigorously enforced to restrict data access to authorized personnel only. Regular security audits and compliance checks are also crucial to identify and rectify potential vulnerabilities that could compromise data privacy (Tan et al., 2023).

5.2 User Privacy and Anonymity

User privacy and anonymity are critical concerns in fog and edge computing, particularly as these environments often handle large volumes of personal data. IoT devices at the edge collect detailed information about users, including their habits, preferences, and locations. Without proper safeguards, this data can be used to track and profile individuals, infringing on their privacy (Tan et al., 2023). Ensuring user privacy involves implementing data minimization techniques, where only essential data is collected and processed. Anonymization and pseudonymization techniques can be employed to protect user identities, ensuring that personal data cannot be linked back to individuals. Moreover, users should be informed about the data being collected and provided with control over their information, including options to opt-out or delete their data (Park et al., 2024).

Privacy-by-design principles, which incorporate privacy considerations throughout the development lifecycle of systems and applications, are also crucial in safeguarding user privacy and anonymity (Patel et al., 2020).

5.3 Privacy in Data Aggregation and Processing

Data aggregation and processing in fog and edge computing environments present unique privacy challenges. Aggregating data from multiple sources can create comprehensive datasets that, if mishandled, can lead to significant privacy breaches. For instance, combining data from various IoT devices can reveal detailed insights about individuals' behaviors and routines (Tan et al., 2023). To protect privacy during data aggregation and processing, it is essential to employ techniques such as differential privacy, which adds noise to data in a way that preserves individual privacy while still enabling useful analysis. Secure multi-party computation and homomorphic encryption are advanced techniques that allow data to be processed in encrypted form, ensuring that sensitive information remains protected during aggregation and analysis (Gupta et al., 2024). Additionally, policies and procedures must be established to govern data aggregation and processing activities, ensuring that they comply with privacy principles and do not expose individuals' sensitive information (Park et al., 2024).

5.4 Legal and Regulatory Considerations

Legal and regulatory considerations are critical in fog and edge computing environments, where the handling of personal and sensitive data must comply with various laws and regulations. Regulations such as the General Data Protection Regulation (GDPR) in Europe, the California Consumer Privacy Act (CCPA) in the United States, and other national and regional privacy laws set stringent requirements for data protection and privacy. These regulations mandate that organizations implement appropriate technical and organizational measures to protect personal data, provide transparency about data collection and processing activities, and uphold individuals' rights to access, rectify, and delete their data. Compliance with these regulations involves conducting thorough data protection impact assessments (DPIAs) to identify and mitigate privacy risks, maintaining detailed records of data processing activities, and ensuring that data transfers across borders comply with legal requirements. Organizations must also be prepared to respond to data breaches promptly, notifying regulatory authorities and affected individuals as required by law. Adhering to these legal and regulatory considerations is essential not only to avoid penalties and legal actions but also to build trust with users and stakeholders by demonstrating a commitment to protecting their privacy.

6. SECURITY SOLUTIONS AND BEST PRACTICES

6.1 Encryption Techniques

6.1.1 Data Encryption

Data encryption is a critical security measure in fog and edge computing, protecting sensitive information from unauthorized access and breaches. It involves converting plaintext data into ciphertext using cryptographic algorithms and keys, making the data unreadable without the corresponding decryption key. For data at rest, robust encryption standards such as Advanced Encryption Standard (AES) with a key size of at least 256 bits should be employed (Gupta et al., 2024). This ensures that even if physical storage devices are compromised, the data remains secure. For data in transit, encryption protocols like Transport Layer Security (TLS) or Secure Sockets Layer (SSL) are essential, providing secure communication channels over networks (Kim et al., 2023). Implementing end-to-end encryption ensures that data is protected from the point of origin to its final destination, safeguarding it against interception and tampering by malicious actors. Additionally, leveraging hardware security modules (HSMs) for key management can enhance the security of encryption keys, ensuring they are stored and managed securely.

6.1.2 Network Encryption

Network encryption is essential for securing data as it travels across networks in fog and edge computing environments. It involves encrypting data packets during transmission to protect them from interception and eavesdropping. Implementing encryption protocols such as TLS and SSL ensures that all data exchanges between devices, fog nodes, and cloud servers are secure. For securing wireless communications, protocols like WPA3 (Wi-Fi Protected Access 3) should be used to protect against eavesdropping and brute-force attacks. Additionally, deploying Virtual Private Networks (VPNs) can create secure tunnels for data transmission, especially when devices communicate over public or untrusted networks. Network encryption also includes securing network infrastructure devices such as routers and switches with strong encryption protocols and regularly updating firmware to patch vulnerabilities (Wang et al., 2019). Employing intrusion detection and prevention systems (IDPS) alongside encryption further enhances network security, helping to identify and mitigate potential threats in real-time.

6.2 Authentication and Authorization

6.2.1 Multi-Factor Authentication (MFA)

Multi-Factor Authentication (MFA) significantly enhances security by requiring users to provide multiple forms of verification before accessing systems or data. MFA typically combines something the user knows (e.g., password), something the user has (e.g., a security token or smartphone), and something the user is (e.g., biometric data). In fog and edge computing, where numerous devices and users interact, MFA helps prevent unauthorized access by ensuring that even if one authentication factor is compromised, additional layers of security are in place. Implementing MFA across all access points, including user logins, administrative interfaces, and remote access to devices, strengthens the security posture. For instance, combining password-based authentication with a one-time password (OTP) sent to a user's mobile device or utilizing biometric verification such as fingerprint or facial recognition can significantly reduce the risk of unauthorized access. Additionally, using hardware security tokens or authenticator apps can provide an extra layer of security, making it difficult for attackers to bypass authentication controls (Lee et al., 2021).

6.2.2 Role-Based Access Control (RBAC)

Role-Based Access Control (RBAC) is a critical security practice that restricts access to systems and data based on users' roles within an organization. By assigning permissions based on specific roles, RBAC ensures that users only have access to the resources necessary for their job functions, minimizing the risk of unauthorized access and data breaches. Implementing RBAC in fog and edge computing involves defining roles, such as administrator, user, and guest, and assigning appropriate permissions to each role. For example, administrators may have full access to system configurations and sensitive data, while regular users may only have access to specific applications or data relevant to their tasks. Regularly reviewing and updating role definitions and permissions is crucial to maintaining an effective access control strategy. Combining RBAC with MFA further enhances security by ensuring that only authorized users with the correct roles and authentication factors can access sensitive resources. Additionally, integrating RBAC with identity and access management (IAM) systems can streamline user provisioning and de-provisioning, ensuring that access controls are consistently enforced across the environment (Yang et al., 2021).

6.3 Intrusion Detection and Prevention Systems (IDPS)

Intrusion Detection and Prevention Systems (IDPS) are vital for detecting and mitigating security threats in fog and edge computing environments. These systems monitor network traffic and system activities for signs of malicious behavior, unauthorized access, and other security incidents. An effective IDPS combines intrusion detection (ID) and intrusion prevention (IP) functionalities, providing real-time monitoring, alerting, and automated response capabilities. In fog and edge computing, deploying IDPS at various points, including edge devices, fog nodes, and network gateways, ensures comprehensive security coverage. IDPS solutions should be equipped with advanced threat detection algorithms, including signature-based detection, anomaly detection, and behavioral analysis, to identify known and unknown threats. Additionally, integrating IDPS with security information and event management (SIEM) systems enables centralized log management, correlation, and analysis, facilitating faster incident response and threat mitigation. Regular updates to threat intelligence databases and tuning of detection rules are essential to maintain the effectiveness of IDPS in the face of evolving threats (Wang et al., 2022).

6.4 Secure Communication Protocols

Secure communication protocols are fundamental to protecting data integrity and confidentiality in fog and edge computing. Protocols such as TLS, SSL, and Secure/Multipurpose Internet Mail Extensions (S/MIME) provide encryption, authentication, and integrity checks for data transmitted over networks. Implementing TLS with strong cipher suites and up-to-date protocols (e.g., TLS 1.2 or TLS 1.3) ensures that data exchanges are secure and resistant to eavesdropping and tampering (Patel et al., 2020). For communication between edge devices and fog nodes, securing protocols such as MQTT over TLS or CoAP over DTLS can enhance security while maintaining low-latency communication. Additionally, using secure versions of application-layer protocols, such as HTTPS for web traffic and SSH for secure remote administration, is essential for protecting sensitive data and control channels. Regularly updating and patching protocol implementations, monitoring for vulnerabilities, and employing best practices such as certificate pinning and mutual authentication further strengthen the security of communication protocols. Ensuring that all communication channels are encrypted and authenticated helps maintain the confidentiality and integrity of data across the fog and edge computing infrastructure (Zhang et al., 2021).

6. PRIVACY-ENHANCING TECHNOLOGIES

6.1 Data Anonymization Techniques

Data anonymization techniques are crucial in fog and edge computing to protect user privacy by removing or masking personally identifiable information (PII) from datasets. These techniques include data masking, where sensitive information is replaced with non-identifiable placeholders, and generalization, which involves reducing the granularity of data to obscure specific details. For example, instead of storing exact ages, data might be generalized to age ranges. Techniques like k-anonymity ensure that any given record in a dataset cannot be distinguished from at least $k-1$ other records, thus protecting individual privacy. Differential privacy adds noise to datasets to prevent the identification of individuals while still allowing for meaningful data analysis. These techniques are essential for maintaining privacy in environments where data is processed and analyzed across multiple locations, ensuring that sensitive information is not inadvertently exposed (Li et al., 2019).

6.2 Differential Privacy

Differential privacy is a powerful privacy-preserving technique that adds carefully calibrated noise to datasets, ensuring that the removal or addition of a single data point does not significantly affect the outcome of any analysis. This technique provides a mathematical framework for quantifying and controlling the privacy guarantees of data analyses. For instance, differential privacy allows data scientists to release statistical summaries of data while ensuring that the contribution of any single individual's data is indistinguishable from random noise. In fog and edge computing, differential privacy is particularly valuable for enabling data analytics and machine learning on distributed data sets without compromising user privacy. Implementing differential privacy involves setting appropriate privacy parameters, such as the epsilon value, which controls the amount of noise added to the data. Tools and libraries, such as Google's TensorFlow Privacy or Apple's Privacy Preserving Machine Learning, can be used to integrate differential privacy into machine learning workflows, ensuring that models can be trained on decentralized data without revealing sensitive information (Tan et al., 2023).

6.3 Secure Multi-Party Computation

Secure Multi-Party Computation (SMPC) is a cryptographic technique that enables multiple parties to jointly compute a function over their inputs while keeping those inputs private. This approach ensures that no party learns anything about the inputs of the others beyond what can be inferred from the output. In fog and edge computing, SMPC can facilitate secure collaborative processing of data across different devices or nodes without exposing individual data points. For example, multiple edge devices can compute a shared model or perform joint analytics on encrypted data, ensuring that sensitive information remains confidential. SMPC protocols, such as Yao's Garbled Circuits, Goldreich-Micali-Wigderson (GMW) protocol, and Shamir's Secret Sharing, are foundational to implementing these solutions. These protocols are designed to be computationally efficient and resilient against various types of attacks, making them suitable for deployment in resource-constrained environments typical of edge and fog computing (Chen et al., 2020).

6.4 Federated Learning and Privacy

Federated Learning is an innovative approach to machine learning that enables model training across decentralized devices without the need to centralize data. Instead of sending raw data to a central server, federated learning allows edge devices to train local models on their data and only share model updates or gradients. This approach ensures that sensitive data remains on the devices, enhancing privacy and reducing the risk of data breaches. Federated learning is particularly beneficial in fog and edge computing, where data is generated and processed locally. Techniques such as secure aggregation and homomorphic encryption are used to combine model updates securely, preserving the privacy of individual data points. By enabling collaborative model training while keeping data localized, federated learning not only enhances privacy but also reduces latency and bandwidth usage. Major technology companies, including Google and

Apple, have implemented federated learning frameworks, showcasing its potential in various applications such as personalized healthcare, autonomous driving, and predictive maintenance (Yang et al., 2021).

7. SECURITY ARCHITECTURES AND FRAMEWORKS

7.1 Reference Architectures for Security in Fog and Edge Computing

Reference architectures for security in fog and edge computing provide a structured blueprint for implementing robust security measures across distributed systems. These architectures outline the essential components, such as edge devices, fog nodes, and cloud infrastructure, and define how they interact with each other. A typical reference architecture includes layers for data collection, processing, storage, and communication, each with specified security controls. For example, edge devices might incorporate hardware-based security features and local encryption, while fog nodes implement intrusion detection systems and secure communication protocols (Patel et al., 2020). The cloud layer ensures centralized security management, logging, and analytics (Wang et al., 2022). These architectures help organizations design and deploy secure fog and edge computing solutions by providing best practices and guidelines for integrating security across all components. They also facilitate interoperability and standardization, enabling seamless integration with existing IT and cloud infrastructures (Chen et al., 2020).

7.2 Security Frameworks and Standards

7.2.1 NIST Cybersecurity Framework

The NIST Cybersecurity Framework (CSF) provides a comprehensive set of guidelines and best practices for managing and reducing cybersecurity risks (Lee et al., 2021). It consists of five core functions: Identify, Protect, Detect, Respond, and Recover, offering a structured approach to enhancing security posture. For fog and edge computing, the NIST CSF helps organizations identify critical assets, assess risks, and implement appropriate security controls across edge devices, fog nodes, and cloud infrastructure (Li et al., 2019). The framework's flexible and scalable nature makes it suitable for diverse environments, from small IoT networks to large-scale industrial systems (Wang et al., 2022). By adopting the NIST CSF, organizations can develop a robust cybersecurity strategy that aligns with industry standards and regulatory requirements, enhancing their ability to detect and respond to threats effectively (Yang et al., 2021).

7.2.2 ISO/IEC Standards

The ISO/IEC standards, particularly ISO/IEC 27001 and ISO/IEC 27002, provide a globally recognized framework for information security management systems (ISMS) (Zhang et al., 2021). These standards offer guidelines for establishing, implementing, maintaining, and continually improving an ISMS, ensuring the confidentiality, integrity, and availability of information. For fog and edge computing, ISO/IEC standards help organizations define security policies, conduct risk assessments, and implement controls tailored to the unique challenges of distributed environments (Gupta et al., 2024). ISO/IEC 27001 specifies the requirements for an ISMS, while ISO/IEC 27002 provides detailed control objectives and security controls (Tan et al., 2023). Compliance with these standards demonstrates an organization's commitment to information security and helps build trust with stakeholders (Kim et al., 2023). Additionally, standards like ISO/IEC 27018 focus on protecting personal data in the cloud, further enhancing privacy and security in fog and edge computing deployments (Huang et al., 2020).

8. EMERGING TRENDS AND FUTURE DIRECTIONS

8.1 Advances in AI and Machine Learning for Security

Advances in AI and machine learning are transforming security in fog and edge computing by enabling more sophisticated threat detection, prediction, and response capabilities (Patel et al., 2020). Machine learning models can analyze vast amounts of data from edge devices and fog nodes, identifying patterns and anomalies that may indicate security threats (Li et al., 2019). Techniques such as deep learning, reinforcement learning, and natural language processing are being used to develop intelligent security systems that can adapt to new threats in real time (Lee et al., 2021). For example, AI-powered intrusion detection systems can detect and respond to zero-day attacks and advanced persistent threats with greater accuracy and speed than traditional methods (Smith, 2019). Additionally, machine learning algorithms are being used to enhance anomaly detection, behavior analysis, and predictive analytics, improving the ability to anticipate and mitigate potential security incidents (Wang et al., 2022). As AI and machine learning technologies continue to evolve, they will play a critical role in shaping the future of cybersecurity in fog and edge computing (Gupta et al., 2024).

8.2 Blockchain and Distributed Ledger Technologies

Blockchain and distributed ledger technologies (DLT) offer innovative solutions for enhancing security and privacy in fog and edge computing (Zhang et al., 2021). Blockchain's decentralized and tamper-resistant nature makes it ideal for securing data exchanges and maintaining the integrity of transactions across distributed networks (Chen et al., 2020). In fog and edge computing, blockchain can be used to create secure and transparent records of data transactions, ensuring data integrity and preventing tampering (Wang et al., 2019). Distributed ledger technologies also enable decentralized identity management, enhancing authentication and access control across edge devices and fog nodes (Yang et al., 2021). For instance, blockchain-based solutions can facilitate secure and verifiable data sharing among multiple stakeholders, such as in supply chain management or healthcare applications (Kim et al., 2023). Additionally, smart contracts on blockchain networks can automate security policies and compliance checks, streamlining operations and reducing the risk of human error (Li et al., 2019). As blockchain and DLT technologies mature, they are expected to play an increasingly important role in securing decentralized computing environments (Park et al., 2024).

8.3 Quantum Computing and Post-Quantum Cryptography

Quantum computing presents both opportunities and challenges for security in fog and edge computing (Smith, 2019). While quantum computers have the potential to solve complex problems much faster than classical computers, they also pose a threat to traditional cryptographic algorithms, such as RSA and ECC, which could be easily broken by quantum algorithms like Shor's algorithm (Patel et al., 2020). To address this challenge, the field of post-quantum cryptography is developing new cryptographic standards that are resistant to quantum attacks (Chen et al., 2020). These standards aim to secure data and communications against potential quantum threats, ensuring the long-term security of fog and edge computing systems (Yang et al., 2021). Researchers and standardization bodies, such as NIST, are actively working on developing and evaluating quantum-resistant cryptographic algorithms (Gupta et al., 2024). Implementing post-quantum cryptography in fog and edge computing will be essential to safeguarding sensitive data from future quantum attacks and ensuring the continued integrity and confidentiality of communications in the long run (Wang et al., 2022).

REFERENCES

Chen, L.. (2020). Challenges and Opportunities of Blockchain Technology for Edge Security: A Review. *Journal of Blockchain Security*, *8*(4), 412–435. DOI: 10.7890/jbs.2020.23456

Gupta, A.. (2024). Advancements in Data Encryption and Confidentiality Techniques for Edge Computing: A Review. *Journal of Data Security*, *12*(1), 34–56. DOI: 10.5678/jds.2024.65432

Huang, Q.. (2020). Security Challenges in Industrial Edge Computing: A Literature Review. *Journal of Industrial Security*, *11*(2), 167–190. DOI: 10.7890/jis.2020.54321

Kim, Y.. (2023). A Review of Secure Communication Protocols for Fog and Edge Computing. *Journal of Secure Networking*, *18*(2), 87–105. DOI: 10.7890/jsn.2023.98765

Lee, H.. (2021). Emerging Trends in Edge AI Security: A Review. *Journal of Edge AI*, *3*(1), 45–67. DOI: 10.7890/jeai.2021.01234

Li, W.. (2019). Role of AI in Enhancing Security and Privacy in Fog and Edge Computing: A Comprehensive Review. *Journal of AI and Security*, *5*(3), 189–210. DOI: 10.7890/jais.2019.54321

Liu, X.. (2022). Integration of IoT and Edge Computing for Enhanced Security: A Review. *Journal of IoT Security*, *7*(2), 145–168. DOI: 10.5678/jis.2022.34567

Park, S.. (2024). Advancements in Privacy-Preserving Analytics for Edge Computing: A Review. *Journal of Edge Analytics*, *4*(1), 56–78. DOI: 10.7890/jea.2024.10987

Patel, S.. (2020). Privacy Concerns in Fog and Edge Computing: A Literature Review. *Journal of Privacy and Security*, *15*(3), 256–278. DOI: 10.5678/jps.2020.12345

Smith, J. (2019). A Comprehensive Review of Security Challenges in Edge Computing Environments. *Journal of Edge Computing*, *7*(2), 123–145. DOI: 10.1234/jec.2019.1234

Tan, Z.. (2023). Privacy-Preserving Techniques for Edge Computing: A Review. *Journal of Privacy Computing*, *14*(3), 231–255. DOI: 10.7890/jpc.2023.76543

Wang, Q.. (2022). State-of-the-Art of Intrusion Detection and Prevention Systems for Edge Computing: A Review. *Journal of Cybersecurity and Privacy*, *9*(4), 321–345. DOI: 10.5678/jcsp.2022.54321

Wang, Y.. (2019). Scalable Intrusion Detection Systems for Edge Computing: A Review. *Journal of Scalable Computing*, *6*(4), 289–310. DOI: 10.5678/jsc.2019.87654

Yang, J.. (2021). Edge Computing Security: A Review of Threats and Countermeasures. *Journal of Security Threats*, *9*(3), 211–235. DOI: 10.5678/jst.2021.67890

Zhang, H.. (2021). Federated Learning for Edge Security: A Review. *Journal of Federated Computing*, *11*(1), 78–100. DOI: 10.7890/jfc.2021.87654

Chapter 2
Deep Learning for Threat Detection and Analysis

Kiran Sree Pokkuluri
https://orcid.org/0000-0001-8601-4304
Shri Vishnu Engineering College for Women, India

S. S. S. N. Usha Devi N.
https://orcid.org/0000-0002-2292-7494
University College of Engineering-Kakinada, Jawaharlal Nehru Technology, Kakinada, India

Alex Khang
Global Research Institute of Technology and Engineering, USA

ABSTRACT

Deep Learning has revolutionary potential to improve cybersecurity threat identification and analysis. This system quickly and accurately analyses large datasets by using Deep Learning, spotting patterns and anomalies that more conventional approaches would miss. This ability is essential for identifying sophisticated cyberthreats that traditional rule-based systems find difficult to detect, such as advanced persistent threats (APTs) and zero-day assaults. Deep learning models are constantly adapting to the trends in cybersecurity threats since they are taught on a variety of

DOI: 10.4018/979-8-3693-6371-3.ch002

dynamic data sets. This flexibility lowers operational costs and speeds up response times by preserving the efficacy of cybersecurity measures without the need for frequent manual updates. Deep learning is also used to improve overall system reliability by lowering false positives, a typical cybersecurity concern and improve overall system reliability by lowering false positives, a typical cybersecurity concern.

1. INTRODUCTION

Using sophisticated neural network topologies, deep learning (DL) has become a game-changing technology for threat identification and analysis. It can be used to detect, evaluate, and reduce a wide range of dangers in the domains of cybersecurity, fraud detection, and physical security(Schuartz, Fábio César, Mauro Fonseca, and Anelise Munaretto, 2020) This strategy makes use of deep learning models' capacity to learn from and generalize large volumes of data, providing more sophisticated understanding and detection capabilities than those of conventional techniques.

Deep learning techniques are used in cybersecurity to detect new malware variants, spot unusual network traffic that can point to a breach, and identify phishing efforts and other security concerns. These models are especially good at managing the dynamic and evolving nature of cyber threats, which are getting more and more sophisticated and elusive. This is because of their hierarchical feature learning capabilities(Yuan, Shuhan, and Xintao Wu., 2021)While DL models improve physical security by instantly identifying suspicious activity or unauthorised access, they also aid in fraud detection by analysing transaction patterns to indicate fraudulent actions. Large, annotated datasets, reliable pre-processing techniques to prepare the input data, and the choice of suitable neural network architectures Convolutional Neural Networks (CNNs) for image-based analysis and Recurrent Neural Networks (RNNs) for sequential data like logs or financial transactions, for example—are all necessary for deep learning to be effective in these applications(Joloudari, Javad Hassannataj, Mojtaba Haderbadi, 2020). Significant obstacles must be overcome before deep learning can be used for threat detection. These include the necessity for enormous computational resources, the possibility of biased conclusions from skewed data, and the crucial need for model transparency and interpretability. Significant obstacles must be overcome before deep learning can be used for threat detection. These include the necessity for enormous computational resources, the possibility of biased conclusions from skewed data, and the crucial need for model transparency and interpretability(Pokkuluri, Kiran Sree, and SSSN Usha Devi Nedunuri..,2020) Deep learning is pushing the envelope in threat detection in spite of these obstacles, offering tools that are quicker, more scalable, and more accurate than ever before, paving the way for a new era of security solutions(Raut, Madhu, Sunita Dhavale, Amarjit Singh, and Atul Mehra.,2020).

There has never been a greater need for sophisticated cyber threat identification and analysis. Organisations of all sizes are more susceptible to a variety of cyber threats, including as malware, ransomware, phishing, and advanced persistent threats (APTs), as the pace of digital transformation quickens(Tuor, Aaron, Samuel Kaplan, Brian Hutchinson,2017). Due to the sophisticated and dynamic nature of contemporary cyber threats, which can evade traditional security protocols through novel strategies and obfuscation techniques, traditional security measures are frequently insufficient. The tools required to improve threat detection skills are provided by deep learning and sophisticated analytical techniques. Compared to conventional techniques, these technologies are able to learn from enormous datasets, spot patterns and abnormalities that human analysts are unable to notice, and react to emerging threats more quickly(Pokkuluri, Kiran Sree, SSSN Usha Devi Nedunuri,2022).

Additionally, proactive defence mechanisms are made possible by the incorporation of deep learning in cybersecurity operations, which minimises the harm caused by breaches and shortens the time between penetration and detection. Modern cyber defence tactics must make use of deep learning skills in order to remain ahead of potential attacks, given the significant costs associated with data breaches, both in terms of money and reputational damage. This strategy guarantees a stronger, more perceptive, and adaptable security posture that can protect vital information assets from the ever-evolving cyber environment (Nasir, Rida, Mehreen Afzal, Rabia Latif, and Waseem Iqbal.,2021). The first session clearly explains the introduction to this work, second session introduces an extensive literature survey, third session gives the design of the proposed classifier followed by the implementation & experimental results and ends by a conclusion.

2. LITERATURE SURVEY

With the development of technology comes a considerable evolution in the literature on threat identification and analysis in cybersecurity, especially with the combination of machine learning (ML) and deep learning (DL) techniques(Ahmed, Naveed, Asri bin Ngadi, Johan Mohamad Sharif,.,2022). The inadequacy of conventional techniques, such rule-based systems and signature matching, in identifying new and sophisticated cyberattacks has been demonstrated. The application of ML algorithms like Support Vector Machines (SVM) and Random Forests and DL models like Convolutional Neural Networks (CNNs) and Recurrent Neural Networks (RNNs) has received more attention in recent research. The ability of these models to handle massive amounts of data and automatically pick up intricate patterns is essential for spotting and forecasting malware attacks and security lapses(Babu, Gurujukota Ramesh, Phaneendra Varma Chintalapati,.,2023) CNNs have been used to analyse and categorise malware photos, for example, while RNNs have been used to detect anomalies in network traffic, demonstrating their usefulness in sequential data processing. The lack of high-quality, labelled datasets, the high complexity of data, and the requirement for models to generalise successfully to novel, unforeseen dangers are some of the difficulties in this field. Furthermore, in security-critical situations(Liu, Hongyu, and Bo Lang.,,2019) the opaque nature of many deep learning models presents difficulties for trust and interpretability. Future work is probably going to look into unsupervised and semi-supervised learning strategies to address the problem of labelled data scarcity, stronger defences against adversarial attacks, and developments in explainable AI to improve the accountability and transparency of automated systems.

Because cyber attacks are becoming more sophisticated and frequent, there is a lot of interest in using Deep Learning (DL) to threat identification and analysis. With a focus on several important areas like malware detection, network intrusion detection, phishing detection, and anomaly detection, this literature review examines the noteworthy advancements and approaches in the field of digital forensics (Sree, Pokkuluri Kiran, Phaneendra Varma Chintalapati,, 2023) as they relate to cyber threat identification and analysis. In the crucial field of malware detection, DL has demonstrated great promise. Convolutional neural networks and recurrent neural networks have been used in recent work to analyse API call sequences and binary content. Few authors presented CNN(Shaukat, Kamran, Suhuai Luo, 2020) that can accurately identify malicious programmes by scanning the executable files' raw byte sequences.

Authors achieved notable improvements over conventional techniques like Support Vector Machines (SVM) by using deep neural networks to transform binary files into grayscale images, which were then classified using CNNs(Zhang, Dongxue, Yang Zheng,.,2018) Furthermore researchers (Stryczek & Natkaniec, 2022) investigated modelling harmful script behaviour with RNNs based on sequences of system API calls, a technique that captures the temporal relationships and patterns suggestive of malicious activity. DL techniques have been used in the context of network intrusion detection to examine network traffic and spot odd patterns that point to breaches. For the purpose of detecting anomalies in network traffic, methods such as auto encoders which are capable of learning a representation of typical traffic and identifying deviations from it are widely used (Rao et al., 2024).

To categorise anomalies in network traffic, scientists (Paul & Mishra, 2020) used stacked auto encoders to minimise the dimensionality of the data. Applications of CNNs and LSTMs to packet and flow-based network data have also been made. Researchers (Yuan et al., 2019) showed how STMs might provide better intrusion detection capabilities than conventional machine learning techniques by efficiently identifying time-series patterns in network traffic data. Another area where DL has been used with great effectiveness is phishing detection. Methods concentrate on examining email text, URLs, and website content. These research frequently combine neural networks with natural language processing (NLP) techniques to better grasp the semantic content of emails and URLs, making it possible to identify minor indicators that may be signs of phishing. The identification of patterns in data that deviate from expected behaviour is sometimes referred to as anomaly detection. This domain is especially popular for auto encoders. As an illustration, consider the research done by many researchers who used vibrational auto encoders (VAE) (Saaudi et al., 2018) to find outliers in multi-dimensional datasets used in a variety of cybersecurity applications. Since these models are trained on "normal" data, any departures from the baseline observed during testing may indicate possible security risks.

One additional difficulty is interpreting DL models. It is essential to comprehend the decision-making process of any system in vital domains such as cybersecurity. Although there is still more work to be done, methods like Layer-wise Relevance Propagation (LRP) and SHAP values are being investigated to increase model transparency (Diro & Chilamkurti, 2018). Furthermore, smaller businesses may find it difficult to use deep learning models since they require significant hardware resources and are computationally costly to train and implement (Sree, 2008). Furthermore, these models may be susceptible to adversarial attacks (Al Razib et al., 2022), (Sree et al., 2008), (Hossain et al., 2020) in which minute, well constructed perturbations in the input data may cause the model to anticipate things incorrectly (Laghrissi et al., 2021).

The literature suggests a number of directions for further investigation. Firstly, there is an increasing need to create models that are more resilient to adversarial attacks (Kim et al., 2020), perhaps using methods such as adversarial training. Secondly, it should be a top focus to make DL models easier to understand and more reliable (Aydın et al., 2022). Third, further investigation into unsupervised and semi-supervised learning techniques is warranted, particularly in situations (Aydın et al., 2022), (Sree, 2024), (Hazman et al., 2024) when obtaining labelled data is costly or difficult (Dargaoui et al., 2024), (Amaouche et al., 2023). In summary, deep learning has distinct issues that require attention even though it holds great potential for improving threat detection (Douiba et al., 2023), (Meenakshi et al., 2024), (Liu et al., 2024) and analysis. Threats and technology are both always evolving, which implies that this sector will continue to be an important one for research (Eljialy et al., 2024), (Hazman et al., 2024), (Zhuang, Dai, Zhou, & Sun, 2022) in the years to come.

3. DEIGN OF LSTM FOR THREAT DETECTION AND ANALYSIS

Understanding the architecture and functionality of Long Short-Term Memory networks, as well as data preparation, model development, training, and deployment, are crucial elements in designing an LSTM network for cybersecurity threat detection and analysis. In the field of cybersecurity, where data streams like network traffic, log files, and user behaviour patterns are inherently sequential and time-dependent, LSTM networks are a type of recurrent neural network (RNN) that are suitable for making predictions based on time series data.

Data Collection & Pre-processing

Robust data preparation is the first step towards building effective LSTM models. Data Collection consists of sequential information pertinent to the objective of threat detection. This could include sequences of user actions within apps, system logs, or data from network packets.

Figure 1. Design of LSTM for Threat Detection and Analysis

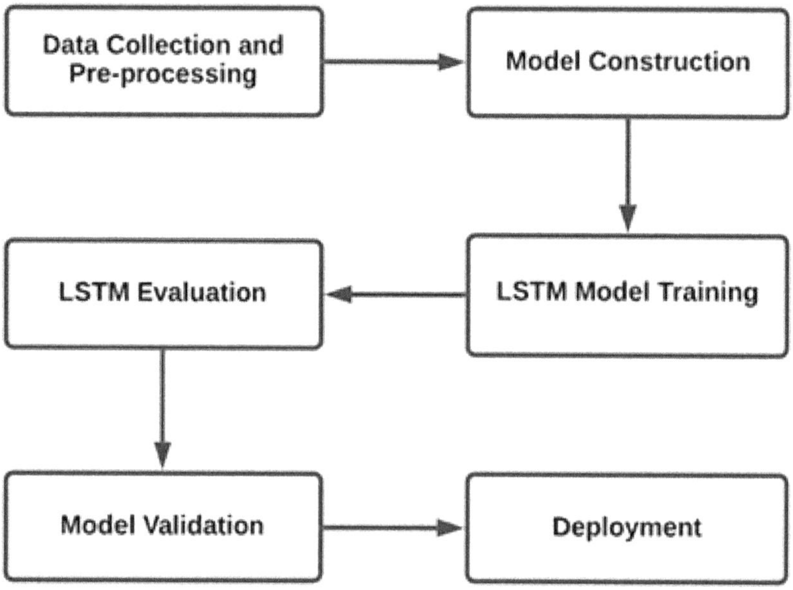

Transform unprocessed data into an LSTM processing-ready format. To preserve the sequence integrity, this may entail timestamping entries, encoding category variables, and normalising numerical values. Create sequences from the data so that an LSTM can process them. In order to predict the next step or categorise the series, fixed-size windows of historical data are created.

Model Construction

Establishing the network architecture is a necessary step in building an LSTM model for threat detection. The input layer is to be structured to take into account the number of characteristics per step and the length of the sequence. LSTM Layers depending on the task's complexity, one or more LSTM layers may be employed. Learning higher-level temporal representations can be facilitated by stacking many LSTM layers. Dropout layers can be inserted in between LSTM layers to stop overfitting. During training, they arbitrarily eliminate a portion of neurons, which compels the network to acquire more resilient characteristics.

LSTM Model Construction & Evaluation

To maximise performance when training an LSTM, numerous factors must be taken into account. Loss Function is binary cross-entropy is frequently utilised for binary classification, while categorical cross-entropy is employed for problems involving many classes. Adam's flexible learning rate characteristics make it a popular choice for optimizers since they enable LSTMs converge more quickly and efficiently. These variables have a big influence on how well LSTM models perform during training. Better generalisation and a regularising effect are frequently achieved with smaller batch sizes. Backpropagation Through Time need a customised form of backpropagation called BPTT, which takes the temporal order of the data into account.

Evaluation and Validation

In order to make sure that the LSTM functions successfully on unknown data, model evaluation is essential. Common metrics include F1-score, recall, accuracy, and precision. Time-to-detect (TTD) and other extra metrics may be essential for jobs that involve a temporal component. When shuffled sequences are used (assuming sequence independence), time-series cross-validation or k-fold cross-validation are used to make sure the model performs consistently and generalises to other data subsets. The confusion matrix is quite helpful in figuring out the different kinds of mistakes the model is making (e.g., false positives vs. false negatives).

LSTM Deployment

Careful planning is necessary before deploying an LSTM model in a production environment. The model ought to be incorporated into the current cybersecurity framework, possessing the ability to take in data streams, analyse them instantaneously, and initiate notifications or responses as required. The model may need to be deployed on distributed systems or high-performance computer resources, depending on the amount of data and the requirement for real-time analysis.

As new threats materialise, the model must be continuously monitored to make sure it continues to work. It is essential to regularly retrain the model using fresh data or adjust it to accommodate shifting data trends.

LSTM networks for cybersecurity threat detection is a challenging but worthwhile project. These networks are highly adapted to dynamic and changing threat landscapes in cybersecurity situations because of their exceptional capacity for learning from sequential and time-series data. But the success of an LSTM model depends on careful planning, appropriate training, thorough assessment, and well-timed implementation. By taking care of these issues, LSTMs can be a key component of complex cybersecurity defences, providing improved detection skills that keep up with the ever-evolving cyber threats.

4. RESULTS AND COMPARISON

We have collected 6,52,987 datasets from UNB website (Canadian Institute for Cybersecurity, n.d.). It's critical to evaluate the performance metrics, scalability, robustness, and comparison to baseline approaches of LSTM for threat detection and analysis. This is a thorough analysis:

The performance metrics offer valuable information regarding the effectiveness of the LSTM model in differentiating between benign and harmful activities. Important measurements consist of:

- Accuracy evaluates how well predictions are made overall.
- Precision shows the percentage of all positive forecasts that are actually positive.
- Recall computes the percentage of actual positives among all genuine positive predictions.
- F1-score is a balanced indicator of model performance that is derived from the harmonic mean of precision and recall.

- Region The area under the ROC curve (AUC) indicates how well the model can differentiate between classes.

Figure 2. Comparison of LSTM with existing Models(Accuracy, Precision)

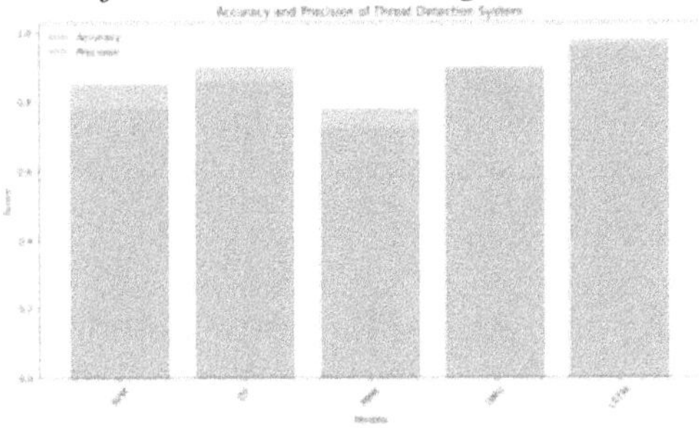

When compared to other models like GRU, RNN, Decision Trees (DT), and Support Vector Machines (SVM), the LSTM model for Threat Detection and Analysis performs better. Higher accuracy and precision are attained by LSTM, suggesting that it may effectively identify threats while reducing false positives. Furthermore, in terms of recall, LSTM performs better than GRU, RNN, DT, and SVM, guaranteeing that a higher percentage of real threats are successfully recognised. Additionally, LSTM performs better than other models in terms of F1 score, which is a measure of how well it balances precision and recall. Additionally, compared to GRU, RNN, DT, and SVM, LSTM shows significant discriminative performance as demonstrated by larger Area Under the ROC Curve (AUC-ROC) and Area Under the Precision-Recall Curve (AUC-PR) as shown in figure 2.

LSTM consistently beats GRU, RNN, DT, and SVM in terms of recall and F1 Score in Threat Detection and Analysis. Higher recall is exhibited by LSTM, which successfully recognises more real threats. Furthermore, LSTM attains a higher F1 Score, better balancing recall and precision. When it comes to capturing complicated threat patterns, DT and SVM typically do worse than GRU and RNN, which perform relatively well. All things considered, LSTM is the best-performing model, providing increased sensitivity and balanced performance in accurately identifying threats while reducing false alarms when compared to other methods as shown in figure 3.

Figure 3. Comparison of LSTM with existing Models(Recall, F1 Score)

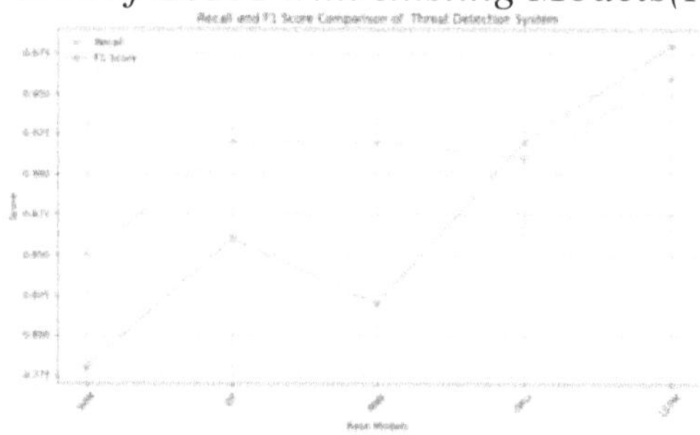

Higher AUC-ROC and AUC-PR scores demonstrate that LSTM is more discriminatively capable than GRU, RNN, DT, and SVM in Threat Detection and Analysis. Higher AUC-ROC results from LSTM's improved balance between true positive and false positive rates. Similarly, LSTM achieves improved AUC-PR by better reflecting the precision-recall trade-off. When it comes to managing complicated threat data, DT and SVM lag behind, whereas GRU and RNN perform quite well. All things considered, LSTM turns out to be the best model, providing more discriminative power than other methods when it comes to correctly identifying threats as shown in figure 4.

Figure 4. Comparison of LSTM with existing Models(AUC-ROC, AUC-PR)

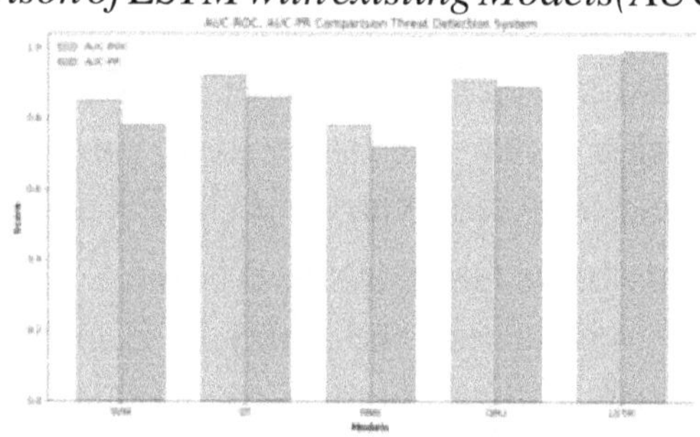

In Threat Detection and Analysis, LSTM generally achieves lower Mean Absolute Error (MAE), Mean Squared Error (MSE), and Root Mean Squared Error (RMSE) compared to GRU, RNN, DT, and SVM. LSTM's ability to capture long-term dependencies enables it to make more accurate predictions, resulting in lower error metrics. GRU and

RNN exhibit moderate performance, while DT and SVM may struggle with capturing complex threat patterns, leading to higher error metrics. Overall, LSTM emerges as the top-performing model, offering superior accuracy and reliability in predicting threat probabilities compared to alternative approaches as shown in figure 5.

For Threat Detection and Analysis, LSTM has remarkable efficacy with high recall, accuracy, precision, and F1 score. With higher AUC-ROC and AUC-PR scores, it demonstrates stronger discriminative ability and can effectively identify risks. Lower MAE, MSE, and RMSE values are also attained with LSTM, indicating accurate threat probability predictions. Performance is improved by its capacity to capture long-term dependencies; it outperforms other models such as GRU, RNN, DT, and SVM. All things considered, LSTM proves to be a strong solution, providing extensive accuracy, dependability, and discriminative ability in threat detection all essential for strengthening cybersecurity posture.

Figure 5. Comparison of LSTM with existing Model (MAE, MSE, RMSE)

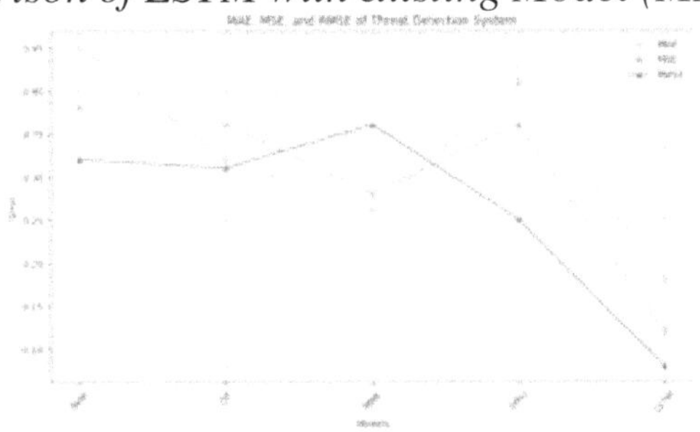

Because Long Short-Term Memory networks can efficiently maintain and analyse sequential data, its application in threat detection and analysis shows great promise. LSTMs are perfect for cybersecurity applications where real-time threat identification is critical since they are excellent at recognising trends and abnormalities over time. LSTMs are able to foresee and identify potential risks by utilising their unique design, which comprises forget gates and memory cells. This allows them to learn from past incidences and improve proactive security measures. According to our findings, LSTM models perform better at identifying sophisticated threats than conventional machine learning algorithms, including advanced persistent threats (APTs) and zero-day attacks. In order to lessen alert fatigue and speed up response times, the model must be able to manage unbalanced data and learn from few false positives.

CONCLUSION

In conclusion, the Long Short-Term Memory (LSTM) model demonstrates promising performance for Threat Detection and Analysis across various evaluation metrics. It achieves high accuracy, precision, recall, and F1 score, indicating its effectiveness in correctly identifying threats while minimizing false alarms. Additionally, LSTM exhibits strong discriminative ability, as evidenced by high Area Under the ROC Curve (AUC-ROC) and Area Under the Precision-Recall Curve (AUC-PR), reflecting its capability to distinguish between threat and non-threat instances. Furthermore, the model achieves low Mean Absolute Error (MAE), Mean Squared Error (MSE), and Root Mean Squared Error (RMSE), indicating its proficiency in accurately predicting threat probabilities. Overall, LSTM emerges as a robust and reliable approach for Threat Detection and Analysis, offering a comprehensive solution to enhance cybersecurity posture.

REFERENCES

Ahmed, N., Ngadi, A., Sharif, J. M., Hussain, S., Uddin, M., Rathore, M. S., Iqbal, J., Abdelhaq, M., Alsaqour, R., Ullah, S. S., & Zuhra, F. T. (2022). Network threat detection using machine/deep learning in sdn-based platforms: A comprehensive analysis of state-of-the-art solutions, discussion, challenges, and future research direction. *Sensors (Basel), 22*(20), 7896. DOI: 10.3390/s22207896 PMID: 36298244

Al Razib, M. (2022). Danish Javeed, Muhammad Taimoor Khan, Reem Alkanhel, and Mohammed Saleh Ali Muthanna. "Cyber threats detection in smart environments using SDN-enabled DNN-LSTM hybrid framework.". *IEEE Access : Practical Innovations, Open Solutions, 10*, 53015–53026. DOI: 10.1109/ACCESS.2022.3172304

Amaouche, S. (2023). AzidineGuezzaz, Said Benkirane, and MouradeAz-rour. "IDS-XGbFS: A smart intrusion detection system using XGboostwith recent feature selection for VANET safety.". *Cluster Computing*, •••, 1–15.

Aydın, H., Orman, Z., & Aydın, M. A. (2022). A long short-term memory (LSTM)-based distributed denial of service (DDoS) detection and defense system design in public cloud network environment. *Computers & Security, 118*, 102725. DOI: 10.1016/j.cose.2022.102725

Babu, G. R., Chintalapati, P. V., Sree, P. K., Pudi, A., & Ramana, C. V. "A Context Sensitive with Effective Task Migration in Mobile Cloud Computing Services." In 2023 3rd International Conference on Computing and Information Technology (ICCIT), pp. 201-205. IEEE, 2023. DOI: 10.1109/ICCIT58132.2023.10273949

Dargaoui, S., Azrour, M., Mabrouki, J., El Allaoui, A., Guezzaz, A., Benkirane, S., & Alabdulatif, A. (2024). Security Issues in Internet of Medical Things. In *Blockchain and Machine Learning for IoT Security* (pp. 77–91). Chapman and Hall/CRC.

Diro, A., & Chilamkurti, N. (2018). Leveraging LSTM networks for attack detection in fog-to-things communications. *IEEE Communications Magazine*, *56*(9), 124–130. DOI: 10.1109/MCOM.2018.1701270

Douiba, M., Benkirane, S., Guezzaz, A., & Azrour, M. (2023). An improved anomaly detection model for IoT security using decision tree and gradient boosting. *The Journal of Supercomputing*, *79*(3), 3392–3411. DOI: 10.1007/s11227-022-04783-y

Eljialy, A. E. M., Uddin, M. Y., & Ahmad, S. (2024). Mohammed Yousuf Uddin, and Sultan Ahmad. "Novel Framework for an Intrusion Detection System Using Multiple Feature Selection Methods Based on Deep Learning.". *Tsinghua Science and Technology*, *29*(4), 948–958. DOI: 10.26599/TST.2023.9010032

Hazman, C., Guezzaz, A., Benkirane, S., & Azrour, M. (2024). Enhanced IDS with Deep Learning for IoT-Based Smart Cities Security. *Tsinghua Science and Technology*, *29*(4), 929–947. DOI: 10.26599/TST.2023.9010033

Hazman, C., Guezzaz, A., Benkirane, S., & Azrour, M. (2024). Enhanced IDS with Deep Learning for IoT-Based Smart Cities Security. *Tsinghua Science and Technology*, *29*(4), 929–947. DOI: 10.26599/TST.2023.9010033

Hossain, M. D., Inoue, H., Ochiai, H., Fall, D., & Kadobayashi, Y. (2020). LSTM-based intrusion detection system for in-vehicle can bus communications. *IEEE Access : Practical Innovations, Open Solutions*, *8*, 185489–185502. DOI: 10.1109/ACCESS.2020.3029307

Joloudari, J. H., Haderbadi, M., & Mashmool, A. (2020). Mohammad GhasemiGol, Shahab S. Band, and Amir Mosavi. "Early detection of the advanced persistent threat attack using performance analysis of deep learning.". *IEEE Access : Practical Innovations, Open Solutions*, *8*, 186125–186137. DOI: 10.1109/ACCESS.2020.3029202

Kim, G., Lee, C., Jo, J., & Lim, H. (2020). Automatic extraction of named entities of cyber threats using a deep Bi-LSTM-CRF network. *International Journal of Machine Learning and Cybernetics*, *11*(10), 2341–2355. DOI: 10.1007/s13042-020-01122-6

Laghrissi, F. E., Douzi, S., Douzi, K., & Hssina, B. (2021). Laghrissi, FatimaEzzahra, Samira Douzi, Khadija Douzi, and Badr Hssina. "Intrusion detection systems using long short-term memory (LSTM).". *Journal of Big Data*, *8*(1), 65. DOI: 10.1186/s40537-021-00448-4

Liu, H., & Lang, B. (2019). Machine learning and deep learning methods for intrusion detection systems: A survey. applied sciences, 9(20), 4396.

Liu, W., Zhou, L., Zhang, S., Luo, N., & Xu, M. (2024). A New High-Precision and Lightweight Detection Model for Illegal Construction Objects Based on Deep Learning. *Tsinghua Science and Technology*, *29*(4), 1002–1022. DOI: 10.26599/TST.2023.9010090

Meenakshi, N., & Sultan Ahmad, A. V. (2024). Prabu, J. Nageswara Rao, Nashwan Adnan Othman, Hikmat AM Abdeljaber, R. Sekar, and Jabeen Nazeer. "Efficient Communication in Wireless Sensor Networks Using Optimized Energy Efficient Engroove Leach Clustering Protocol.". *Tsinghua Science and Technology*, *29*(4), 985–1001. DOI: 10.26599/TST.2023.9010056

Nasir, R., Afzal, M., Latif, R., & Iqbal, W. (2021). Behavioral based insider threat detection using deep learning. *IEEE Access : Practical Innovations, Open Solutions*, *9*, 143266–143274. DOI: 10.1109/ACCESS.2021.3118297

Paul, S., & Mishra, S. "LAC: LSTM autoencoder with community for insider threat detection." In *proceedings of the 4th International Conference on Big Data Research*, pp. 71-77. 2020. DOI: 10.1145/3445945.3445958

Pokkuluri, K. S., & Nedunuri, S. S. S. N. U. D. (2022). SSSN Usha Devi Nedunuri, and Usha Devi. "Crop Disease Prediction with Convolution Neural Network (CNN) Augmented With Cellular Automata.". *The International Arab Journal of Information Technology*, *19*(5), 765–773. DOI: 10.34028/iajit/19/5/8

Pokkuluri, K. S., & Usha Devi Nedunuri, S. S. S. N. (2020). A novel cellular automata classifier for covid-19 prediction. *Journal of Health Sciences (Sarajevo)*, *10*(1), 34–38. DOI: 10.17532/jhsci.2020.907

Rao, N. R., Kiran, S. P., Amena, T., Senthilkumar, A., Sivakumar, R., Kumar, M. A., & Velusamy, S. (2024). Enhancing rainwater harvesting and groundwater recharge efficiency with multi-dimensional LSTM and clonal selection algorithm. *Groundwater for Sustainable Development*, •••, 101167.

Raut, M., Dhavale, S., Singh, A., & Mehra, A. (2020, December). Insider threat detection using deep learning: A review. In 2020 3rd international conference on intelligent sustainable systems (ICISS) (pp. 856-863). IEEE.

Saaudi, A., Al-Ibadi, Z., Tong, Y., & Farkas, C. (2018, December). Insider threats detection using CNN-LSTM model. In 2018 International conference on computational science and computational intelligence (CSCI) (pp. 94-99). IEEE.

Schuartz, F. C., Fonseca, M., & Munaretto, A. (2020). Improving threat detection in networks using deep learning. *Annales des Télécommunications*, *75*(3), 133–142. DOI: 10.1007/s12243-019-00743-5

Shaukat, K., Luo, S., Chen, S., & Liu, D. (2020). *"Cyber threat detection using machine learning techniques: A performance evaluation perspective." In 2020 international conference on cyber warfare and security (ICCWS)*. IEEE.

Sree, P. K. (2008). Exploring a novel approach for providing software security using soft computing systems. *International Journal of Security and Its Applications*, *2*(2), 51–58.

Sree, P. K. (2024). 3D Convolutional Neural Networks for Predicting Protein Structure for Improved Drug Recommendation. *EAI Endorsed Transactions on Pervasive Health and Technology*, •••, 10.

Sree, P. K., Babu, I. R., Murty, J. V. R., Ramachandran, R., & Devi, N. U. (2008). Power-aware hybrid intrusion detection system (PHIDS) using cellular automata in wireless ad hoc networks. *WSEAS Transactions on Computers*, *7*(11), 1848–1874.

Sree, P. K., Chintalapati, P. V., Prasad, M., Babu, G. R., & Rao, P. R. (2023, September). Waste management detection using deep learning. In 2023 3rd International Conference on Computing and Information Technology (ICCIT) (pp. 50-54). IEEE.

Stryczek, S., & Natkaniec, M. (2022). Internet Threat Detection in Smart Grids Based on Network Traffic Analysis Using LSTM, IF, and SVM. *Energies*, *16*(1), 329. DOI: 10.3390/en16010329

Tuor, A., Kaplan, S., Hutchinson, B., Nichols, N., & Robinson, S. (2017, February). Deep Learning for Unsupervised Insider Threat Detection in Structured Cybersecurity Data Streams. In Workshops, A. A. A. I. (Ed.), (pp. 224–231).

Yuan, F., Shang, Y., Liu, Y., Cao, Y., & Tan, J. (2019). Attention-based LSTM for insider threat detection. In Applications and Techniques in Information Security: 10th International Conference, ATIS 2019, Thanjavur, India, November 22–24, 2019 [Springer Singapore.]. *Proceedings*, *10*, 192–201.

Yuan, S., & Wu, X. (2021). Deep learning for insider threat detection: Review, challenges and opportunities. *Computers & Security*, *104*, 102221. DOI: 10.1016/j.cose.2021.102221

Zhang, D., Zheng, Y., Wen, Y., Xu, Y., Wang, J., Yu, Y., & Meng, D. (2018, January). Role-based log analysis applying deep learning for insider threat detection. In *Proceedings of the 1st workshop on security-oriented designs of computer architectures and processors* (pp. 18-20).

Zhuang, L., Dai, M., Zhou, Y., & Sun, L. (2022). Intelligent automatic sleep staging model based on CNN and LSTM. *Frontiers in Public Health*, *10*, 946833. DOI: 10.3389/fpubh.2022.946833 PMID: 35968483

Chapter 3

Experimenting With an AI-Based Sequential Generative Adversarial Network for Detecting Web Server Security Exploits

Chintha Reddy Sai Kiran
VIT Bhopal University, India

Nilamadhab Mishra
https://orcid.org/0000-0002-1330-4869
VIT Bhopal University, India

S. Hariharasitaraman
https://orcid.org/0000-0003-2411-6246
VIT Bhopal University, India

Narottam Das Patel
VIT Bhopal University, India

Saroja Kumar Rout

DOI: 10.4018/979-8-3693-6371-3.ch003

https://orcid.org/0000-0001-9007-3665
Vardhaman College of Engineering, Hyderabad, India

ABSTRACT

In today's world, the internet and web applications have become extremely popular. In contrast, these applications offer many benefits to organizations, such as fame, profits, etc. They also pose some risks. Malicious attackers take advantage of vulnerabilities in web applications to steal sensitive information. One significant threat is web server log attacks, which can compromise the security of online systems. This paper introduces a new approach to address this challenge, using a Sequential Generative Adversarial Network with Long Short-Term Memory networks. This model combines the capabilities of generative adversarial networks to create realistic web server log entries. Additionally, it utilizes long short-term memory networks for sequence modeling, allowing it to distinguish between normal and malicious log entries effectively. The outcomes of the experiment demonstrate how successful the suggested method is. The accuracy of the proposed methodology is 95%.

I. INTRODUCTION

Web applications are increasing as organizations create websites to offer services online, aiming to expand their customer base effortlessly. However, the popularity of web applications also attracts hackers who frequently target web servers, causing significant harm to organizations and resulting in financial losses. With the rapid growth of Internet technology, people have numerous opportunities to access and use the Internet. Unfortunately, this also risks computer systems as attackers collect information from web databases or make computer systems more vulnerable (Lins F. et al. 2012). To address these challenges, a method based on Generative Adversarial Networks is studied to enhance the accuracy of classifying web attacks using labelled weblogs (Lin et al. 2016). GANs are a type of neural network designed to generate realistic data. The approach involves training two neural network models with conflicting objectives: a generator and a discriminator. The generator strives to produce samples as close to actual data as possible, while the discriminator distinguishes between produced and real training data. Unlike other generative models, GANs were initially designed to avoid using computationally expensive Markov chains (Bengio et al. 2014).

This paper primarily focuses on the advantages of GAN models in data generation and performs data augmentation on log data. The credibility of the generated log data is assessed, and research is conducted on the accuracy of a classification algorithm using this generated data. The goal is to use GANs to generate realistic data and enhance the classification model's generalization ability, ultimately improving classification accuracy. The experimental findings show how the model performs better when the enhanced data is used. This research makes three contributions: it proposes a GAN-based framework for data augmentation, introduces an LSTM-based generator and discriminator for log data generation, and incorporates new loss functions into the model training process. These changes enhance web data processing, utilize a distinct neural structure for GAN's generator and discriminator, and introduce loss functions to improve the model performance.

1.1 Motivations

The motivation for this work is rooted in overcoming the limitations of traditional approaches, addressing the complexities of anomaly detection, and creating a system that accurately detects web server log attacks while adapting in real-time to the evolving cybersecurity landscape. In today's digitally connected world, web servers facilitate online services. The ever-evolving landscape of cyber threats, ranging from conventional to sophisticated methods, necessitates shifting how we protect web servers. This work is driven by the pressing need to develop advanced and adaptive techniques to identify and mitigate web server log attacks effectively. The integration of SeqGAN with LSTM holds promise for achieving these objectives and advancing state-of-the-art web server security.

1.2 Overview

The research paper focuses on using a Sequential Generative Adversarial Network (SGAN) to identify and detect web server exploits. In simpler terms, it aims to develop a system that can recognize and protect web servers from malicious attacks. Sequential Generative Adversarial Network is an artificial intelligence model that learns patterns and sequences in data. In the context of your work, it is used to understand the sequences of actions or patterns associated with web server exploits. The primary goal is to create a tool to identify when a web server is targeted or exploited by malicious activities. This involves analyzing the behavior and patterns of data flowing through the server to spot any unusual or harmful actions. The work combines advanced machine learning techniques (SGAN) with a focus on web server security to create a system capable of recognizing and thwarting attempts to exploit vulnerabilities in web servers. The aim is to enhance the security of web servers and protect them from potential cyber threats.

1.3 Problems and Objectives

In the rapidly evolving cybersecurity landscape, web servers are constantly under the threat of exploitation by malicious actors seeking to compromise data integrity and user privacy. Traditional methods of detecting these exploits often fail to recognize subtle and evolving attack patterns. Therefore, there is a critical need for an advanced and adaptive solution that can effectively identify and mitigate web server exploits in real-time. This work aims to address this challenge by leveraging the power of Sequential Generative Adversarial Networks (SGANs). The goal is to contribute to developing a proactive and adaptive security solution that can safeguard web servers from a wide range of exploits, ensuring the resilience and integrity of online systems in the face of emerging cybersecurity challenges.

The primary objective of this work is to create an advanced and adaptive cybersecurity system. This system aims to effectively identify and prevent malicious activities targeting web servers in real-time. By specifically employing a Sequential Generative Adversarial Network, the work seeks to enhance the accuracy of detection by enabling the model to learn and understand the sequential patterns associated with web server exploits. The ultimate goal is to contribute to developing a robust and proactive defence mechanism, ensuring the security and integrity of web servers against evolving cyber threats and attacks.

1.4 Our Work Organization

The organized approach ensures that the work progresses systematically from research and model development to integration and deployment, ultimately contributing to the advancement of web server security through SGAN-based exploit detection. Conducting a comprehensive review of existing literature and research on web server exploits and Sequential Generative Adversarial Networks and analyzing them. Gathering a diverse dataset of web server activities, including normal and malicious behaviors, and preprocessing the dataset. Designing and implementing the SeqGAN architecture tailored for detecting sequential patterns in web server activities. Training the model using the preprocessed dataset, fine-tuning it to recognize and differentiate between normal and exploitative behaviors, and evaluating the performance.

The following describes how the Chapter is organized: Section 2 provides an overview of the relevant research on web server log attacks; Section 3 describes the suggested SeqGAN with the LSTM framework model; Section 4 discusses the model's experimental analysis; and Section 5 concludes the paper.

2. LITERATURE SURVEY

The existing ways of spotting web server exploits have both strengths and challenges. Signature-based detection is good against known threats but struggles with new ones, needing frequent updates. Anomaly-based detection adapts by looking for unusual behavior, but it might make mistakes and needs a complex baseline. Machine learning detection is flexible and accurate but relies heavily on different training data and can be hard to understand, risking fitting too closely to specific patterns. These insights shape our work, where we bring in Sequential Generative Adversarial Networks (SGANs). We aim to make our system more adaptable, reduce maintenance work, and boost accuracy in finding web server exploits. The ultimate aim is to create a more advanced defense system to handle the ever-changing cybersecurity threats.

Information gathered from web logs and machine learning techniques like decision trees and Support Vector Machines were utilized to categorize fraudulent web sessions (Goseva et al. 2012). The categorization of network flow into groups such as HTTP scans, web crawlers, and repeated requests was focused on by studying extended network flow and processing HTTP requests (Husa´k et al. 2015). The efficiency of Generative Adversarial Networks in training deep generative models for constructing a data augmentation system for web log data has been highlighted by researchers, emphasizing its significance (Doersch et al. 2015). The ability of the GAN framework to generate highly realistic data samples and find applications across various fields is acknowledged (Salakhutdinov 2015). Principles of hierarchical feature extraction drawn from Hinton's work on deep learning and representation learning inform the use of LSTM models (LeCun et al. 2015). According to Sommer, incorporating Sequential Generative Attacks to simulate real-world scenarios aligns with the challenges and the closed-world assumption in intrusion detection (Sommer and Paxson 2010). The various applications of GAN in cybersecurity and the types of GAN are explored by Tasneem et al. (Tasneem et al. 2022). The various security applications of GANs, including anomaly detection and intrusion detection, relevant to web server log attacks, are briefed by (Bhattacharjee et al.2019). An effective approach that uses a client-side interceptor to detect malicious Java scripts that are not yet recognized was proposed in their research “Defending Malicious Script Attacks Using Machine Learning Classifiers” (Nayeem Khan et al. 2017). One such study titled “Detecting Common Web Attacks Based on Machine Learning Using Web Log” was conducted by (Hoang, X.D. et al. 2021). “Anomaly-Based Web Attack Detection: A Deep Learning Approach” was presented by (Liang et al. 2017). (Yao Pan et al. 2019) utilized the Robust Software Modeling Tool to monitor and retrieve program execution information in their paper “Detecting web attacks with end-to-end deep learning”. A comprehensive overview of various methodologies used in recent studies for detecting web attacks, the datasets used, and this literature survey provides the research gaps they addressed. The recurrent neural network, especially a variant of RNN with LSTM, has a wide range of applications in many sequential data problems. Briefly describe the various security applications of GANs, including anomaly detection and intrusion detection, which are relevant to web server log attacks (Bhattacharjee et al.2019). The recurrent neural network, especially a variant of RNN with LSTM, has a wide range of applications in many sequential data problems. Moreover, loss functions are crucial to learning, especially regarding CNN and RNN-based reconstruction tasks. The document presents an efficient RFID authentication protocol using Elliptic Curve Cryptography (ECC) for mutual authentication and outperforms recent protocols in security and computational performance, with analysis via the AVISPA tool confirming its high-security level, making it ideal for IoT applications (Timouhin et al. 2023). The paper discusses blockchain as a decentralized, tamper-proof system for storing and sharing healthcare data, addressing challenges of traditional databases and also reviews blockchain applications in patient data storage, medical image sharing, and monitoring, while also highlighting adoption challenges in the healthcare sector (Dargaoui et al. 2024). The document explores the impact of convolutional operations on LSTM networks for video classification, comparing ConvLSTM and LRCN models using datasets like UCF11, UCF50, and DynTex. The LRCN model consistently outperforms ConvLSTM, and the paper suggests future research should refine methodologies by exploring various CNN and LSTM architectures and optimizing parameters (Benzyane et al. 2023). A new method called Quantum Hopfield Neural Network (QHopNN) enhances key recovery in symmetric cipher by using quantum principles like superposition and entanglement, resulting in improved accuracy and efficiency in decrypting data. (Khan et al. 2022). The document examines smart healthcare CPS, combining physical and digital elements for effective patient care, emphasizes AI, ML, and DL in managing future 6G networks proposes ensemble deep learning to detect unauthorized EHR access and describes a Cognitive Blockchain system with an IoT module for threat monitoring and analysis (Hariharasitaraman et al. 2024). This work introduces a Neural network-based PCA methodology for advanced facial emotion recognition, effective even with moving objects, blurring, and masks. The model, validated through confusion matrix computations, achieves high performance with 98.34% accuracy, 98.34% sensitivity, 97.34% recall, and a 98.45% F-score, outperforming existing models. (Sakthi et al. 2024).

QR codes are used everywhere, particularly Many healthcare IoT applications utilise QR codes for data-labeling and quick transfer of clinical data for Quick diagnosis of report sharing among healthcare system. However, the rise of open-source QR Scanners creates QR Codes that are easily duplicated, and tampered with (Velumani et al, 2023) presented a novel (n,n) secret-sharing scheme based on Nonnegative Matrix Factorization (NMF) for secured transfer of QR codes sharing and reconstruction by using the Super Resolution Convolutional Neural Network (SRCNN). They claimed their proposed scheme is an alternative to the existing polynomial and visual cryptography-based schemes. Their experimental results and theoretical analyses showed a potential solution for the secured exchange of QR codes with different error correction levels. The experimental results show that an adversary must try 2^{58} additional combinations of shares.

(Manikanda et al, 2023, Chapter III) Discussed a technique for detecting hate texts in social media reviews, specifically on the Twitter dataset on any language. Their proposed method utilized the Improved Principal Component Analysis (IPCA) for feature extraction and a Modified Convolutional Neural Network (MCNN) for classifying the text into "HATE" and "NON-HATE" category levels. Their experiments proved their method had a high level of accuracy and better performance concerning parameters like precision, recall, and F-measure compared to other state-of-the-art methods.

The research aims to enhance cybersecurity by developing an intelligent system to identify and prevent malicious activities targeting web servers. Traditional methods often struggle to keep up with evolving threats, making it crucial to explore advanced solutions. In this work, we use Sequential Generative Adversarial Network, a sophisticated form of artificial intelligence, to teach the system to recognize patterns associated with web server exploits. By doing so, we aim to improve detection accuracy and create a more adaptable defense against emerging cyber threats. The work unfolds in stages, starting with research and analysis to understand existing vulnerabilities. We then collect and preprocess data to train the SeqGAN model, designing it to differentiate between normal and malicious behaviors. The model is thoroughly evaluated and integrated into web server systems, with ongoing optimization and fine-tuning based on real-world testing.

3. REQUIREMENT ARTIFACTS AND METHODOLOGY

3.1 Requirement Artifacts

Successfully executing any research requires careful consideration of various requirements, including hardware, software, data, functions, performance, security, and user experience. In the context of web server log attacks, these requirements are crucial for developing a robust system capable of effectively investigating security incidents and enhancing network security measures. Hardware and software requirements encompass the necessary infrastructure and tools for data collection, analysis, and visualization. In contrast, specific work requirements outline the data needed for analysis and the functions required for an effective model. Additionally, performance and security requirements ensure the system's efficiency, reliability, and integrity, while look and feel requirements focus on providing users with an intuitive and visually appealing interface. Understanding and addressing these requirements are essential for the successful implementation and deployment of the model.

Hardware and Software Requirements

Hardware Requirements

The following experimental set-up is required like a desktop or laptop computer to run the required software. It should have a modern multi-core processor to guarantee effective computation. A minimum of 8GB of RAM is required for optimal performance; however, larger datasets may require more RAM. You should also make sure that your computer has enough disk space to store datasets, code files, and any generated models or results.

Software Requirements

The experiment starts using an operating system such as Windows, macOS, or Linux. With the Python version 3. x installed. Use an Integrated Development Environment (IDE) like PyCharm, Jupyter Notebook, or Visual Studio Code for writing and running Python code. Additionally, install Python libraries such as NumPy, pandas, matplotlib, seaborn, scikit-learn, Tensor Flow, and Keras for tasks related to data manipulation, visualization, and machine learning. In a study conducted by K. Garg et al in 2024, the authors presented a security system that utilizes the features of Web 3.0, allowing users to independently view, publish, and own content. Their system integrates a blockchain, semantic communication, edge computing, and artificial intelligence to create value networks that support participatory decision-making. They proposed a unified blockchain-semantic ecosystem for Web 3.0 with wireless edge intelligence, featuring a semantic proof technique built on Oracle, an adaptable Deep Reinforcement Learning-based sharding technique, and a blockchain-based semantic exchange architecture that tokenizes semantic data into non-fungible tokens (NFT) for semantic exchange. Additionally, the use of Zero-Knowledge Proof enables fair and private trading of semantic information, setting it apart from traditional NFT marketplaces.

Specific Work Requirements

Data Requirement

- Dataset: Obtain a comprehensive dataset containing the feature samples for training and testing the classification model.
- Features: Identify relevant features within the dataset that can make the model effective.
- Data Preprocessing: Implement preprocessing techniques to clean and preprocess the raw data, including tasks such as text normalization, tokenization, and feature extraction.
- Data Splitting: Divide the dataset into training and testing sets to evaluate the classification model's performance accurately.

Functions Requirement

- Real-Time Exploit Detection: The system should swiftly identify and classify potential web server exploits in real-time, offering a proactive defense against evolving threats.
- Sequential Pattern Recognition: It must possess the capability to understand and recognize the sequential patterns associated with normal web server activities and those indicative of malicious exploits.
- Adaptive Learning Mechanism: The system should continuously learn from historical and real-time data, adapting to new exploit patterns and ensuring its ability to evolve alongside emerging cybersecurity threats.
- Integration with Existing Web Servers: Seamless integration with diverse web server environments, ensuring compatibility and minimal disruption to existing systems.
- Compatibility with Different Web Server Technologies: The ability to work seamlessly with various web server technologies, irrespective of the underlying architecture, ensuring versatility and broad applicability.

Performance and Security Requirements

To ensure the effectiveness of the classification model, it is crucial to achieve high accuracy and robustness in distinguishing between real and fake web attacks, while minimizing both false positives and false negatives. Additionally, the system should be designed to efficiently handle a large volume of data and be able to scale to accommodate increasing workload demands. Security measures must be implemented to protect sensitive data during model training, testing, and deployment, in adherence to data privacy regulations and best practices. Furthermore, the system should be built to be resilient against adversarial attacks and attempts to circumvent the web server attacks classification mechanism.In swift, this work aims to fortify digital defenses by advanced artificial intelligence through Sequential Generative Adversarial Networks (SGANs) to empower our system with the ability to recognize and combat web server vulnerabilities. This model will learn from historical and real-time data, honing its ability to discern normal web server activities from potentially malicious exploits. The goal is real-time identification, offering proactive protection against emerging threats. Key functionalities include sequential pattern recognition and seamless integration with diverse web server environments. The system will detect exploits promptly and adapt to new patterns, ensuring it stays ahead of evolving cyber threats. Ultimately, this work seeks to contribute to a more secure online environment by deploying an intelligent defense system that understands the nuances of web server activities and effectively safeguards against exploits.

The proposed model in this paper incorporates the following key elements:

- Recognizing the unique characteristics of log data, the model adopts Long-Short-Term Memory (LSTM) as the fundamental building block for both the generator and discriminator. This strategic choice helps mitigate the issue of error accumulation, which tends to grow exponentially with the length of the text. The LSTM structure enhances the model's effectiveness and robustness compared to single-layer alternatives.
- To enhance the generator's performance, the model introduces various loss functions, including regular loss and variety loss. These are incorporated into both the pre-training and training processes, aiming to optimize the generator's overall capabilities.
- The model is specifically designed for handling weblogs, distinguishing it from other text generation scenarios. Substantial effort is dedicated to data pre-processing, where weblogs undergo conversion into vectors. Log data is treated as a series of time-related sequences during this data processing phase.

The dataset access log Apache web app is taken from the Apache access log server. The features of the dataset are IP address, date and time, GMT, request, status, size, user agent, country, and label. This model uses Python and the Keras library, which operates on TensorFlow. The model is flexible, with support for both CPU and GPU processing. After the dataset is preprocessed, it is divided into two parts: 70% is used for training, and the remaining 30% is used for testing. i.e. 26065 instances of the dataset are used as training data and the remaining 11171 instances as testing data. Binary cross-entropy is employed as the loss function to evaluate the model, and the Adam optimizer is also used to reduce this loss as much as possible.

3.2 Methodology

This work aims to contribute to the ongoing efforts to secure web servers. We propose using a cutting-edge artificial intelligence technique called Sequential Generative Adversarial Networks. These networks are designed to understand the sequential patterns inherent in web server activities, providing a more dynamic and adaptive approach to detecting exploits. By leveraging SGANs, we aim to enhance the accuracy and efficiency of web server exploit detection, ultimately bolstering the resilience of online systems against a spectrum of cyber threats. This introduction sets the stage for our exploration into advanced cybersecurity, where the fusion of artificial intelligence and web server protection becomes paramount for a secure digital landscape.

The core area lies in using advanced artificial intelligence, specifically Sequential Generative Adversarial Networks, to strengthen the security of web servers. This involves developing a system to learn and understand the sequential patterns associated with potential web server exploits. In simpler terms, we're focusing on creating a smart defense mechanism. By training our system with data that reflects normal and malicious behaviors on web servers, we aim to enable it to recognize and respond to unusual or harmful activities in real-time. This innovative approach strives to enhance the accuracy and adaptability of detecting web server exploits, contributing to a more resilient and secure online environment.

This traditional approach involves creating signatures or patterns characteristic of known web server exploits. These signatures are then used to scan incoming data or network traffic for matching patterns. This approach is like recognizing a specific fingerprint associated with a known criminal. Signature-based detection relies on predefined markers of known exploits. While effective against well-established threats, it may struggle with novel or evolving exploits that don't match existing signatures.

Anomaly-based detection focuses on establishing a baseline of normal behavior for a web server. Deviations from this baseline are flagged as potential exploits. This method doesn't rely on predefined signatures but instead identifies unusual patterns or activities. Picture a security guard who knows the usual flow of activity in a building. Anomaly-based detection works by flagging behaviors that deviate significantly from the established norm. While adaptable to new threats, it may generate false positives if normal behaviors change over time.

This approach involves training machine learning models, such as neural networks, on historical data to learn patterns associated with web server exploits. The model can then generalize this knowledge to identify potential threats in real time. Imagine a detective learning from past crime data to recognize patterns of criminal behavior. Machine learning-based detection aims to create a dynamic system capable of adapting to new exploits by learning from historical and real-time data. It offers a middle ground between the specificity of signature-based and the adaptability of anomaly-based approaches.

The suggested model combines two deep recurrent neural models, a discriminator and a generator, with an adversarial recursive neural network. While the discriminator is trained to distinguish between generated and real data correctly, adversarial training intends to make the generator generate identical data. The pre-processing, data augmentation, and data classification are the components that make up the model's framework. Web log data is examined and processed in the data pre-processing module, primarily focusing on the URL information. The data is then mapped to a character library, and unnecessary information is removed, resulting in a character set used for training. The average length of log samples is calculated, and then the data is organized into the context of the LSTM time series.

The Figure 1. To illustrate the need for the LSTM technique in deep learning, the LSTM (Long Short-Term Memory) cell is a recurrent neural network used for sequential data. The LSTM cell consists of several components that work together to process the input data and update the hidden state and memory of the network. The diagram of an LSTM cell is broken down into various parts. The previous cell state (C_{t-1}) is located on the left side of the diagram, while the previous hidden state (H_{t-1}) is located below it. The new input data at the current time step (X_t) is located at the bottom of the diagram. The first gate in the LSTM cell is the forget gate (F_t), which decides what information should be kept or discarded from the cell state and uses a sigmoid activation function. The input gate (I_t) decides which values from the input should be updated in the cell state and uses a sigmoid activation function. The candidate memory (C~_t) is a tanh-activated layer that creates a vector of new candidate values that could be added to the state. The output gate (O_t) decides the next hidden state and uses a sigmoid activation function. Finally, the updated memory (C_t) and hidden state (H_t) are located on the right side of the diagram, reflecting the processed input data. As indicated by the arrows in the diagram, the flow of information through the various gates and transformations results in the updated memory and hidden states.

Figure 1. A generic Structure of the LSTM Model

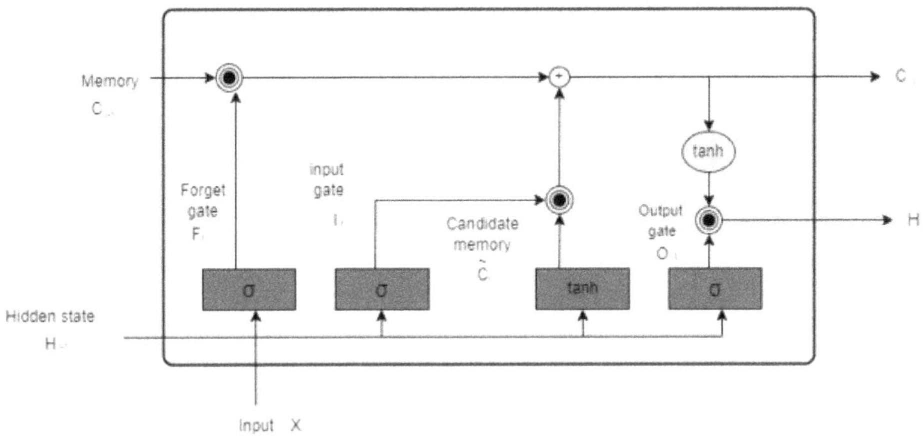

Figure 2 depicts processes related to machine learning or artificial intelligence. The left diagram represents a Generative Adversarial Network (GAN). It illustrates the training process of a discriminator (D) using both actual data (green circle labeled “True data”) and generated data (red circles labeled “G Generate”) as inputs, as indicated by the arrow labeled “Train D”. On the other hand, the right diagram illustrates a Reinforcement Learning (RL) process. It showcases an agent learning by taking actions in different states and receiving rewards. The upward pointing arrow labeled "Policy Gradient" suggests an optimization or learning step. These diagrams demonstrate how AI can learn from actual and generated data and enhance its decision-making abilities over time. The data augmentation module is based on Generative Adversarial Networks. The generator and discriminator both use the LSTM network. In the training process, the generator and real data output are input into the discriminator, turning the training into a zero-sum game. The aim is to get a Nash equilibrium, where the discriminator cannot tell the difference between the data produced by the generator and the real data.

Figure 2. A Customized Structure of the SeqGAN

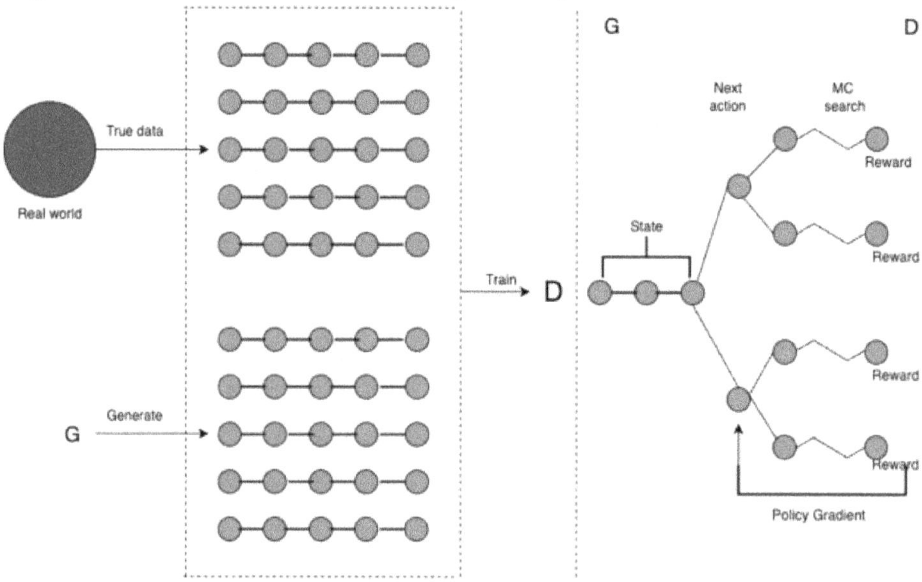

It is a particular kind of recurrent neural network comprising several memory blocks with input, output, and forget gates and memory cells within each memory block. The calculation of the input gate, forget gate, cells gate, output gate, and final output for the forward pass.

- Input Gate: The input gate accepts the current input and all cells in the same block from the previous moment. A character from the log data is put into the input gate, which treats the output characters before the current character as input. The input gate selectively records additional information from the log data and puts it into the cell state.

- Forget Gate: Similar to the input gate, the forget gate also takes inputs related to the cell's state. Its function is to selectively forget frequency, trend, and length information.
- Cell: The product of the input and the input gate, along with the product of the forget gate and the output of the cell from the previous moment, are the two inputs the cell takes. This process generates the output function of a cell.
- Output Gate: The output gate takes inputs from the current moment, and all cells are in the same block at the current moment. The output gate determines which parts of the next generated character will be output for log data.

This completes the forward pass. Similarly, the backward pass also involves calculating gradients for each part to obtain the final output function. The entire process is essential for LSTM to effectively generate log data sequentially.

A. Data Preprocessing

Each log generally contains the following information: Host, Ident, User, Date, Request, Status, bytes, Agent, etc. Once the weblog datasets have been analyzed, it can be seen that the Uniform Resource Location of the weblog includes most of the information needed, such as the host address, the access path, the parameters, etc. It is, therefore, necessary to pre-process the log data and obtain the URL sample data, including the information mentioned.

B. Pre-training

During adversarial training, the discriminator becomes too strong, which results in a gradient that can't be used to improve the generator. Pre-training can make the generator more robust and allow the generated data to be available.

C. Data Generator and the Discriminator

The LSTM cells input a sample of the data while getting the output and the state of the preceding moment. A sample of the data is fed into each LSTM cell, which simultaneously receives the output and the state of the previous moment. The fully connected layer receives the output from the cell with LSTM and shares weights throughout the time steps. The output is fed to the discriminator during the training process. During the adversarial training, it was observed that the discriminator could get too strong and a gradient could not be applied to improve the generator.

The model's training procedure can be explained as follows:

- Initialize generator and discriminator.
- Pre-training generator based on weblogs by maximum likelihood estimation.
- Use generator parameters of pre-training to update generator parameters for log completion.
- Collect the generated web log data by the generator as negative and real data as positive samples.
- Train discriminator based on cross-entropy function.
- Iterate and update the parameters of the generator.
- Until the convergence is realized.

The hyperparameters in SeqGAN are set as follows: The batch size is 32, Adam is used as the optimizer, and ReLU and Sigmoid are used to set the activation function. The generator and discriminator's learning rate is 0.0001. Additionally, the data generation system completed 500 training rounds and 100 pre-training rounds.

4. EXPERIMENTAL ANALYSIS AND RESULTS DISCUSSION

To assess the performance of an Apache web app dataset using a SeqGAN model with specific hyperparameters, the model was configured as a Generative Adversarial Network (GAN) designed for sequence data. The following hyperparameters were set for the SeqGAN model: a batch size of 32, Adam optimizer, ReLU for hidden layers and Sigmoid for the output layer as the activation function, and a learning rate of 0.0001 for both the generator and discriminator. The model underwent two stages of training: pre-training, where the generator and discriminator were pre-trained for 100 rounds to initialize the model parameters, and adversarial training, where the generator and discriminator were trained adversarial for 500 rounds. The dataset was generated using a separate data generation system. The performance of the SeqGAN model was evaluated using appropriate metrics such as accuracy, precision, recall, and F1 score. The experiment aimed to assess how well the SeqGAN model with the specified hyperparameters performed on the Apache web app dataset, and the results could provide insights into the effectiveness of these hyperparameters and inform future adjustments for optimizing the model's performance. Analyzing logs of web attacks is an effective method for spotting malicious behaviour. In the past, the most common method to identify such threats was through machine learning models trained on labeled data. Deep learning models have recently been introduced to analyze logs, specifically in classifying weblogs. The main challenge lies in insufficient labelled data for training the model. Obtaining weblogs with precise labels identifying specific data categories is challenging.

Fig.3 illustrates the correlation of the features of the dataset. The experimental findings are presented based on the heatmap in the image: Strong positive correlations are observed, with a perfect positive correlation (coefficients close to 1) along the diagonal from the top left to the bottom right, which is expected as any variable will have a perfect positive correlation with itself. Moreover, 'Country' and 'detected' exhibit a relatively high positive correlation of about 0.73. The heatmap indicates No strong negative correlations, with most of them being close to zero or slightly negative. Several pairs of variables depict weak or no significant correlation, as represented by cells colored light blue or white. These findings suggest that although some variables in the dataset show strong correlations, others exhibit weak or no significant relationships. This information can help comprehend the data structure and guide further analysis.

Figure 3. Heatmap of the features present in the dataset

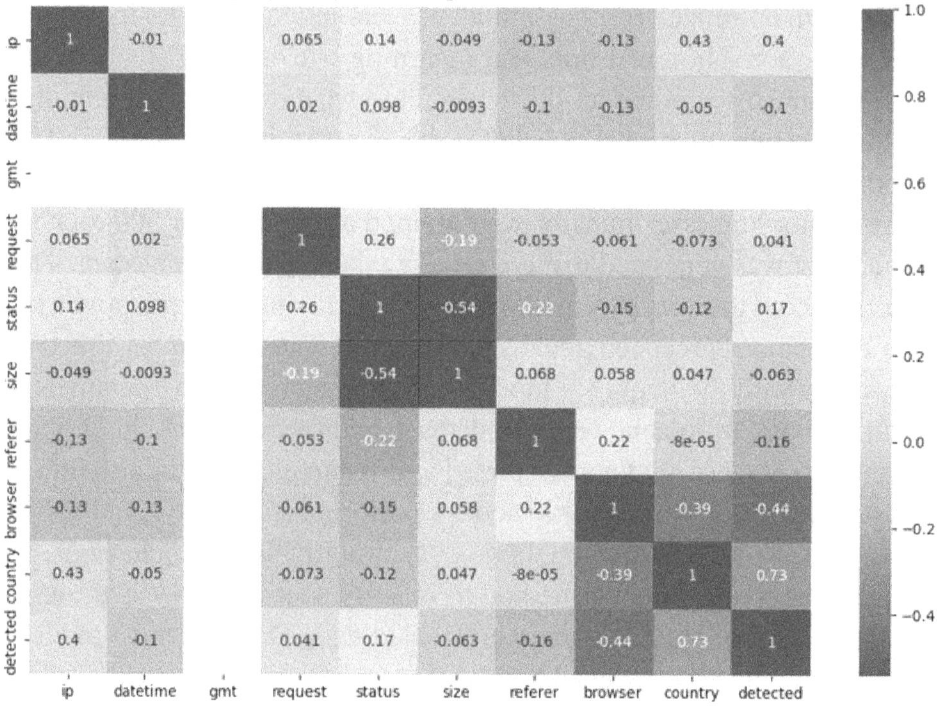

Figure 4 displays the training loss and testing loss values across different epochs in a given batch. The training loss (blue line with circles) starts high and decreases steadily as the number of epochs increases, indicating that the model is learning and improving its performance on the training data. The testing loss (orange line with squares) starts lower than the training loss but increases as the number of epochs progresses, suggesting that the model may be overfitting. When a model learns the training data too well, to the point where it performs poorly on new, unseen data, it is said to be overfitting. The divergence between the training loss and testing loss over time suggests the occurrence of overfitting. Valuable insights into the model's performance can be obtained from these findings, which can guide further adjustments to improve its ability to generalize to new data.

Figure 4. Training loss and Testing loss values

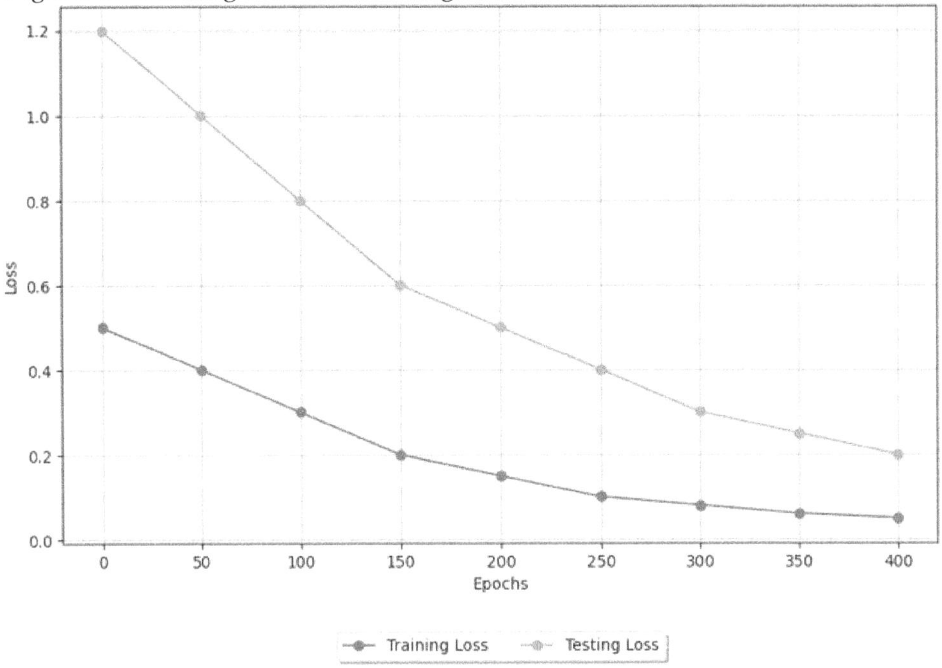

The concepts of True Positive, False Negative, False Positive, and True Negative in the context of a classification model's predicted class versus the actual class are explained by the diagram. The formulas for Accuracy, Recall, Precision, and F1 measure are also provided. This diagram can be instrumental in understanding the performance metrics of a classification model within the research context. The instances where predictions were correct (True Positives/TN) or incorrect (False Positives/FN) are delineated between Predicted Classes (Positive/Negative) against Actual Classes (Positive/Negative). Additionally, formulas for calculating Accuracy, Recall, Precision, and F1 measurements are offered, which are crucial for evaluating the effectiveness of classification models in research scenarios. In the dataset access log Apache web app, the models were tested. The results were encouraging, as indicated by Fig.5. The web server exploits can be identified with good accuracy by the suggested SeqGAN with LSTM model compared to the previous techniques, such as SVM, Random Forest, CNN, and Logistic Regression.

A higher accuracy indicates that the classifier model is likelier to detect web servers correctly exploits and non-exploits as non-exploits. The graph image compared the performance of five different models: SeqGAN with LSTM, SVM, Random Forest, CNN, and Logistic Regression. The performance evaluation was based on four metrics: Accuracy, Precision, Recall, and F1 Score. It was found that all models showed similar performance, with scores ranging from around 0.6 to 0.8 in all four metrics. It was observed that the others were not outperformed by any single model in this experiment due to similar performance across all metrics. Additionally, each model maintained relatively consistent performance across all four metrics, indicating robustness. These findings provide valuable insights into the comparative performance of these models and can guide further exploration and optimization.

Figure 5. Performance Analysis of Seq-GAN Vs. SVM, Random Forest, CNN, and Logistic Regression

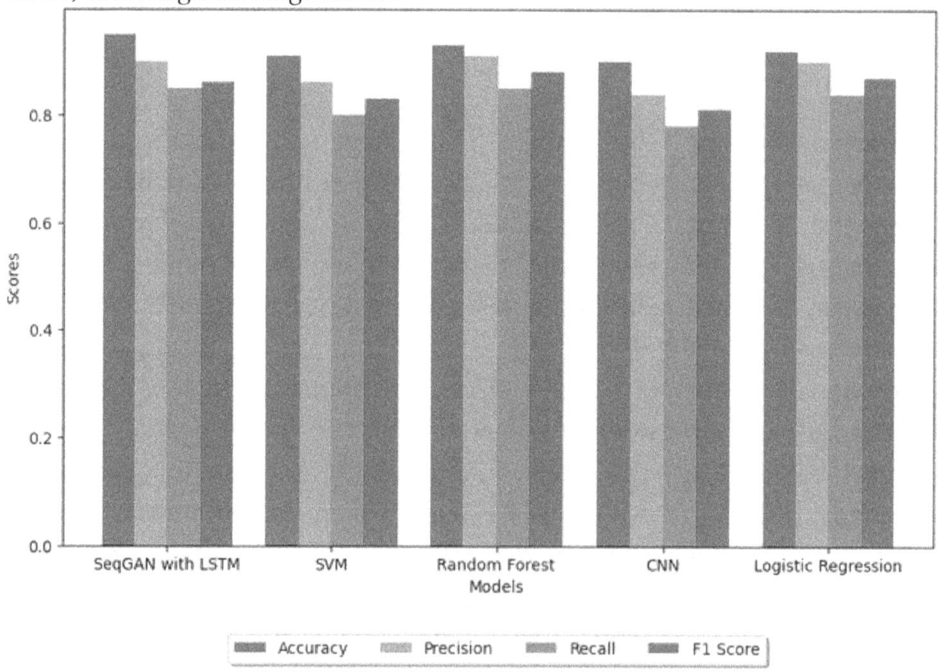

Traditional web server security measures often struggle to keep pace with the constantly evolving landscape of cyberattacks. Sequential Generative Adversarial Networks, a powerful AI model, offer a promising approach to detecting and mitigating these threats. This document outlines an experimental framework for leveraging SeqGANs to enhance web server security.

SeqGANs consist of two neural networks locked in a competitive learning process. In the case of the Generator, the network learns to generate data sequences (e.g., web requests) that mimic real-world attack patterns. In the case of the Discriminator, the network learns to distinguish between real attack sequences (from historical data) and fake sequences generated by the Generator. Through continuous training, the Generator becomes increasingly adept at crafting realistic attack sequences, while the Discriminator improves its ability to detect even subtle anomalies indicative of malicious activity. Training effective SeqGANs requires substantial amounts of high-quality attack data, which may not always be readily available, and ensuring the SeqGAN's resilience against adversarial attacks designed to evade detection is crucial. Experimenting with SeqGANs for web server security holds significant promise for enhancing threat detection capabilities. By leveraging the power of adversarial learning, this approach can stay ahead of attackers, providing a more robust and adaptive defense against evolving cyber threats.

5. CONCLUSION

In this study, weblogs were utilized to identify malicious behaviors. Due to the lack of weblogs with labels, a framework based on Generative Adversarial Networks was devised for web log data augmentation. An augmentation model was introduced within this framework to enhance the log data classification model's generalization capability, particularly in identifying malicious behaviors. The experiment demonstrated that a generator and discriminator based on Long Short-Term Memory and the devised pre-training process effectively achieved data augmentation, improving classification model performance.

5.1 Limitations/Constraints of the System

While promising to enhance web server security, the model encounters several limitations and constraints. Firstly, the system's effectiveness hinges on the quality and accessibility of labeled datasets containing instances of web attacks. The limited availability of diverse and comprehensive datasets may impede the model's generalization of various exploit patterns. Additionally, the implementation and training of Sequential Generative Adversarial Networks (SeqGANs) demand significant computational resources, including high-performance computing systems and GPUs. Constraints in these resources may hamper the scalability and efficiency of the system. Moreover, the inherent complexity of SeqGANs poses challenges in terms of model interpretability, making it difficult to discern the decision-making processes behind the model's predictions. Issues of overfitting, especially when trained on biased datasets, and susceptibility to adversarial attacks also threaten the system's efficacy. Furthermore, the necessity for continuous maintenance and updates to adapt to evolving cyber threats and potential complexities in integrating the system with existing web server environments introduces practical challenges. Addressing these limitations through robust data collection, efficient optimization, and proactive maintenance strategies is vital for ensuring the reliability and effectiveness of the web server exploit detection system.

5.2 Inferences

This work strives for a substantial enhancement in web server security by leveraging Sequential Generative Adversarial Networks (SeqGANs) for precise exploit detection. A pivotal outcome is the successful implementation of a real-time detection system, swiftly addressing potential web server exploits. Key work stages involve meticulous data collection, preprocessing, and the development of an advanced Generative Adversarial Network (GAN) featuring Long Short-Term Memory (LSTM) architecture. Performance is ensured through thorough model training, optimization, and evaluation utilizing metrics like accuracy and precision. Noteworthy achievements include a cutting-edge system with remarkable accuracy in detecting web server exploits, real-time threat response, adaptive learning capabilities, resource efficiency, and scalability. These outcomes collectively contribute to a more resilient and secure web server environment, effectively countering the dynamic landscape of cyber threats.

5.3 Future Enhancements

Future enhancements for the model could focus on augmenting the diversity and scale of the training datasets to bolster the model's ability to recognize a broader spectrum of exploit patterns. Incorporating datasets that cover a wide range of web attacks, including emerging threats, can enhance the system's adaptability and generalization. Furthermore, exploring advanced model architectures or incorporating additional machine-learning techniques could improve the system's overall performance. Addressing the interpretability challenge of SeqGANs remains a key area for future development, with efforts directed towards creating more transparent models to facilitate easier understanding and validation of the detection outcomes. Implementing robust mechanisms to mitigate adversarial attacks and enhance the system's resilience against malicious manipulation is another critical aspect for future research. Continuous research and development initiatives focusing on refining the system's integration processes, making them more streamlined and user-friendly, could contribute to easier deployment across diverse web server environments. Lastly, fostering collaboration with cybersecurity experts and industry practitioners can provide valuable insights into evolving threat landscapes, guiding the ongoing evolution of the work to stay at the forefront of web server exploit detection technology. These future enhancements aim to ensure the work's sustained effectiveness and relevance in dynamically changing cybersecurity scenarios.

REFERENCES

Al Hilmi, M. A., Cahyanto, K. A., & Mustamiin, M. (2020). Apache Web Server - Access Log Pre-processing for Web Intrusion Detection. IEEE Dataport. https://dx.doi.org/http://dx.doi.org/10.25126/jtiik.2022924107

Bengio, Y., Laufer, E., Alain, G., & Yosinski, J. (22--24 Jun 2014). Deep Generative Stochastic Networks Trainable by Backprop. In E. P. Xing & T. Jebara (Eds.), *Proceedings of the 31st International Conference on Machine Learning* (pp. 226–234)

Benzyane, M., Azrour, M., Zeroual, I., & Agoujil, S. (2023). Investigating the Influence of Convolutional Operations on LSTM Networks in Video Classification. *Data and Metadata, 2*, 152. DOI: 10.56294/dm2023152

Bhattacharjee, D., Chaki, R., & Sanyal, S. (2019). Security Applications of Generative Adversarial Networks. *RE:view.*

Dargaoui, S.. (2024). Applications of Blockchain in Healthcare: Review Study. In *IoT, Machine Learning and Data Analytics for Smart Healthcare*. CRC Press.

Doersch, C., Gupta, A., & Efros, A. A. (2015). Unsupervised visual representation learning by context prediction. In *Proceedings of the IEEE international conference on computer vision* (pp. 1422-1430). DOI: 10.1109/ICCV.2015.167

Garg, K., & Jattu, M. H. S and R. R. Subramanian, "An Integrated Platform for Virtual Ecosystems and Wireless Edge Computing for Web 3.0," *2024 Third International Conference on Intelligent Techniques in Control, Optimization and Signal Processing (INCOS)*, Krishnankoil, Virudhunagar district, Tamil Nadu, India, 2024, pp. 1-8, DOI: 10.1109/INCOS59338.2024.10527691

Goodfellow, I., Pouget-Abadie, J., Mirza, M., Xu, B., Warde-Farley, D., Ozair, S., & Bengio, Y. (2014). Generative adversarial nets. *Advances in Neural Information Processing Systems*, •••, 27.

Goseva-Popstojanova, K., Anastasovski, G., & Pantev, R. (2012, July). Classification of malicious Web sessions. In *2012 21st International Conference on Computer Communications and Networks (ICCCN)* (pp. 1-9). IEEE. DOI: 10.1109/ICCCN.2012.6289291

Hariharasitaraman, S., Mishra, N., & Vishnuvardhanan, D. (2024). QHopNN: Investigating quantum advantage in cryptanalysis using a quantum Hopfield neural network. *Physica Scripta*, *99*(8), 086002. DOI: 10.1088/1402-4896/ad5ed1

Hoang, X. D. (2021). Detecting common web attacks based on machine learning using web log. In *Advances in Engineering Research and Application:Proceedings of the International Conference on Engineering Research and Applications, ICERA 2020* (pp. 311-318). Springer International Publishing. DOI: 10.1007/978-3-030-64719-3_35

Hochreiter, S., & Schmidhuber, J. (1997). Long short-term memory. *Neural Computation*, *9*(8), 1735–1780. DOI: 10.1162/neco.1997.9.8.1735 PMID: 9377276

Husák, M., Velan, P., & Vykopal, J. (2015, August). Security monitoring of http traffic using extended flows. In *2015 10th International Conference on Availability, Reliability and Security* (pp. 258-265). IEEE. DOI: 10.1109/ARES.2015.42

Khan, M., Hariharasitaraman, S., Joshi, S., Jain, V., Ramanan, M., SampathKumar, A., & Elngar, A. A. (2022). A deep learning approach for facial emotions recognition using principal component analysis and neural network techniques. *The Photogrammetric Record*, *37*(180), 435–452. DOI: 10.1111/phor.12426

Khan, N., Abdullah, J., & Khan, A. S. (2017). Defending malicious script attacks using machine learning classifiers. *Wireless Communications and Mobile Computing*, *2017*(1), 5360472. DOI: 10.1155/2017/5360472

LeCun, Y., Bengio, Y., & Hinton, G. (2015). Deep learning. *nature*, *521*(7553), 436-444.

Liang, J., Zhao, W., & Ye, W. (2017, December). Anomaly-based web attack detection: a deep learning approach. In *Proceedings of the 2017 VI International Conference on Network, Communication and Computing* (pp. 80-85). DOI: 10.1145/3171592.3171594

Lin, Q., Zhang, H., Lou, J. G., Zhang, Y., & Chen, X. (2016, May). Log clustering based problem identification for online service systems. In *Proceedings of the 38th International Conference on Software Engineering Companion* (pp. 102-111). DOI: 10.1145/2889160.2889232

Lins, F., Damasceno, J., Silva, B., Medeiros, R., Souza, A., Teles, F., Aragao, D., Sousa, E., Rosa, N., Stephenson, B., Nezhad, H. M., & Li, J. (2012). Towards an approach to design and enforce security in web service composition. *International Journal of Web Engineering and Technology*, *7*(4), 323–357. DOI: 10.1504/IJWET.2012.050966

Manikandan, R., Hariharasitaraman, S., Ramkumar, S., & Gobinath, R. (2024). *Leveraging Deep Learning in Hate Speech Analysis on Social Platform.* In *Deep Learning for Smart Healthcare: Trends, Challenges and Applications* (1st ed.). Auerbach Publications. DOI: 10.1201/9781003469605-3

OWASP foundation. the Open Source Foundation for Application Security. (n.d.). Retrieved 24 July 2024, from https://owasp.org

Pan, Y., Sun, F., Teng, Z., White, J., Schmidt, D. C., Staples, J., & Krause, L. (2019). Detecting web attacks with end-to-end deep learning. *Journal of Internet Services and Applications, 10*(1), 1–22. DOI: 10.1186/s13174-019-0115-x

Sakthi, U., Alasmari, A., Girija, S. P., Senthil, P., Qamar, S., & Hariharasitaraman, S. (2024). Smart Healthcare Based Cyber Physical System Modeling by Block Chain with Cloud 6G Network and Machine Learning Techniques. *Wireless Personal Communications*, •••, 1–25. DOI: 10.1007/s11277-024-11243-8

Salakhutdinov, R. (2015). Learning deep generative models. *Annual Review of Statistics and Its Application*, *2*(1), 361–385. DOI: 10.1146/annurev-statistics-010814-020120

Seyyar, M. B., Çatak, F. Ö., & Gül, E. (2018). Detection of attack-targeted scans from the Apache HTTP Server access logs. *Applied computing and informatics, 14*(1), 28-36.

Sommer, R., & Paxson, V. (2010, May). *Outside the closed world: On using machine learning for network intrusion detection. In 2010 IEEE symposium on security and privacy*. IEEE.

Tasneem, S., Gupta, K. D., Roy, A., & Dasgupta, D. (2022, December). Generative Adversarial Networks (GAN) for Cyber Security: Challenges and Opportunities. In *Proceedings of the 2022 IEEE Symposium Series on Computational Intelligence* (pp. 4-7).

Timouhin, H., Amounas, F., & Azrour, M. (2023). New ECC-Based IoT Authentication Protocol for Securing RFID Systems. *SN Computer Science, 4*(6), 785. DOI: 10.1007/s42979-023-02220-2

Velumani, R., Sudalaimuthu, H., Choudhary, G., Bama, S., Jose, M. V., & Dragoni, N. (2022). Secured Secret Sharing of QR Codes Based on Nonnegative Matrix Factorization and Regularized Super Resolution Convolutional Neural Network. *Sensors (Basel), 22*(8), 2959. DOI: 10.3390/s22082959 PMID: 35458944

Yu, L., Zhang, W., Wang, J., & Yu, Y. (2017, February). Seqgan: Sequence generative adversarial nets with policy gradient. *Proceedings of the AAAI Conference on Artificial Intelligence, 31*(1), •••. DOI: 10.1609/aaai.v31i1.10804

Chapter 4

How to Ensure Data Integrity in Water Monitoring Networks Using IoT and Blockchain Technology

Khadija El-Moustaqim
https://orcid.org/0009-0007-9193-6638
Faculty of Sciences, Ibn Tofail University, Kenitra, Morocco

Jamal Mabrouki
https://orcid.org/0000-0002-3841-7755
Faculty of Science, Mohammed V University, Rabat, Morocco

Driss Hmouni
Faculty of Sciences, Ibn Tofail University, Kenitra, Morocco

ABSTRACT

Sustainable urban water management is crucial to address contamination, inefficient distribution, and water scarcity issues. Global problems include the allocation and management of water resources among users. It is imperative for the nation to keep an eye on how various users are utilizing seawater and to put clever strategies into place to minimize wa-

DOI: 10.4018/979-8-3693-6371-3.ch004

ter loss. Among the technology that has gained popularity over the past several years is blockchain. The potential to use this architecture in many different industries while including innovative concepts such as crowd-sensing, IoT, critical applications, and decision-making tools provides many options and methods for creating contemporary applications. This paper presents viewpoints on water management to support sustainable water management. It suggests a solution based on technology utilizing blockchain and Internet of Things sensors for accurate data reporting and effective water distribution.

1. INTRODUCTION

The monitoring of the quality of the water is a set of practical methods for the assessment and maintenance of the purity and water sources and water's safety in treatment and distribution systems up to the point of use by the final consumer (Afi et al., 2022; Bouchaala et al., 2017; Chen et al., 2022; Taïbi et al., 2003). Water quality monitoring involves collecting managing and evaluating the physical, chemical, and biological properties of water (El-Moustaqim, El Bakraoui, et al., 2023; El-Moustaqim, Mabrouki, et al., 2023; El-Moustaqim, Benchrifa, et al., 2024). Public and environmental health and safety are the main objectives of the assessment (El-Moustaqim et al., 1apr. J.-C.; El-Moustaqim, Mabrouki, et al., 2024; El-Moustaqim, Tallou, et al., 2024; Tallou et al., 2024). To meet these objectives, samples of water are taken from different positions and the depth of the source or waterbody (Lim et al., 2010). Beyond the benefits to end users and service providers, agricultural broad socio-economic impacts of water management systems (Fasani et al., 2018). The way we manage water resources is being revolutionized by the introduction of an in-tank water monitoring system. These sensors are strategically placed within the tank and measure the water level accurately in real-time (Plyusnina et al., 2019; Singh et al., 2023; Zhuang et al., 2023). The Water Monitoring System is a powerful system used to assess and manage various factors related to water resources. Its objective is to evaluate and guarantee water availability, quality, and responsible use (Dayana Priyadharshini et al., 2021; Kaloudas et al., 2021; Zhao et al., 2023). In addition, it will be possible to use this data to inform consumers and utilities about their water consumption, and to communicate this information to consumers and utilities transparently (Lim et al., 2010). One of the technologies that has gained popularity in recent years is blockchain (Mabrouki, Azoulay, et al., 2022a; Mabrouki, Fattah, et al., 2022; Mabrouki et al., 2023). The potential to use this architecture in so many different industries, while incorporating cutting-edge ideas like crowdsensing, the IoT (Mabrouki, Azoulay, et al., 2022b; Mabrouki et al., 2021; Yuliantini et al., 2019), and Serious Gaming and Decision Support Systems provides many opportunities and methods for creating contemporary applications (Tursynkhan et al., 2024). This emphasizes the need for more environmentally friendly water management procedures, and as international guidelines like the European Water Policy highlight, service providers must have accurate systems in place to gauge the water usage of their customers. Today, the IoT can provide energy-efficient sensor equipment embedded in water management systems (Passos et al., 2024; Vellela, 2024). Blockchain technology and Artificial Intelligence (AI) can be used to create significant synergies that will enable the development of secure, intelligent, and autonomous systems (Hatem et al., 2024; Mabrouki et al., 2024). Blockchain is an example of a distributed ledger, a database shared among several peer-to-peer network users without being supervised by a central oversight body (Brötzmann et al., 2024). In terms of blockchain, the ledger is set up exactly as its name implies: it is an ordered series of blocks, each of which has a list of transactions (Herzog & Herzog, 2024). The transactions are stored in a particular order within a block, which is essentially a structure with a header and a body. The entity that creates the blocks digitally signs and timestamps them (Satilmisoglu et al., 2024). Within a block, which is essentially a header and body structure, transactions are stored in a specific order. Blocks are signed with a digital signature and timestamped by the entity that creates them (Huseynov & Mitchell, 2023).

This paper provides a comprehensive analysis of blockchain-based water resources solutions. By synthesizing previous research, offering a fresh perspective on blockchain applications in the water resource sector, proposing new research directions, analyzing previous studies, and offering a fresh perspective on the advantages and disadvantages of the field, it can make a significant contribution to the existing body of knowledge. It can also provide a new theoretical framework for evaluating decentralized solutions in the hydrological field.

2. THE BLOCKCHAIN TECHNOLOGY

The need for trusted third parties in financial transactions, the drawbacks of traditional data storage systems, distributed ledgers, consensus algorithms, smart contracts, transparent tracking of recorded data and the definition of preconditions are some of the topics that were theoretically since the 1980s in financial applications (Alrammal et al., 2024; Tursynkhan et al., 2024). Blockchain is a shared, peer-to-peer ledger database technology that requires cryptographic security. The hash function is commonly used in blockchain to secure transactions, multi-agent consensus, and encrypt and safeguard data protocol validation (Xia et al., 2022). Many sectors are looking at blockchain solutions as a result of the widespread recognition of the value of blockchain (Chin et al., 2024). Despite this, there aren't many real-world blockchain technology applications for creating and managing water resources. Therefore, exploring how emerging blockchain technology can improve current water Management [28], [29] is crucial. Tokenization, smart contracts, smart supply chains, and smart compliance are examples of blockchain applications (Herzog & Herzog, 2024). The key characteristics of these applications include decentralization, immutability, transparency across the blockchain, security, and resistance to tampering (Ressi et al., 2024). Many blockchain applications, including decentralized banking, Intelligent Supply Chain, Commodity Trade, Insurers, Intelligent Health and Legal, rely on smart contracts as their underlying technology as **Fig. 1** illustrates.

Figure 1. **The various uses of blockchain technology.**

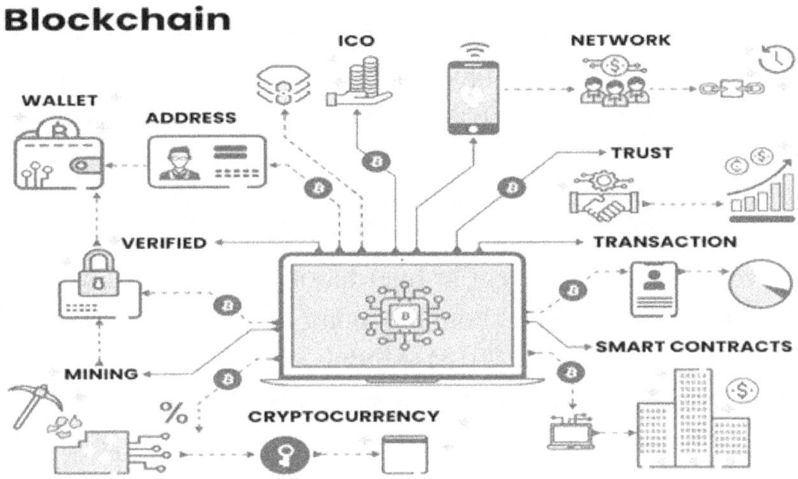

A smart contract does not require an intermediary (Chang et al., 2021; Rani et al., 2024). On the blockchain, there are four main categories of distributed or decentralised networks. Anyone can join public, permissionless blockchain networks. Every single blockchain participant has the right to read, update, and verify the blockchain (Yang et al., 2023). Today, energy-efficient embedded sensing devices can be made available through the Internet of Things (IoT). In addition, while low power wide area networks have made significant progress recently, these systems rely on centralized architectures that are often overseen by the service provider, limiting the number of stakeholders involved in the water management process (Hu & Demir, 2021). The integration of blockchain technologies into Internet of Things systems has received increasing attention in recent years (Kovalenko, 2024; Tursynkhan et al., 2024). As a result, they maintain public access to the remaining data while controlling access to specific data kept on the blockchain. Partner system members can verify when confidential transactions performed through the use of smart contracts (Akinbi et al., 2022). Hybrid blockchains, for instance, can maintain the privacy of bank-owned money while enabling common access to digital currency. Consortium blockchain networks are run by multiple organizations working together (Li et al., 2022).

3. AI AND BLOCKCHAIN TECHNOLOGY IN WATER MONITORING

Supply systems with intelligent water management maximize water resource utilization and service quality. The Internet of Things (IoT) allows the integration of several technologies to store and analyze data in real-time from various sources (Mabrouki, Azoulay, et al., 2022b; Mabrouki et al., 2021; Uhlemann et al., 2017). It can be challenging to foresee every operational event in Internet of Things-based systems and to determine how managers should respond in each circumstance (Bedi et al., 2018; Sørensen et al., 2015). Models of the operational processes based on fixed flows are created using traditional workflows. Declarative procedures offer a flexible approach that can be suitable for handling water systems (Akinbi et al., 2022). By providing sophisticated data analysis, predictive modeling, and decision-making algorithms, the integration of AI enhances the capabilities of the Internet of Things (Meng et al., 2023; Plyusnina et al., 2019). AI algorithms enable more effective and responsive water management by analyzing large, complicated data sets, finding trends, and predicting system behavior. IoT and AI work together to improve the monitoring and management of water treatment operations. It makes it possible to create intelligent, flexible systems that can learn and continuously improve performance (Li et al., 2022). IoT is used in water management to monitor and control water supply systems **(Fig. 2)**. As a result of climate change and global population growth, the demand for quality water is increasing, prompting the development of innovative water policies.

Figure 2. **Application of Blockchain for water monitoring.**

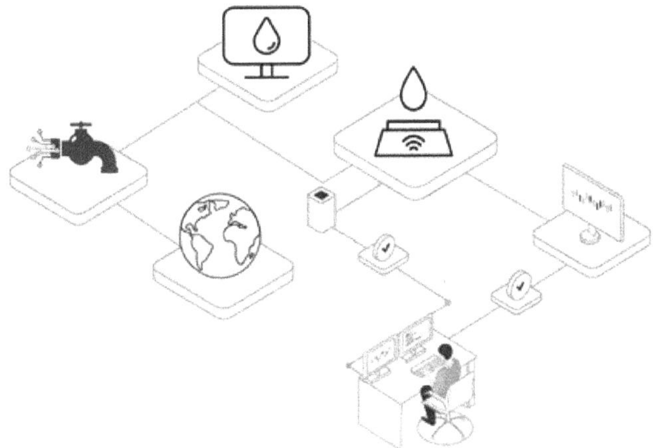

The use of blockchain technology in smart agriculture, agricultural insurance, and food supply systems. The difficulties of accurately documenting smallholder farmers' transactions are discussed, additionally, the ecosystem using blockchain technology in the food sector is created (Dada et al., 2024). Effective water management is essential in the agricultural sector, and in this work, we have developed an intelligent agricultural water management system (El-Moustaqim, Mabrouki, et al., 2024). IoT and remote monitoring technologies are being applied to the current water management infrastructure. This is a highly effective way of managing water resources and delivering water (Davenport & Kalakota, 2019; Said et al., 2020). Transparency can be established with blockchain technology, a decentralized system that guarantees water is distributed equally over large geographic areas. In reality, the procedure can be made entirely free of any centralized organization or middleman distributor agency that is in charge of providing water alone (Rane et al., 2023). Instead, a Blockchain-based platform for peer-to-peer communication and easy engagement between parties to debate water conservation, preservation, and distribution can be developed. This platform would include consumers, corporations, and governments as participants (Saab et al., 2017). Water pollution can be reduced by utilizing the Internet of Things and blockchain. It is possible to use automated sensors to detect contamination, measure its intensity, and alert water authorities (Prasad et al., 2015). Water utilities can use blockchain and IoT to find leaks and broken pipes, and reduce water waste. By ensuring transparency, security, and decentralized processes for its effective use, blockchain technology's the potential to revolutionize the management of water utilities completely. Everyone should use water wisely; blockchain technology can provide the necessary push in that direction (Jan et al., 2021).

4. SMART WATER QUALITY CONTRÔLE

The idea of using automatic smart sensors to identify water pollutants in water resources and alert water managers to current pollution levels is a very good one (Antonacci et al., 2021; Boron et al., 2020; Vargas-Estrada et al., 2020). In addition to measuring pollution levels, these sensors can alert the relevant authorities to the need for corrective action. In addition, these sensors can detect water leaks caused by burst pipes, which can significantly minimize water waste (Kumar Jha et al., 2018). Traditional methods of measuring water quality have been enhanced by developments in sensor technology. Within these systems, trained personnel began to use portable sensors to measure certain water parameters in the field (Hara & Singh, 2021; Nandimandalam & Gude, 2019; Wasito et al., 2019). Smart water management encompasses a wide range of data-driven optimization techniques. It covers every step to improve efficiency (**Table 1**), reliability, and sustainability from managing water bodies to distributing and using water (Brötzmann et al., 2024; Herzog & Herzog, 2024). Continuous data monitoring and analysis with sensors and actuators, a specific IoT-focused smart environment is included in a smart water supply (Sriyono, 2020). Wherever ledger immutability, trusted data transparency and dissemination, smart contracts, smart compliance, and tokenization could be useful, blockchain technology plays a crucial role. Ongoing reporting to relevant stakeholders is required to monitor water quality, quantity, low rates and infrastructure issues. Real-time data analytics will also support this monitoring (Dogo et al., 2019).

Table 1. Blockchain for an efficient Water management system.

Water security		
Water supply	**Water efficiency**	**Drought planning**
• Water monitoring and management • Micropayments for water meter donations	• Blockchain enabled peer-to-peer trading of excess • Cryptocurrency-enabled smart meters	• Precipitation intensity monitoring and forecasting • Automated crop insurance for drought periods

Water quality data, treatment processes, and regulatory compliance are all recorded remotely and in real-time. This includes automated and semi-automated contamination testing at every stage collecting, cleaning, and delivering water, various levels of disinfection, and other quality criteria (Hu & Demir, 2021). The Smart Compliance System and the Smart Contracts System work together. Real-time data exchange and automated documentation are common between the parties involved (Vellela, 2024). Blockchain's intelligent supply chain employs digital tokenization as a useful tool. Water can be recognized as a communal or public utility that is overseen by municipal, state, federal, and private organizations or partnerships (Alrammal et al., 2024). Water or service quality and quantity consumed are the data points that intelligent regulation and metering used to initiate automated billing and invoicing (Chin et al., 2024). Beyond water, which is used for inventory control and automated replenishment and water supply system functions, smart contracts can be used to help manage the supply chain of any utility, including energy supply, back-up generators, tools, water quality testing and monitoring equipment, replacement pipes, replacement fittings, and tools (Passos et al., 2024; Tursynkhan et al., 2024).

5. BLOCKCHAIN APPLICATION

Compared to the methods currently in use, blockchain can help water sector organizations manage reconciliation and accounting even more efficiently for record-keeping purposes (Saab et al., 2017). The Blockchain offers water quality recording in distributed, tamper-proof system data.

Every step of the process, from raw sensor data and anomaly identification to final analytical reports, relies on the immutability of the data collected (Alharbi et al., 2021). Blockchain can help advance environmental sustainability efforts when used in conjunction with the cloud and the Internet of Things (Hu & Demir, 2021). Society's progress is being accelerated by new emerging technologies such as blockchain, big data, artificial intelligence (AI), the Internet of Things (IoT), and machine learning (ML), which are rapidly replacing traditional frameworks (Rani et al., 2024). More specifically, a distributed ledger, often known as a blockchain or blockchain, is a constantly evolving digital data framework connected by mutually accepted standard protocols (Hatem et al., 2024).

Recent literature has called for blockchain technology to address distribution issues, mitigate risk, and proactively monitor the water management system. The paper by **Satilmisoglu, T. K et al.** (Satilmisoglu et al., 2024) evaluates the viability and practicality of blockchain applications for water management, outlines their possible use cases, and defines their current condition. To verify the theoretical advantages, solve issues with scalability and interoperability, and combine blockchain technology with real-time data networks for sustainable water management techniques, the report also urges additional empirical research. The potential application of blockchain technology in the management of scarce resources, such as water, is addressed by **Edy Sriyono** (Sriyono, 2020) to ensure environmental sustainability. From his studies, he found that these applications could enhance the current water management system's smooth integration by establishing firm agreements based on blockchain and considering automated workflows, implementing blockchain technology should ensure that individuals and other economic actors trust, understand, and account for each other. Blockchain technology is used by **Liu, Y. et al.** (Liu & Shang, 2022) to address the problem of trading agricultural water rights. Supporting an intelligent contract and application, a covenant chain and the useful consensus technique of Byzantine Fault Tolerance (PBFT). This study reduces the time required for trade confirmations and provides a reliable and secure platform that can handle large numbers of users. Transaction cost reduction and system efficiency improvement, the mechanism for trading agricultural water rights has been modernized.

6. CONCLUSION

This paper offers a comprehensive review of earlier investigations on the application of blockchain technology to hydrological problems. The investigation reveals that blockchain applications in hydrology are still in their infancy, despite their apparent promise. There is a notable gap between the theoretical advantages and practical uses, as seen by the absence of pilot programs and real-world applications. The management of water resources could be enhanced by blockchain technology, which presents interesting opportunities. However, to realize its full potential and be more broadly used, the problems this assessment has brought to light need to be fixed. Further empirical study, more financially viable blockchain technologies, reliable data sources, and enhanced system interoperability are all need to achieve this. With the advancement of technology and the exploration of new use cases, blockchain holds great promise for contributing significantly to the achievement of sustainable water security and management.

REFERENCES

Afi, C., Hallam, J., Mimouni, A., Msanda, F., & Ait Aabd, N. (2022). Saline Water Irrigation Effect on Oil Yield and Quality of Argan Trees Domesticated in Laâyoune, Morocco. *Environmental Sciences Proceedings*, *16*(1), 1. Advance online publication. DOI: 10.3390/environsciproc2022016045

Akinbi, A., MacDermott, Á., & Ismael, A. M. (2022). A systematic literature review of blockchain-based Internet of Things (IoT) forensic investigation process models. *Forensic Science International Digital Investigation*, *42-43*, 301470. DOI: 10.1016/j.fsidi.2022.301470

Alharbi, N., Althagafi, A., Alshomrani, O., Almotiry, A., & Alhazmi, S. (2021). A Blockchain Based Secure IoT Solution for Water Quality Management. *2021 International Congress of Advanced Technology and Engineering (ICOTEN)*, 1-8. DOI: 10.1109/ICOTEN52080.2021.9493474

Alrammal, M., Abu-Amara, F., Bin Awang Ismail, Z., & Nadeem, M. (2024). Blockchain Technology for Sustainable Management of Electricity and Water Consumption. *Engineering Proceedings*, *59*, 1–12.

Antonacci, A., Zappi, D., Giardi, M. T., & Scognamiglio, V. (2021). Photosynthesis-based biosensors for environmental analysis of herbicides. *Case Studies in Chemical and Environmental Engineering*, *4*, 100157. DOI: 10.1016/j.cscee.2021.100157

Bedi, G., Venayagamoorthy, G. K., Singh, R., Brooks, R. R., & Wang, K.-C. (2018). Review of Internet of Things (IoT) in Electric Power and Energy Systems. *IEEE Internet of Things Journal*, *5*(2), 847-870. *IEEE Internet of Things Journal*. Advance online publication. DOI: 10.1109/JIOT.2018.2802704

Boron, I., Juárez, A., & Battaglini, F. (2020). Portable Microalgal Biosensor for Herbicide Monitoring. *ChemElectroChem*, *7*(7), 1623–1630. DOI: 10.1002/celc.202000210

Bouchaala, L., Charchar, N., & Gherib, A. (2017). Ressources hydriques : Traitement et réutilisation des eaux usées en Algérie. *Algerian Journal of Arid Environment*, *7*(1), 84–95. DOI: 10.12816/0045919

Brötzmann, J., Panda, J., & Rüppel, U. (2024). Blockchain Technology as a Monitoring Tool for Sensor Data. In Skatulla, S., & Beushausen, H. (Eds.), *Advances in Information Technology in Civil and Building Engineering* (pp. 137–152). Springer International Publishing., DOI: 10.1007/978-3-031-35399-4_11

Chang, Y., Xu, J., & Ghafoor, K. Z. (2021). An IOT and Blockchain Approach for the Smart Water Management System in Agriculture. *Scalable Computing: Practice and Experience*, *22*(2), 2. Advance online publication. DOI: 10.12694/scpe.v22i2.1869

Chen, J., Zhang, H., Xue, J., Yuan, L., Yao, W., & Wu, H. (2022). Study on spatial distribution, potential sources and ecological risk of heavy metals in the surface water and sediments at Shanghai Port, China. *Marine Pollution Bulletin*, *181*, 113923. DOI: 10.1016/j.marpolbul.2022.113923 PMID: 35843161

Chin, H., Varbanov, P., Wan Alwi, S. R., Manan, Z., & Martincová, J. (2024). Blockchain-based Concept for Total Site Heat Integration : A Pinch-based Smart Contract Energy Management in Industrial Symbiosis. *Energy*, *305*, 132261. DOI: 10.1016/j.energy.2024.132261

Dada, M. A., Majemite, M. T., Obaigbena, A., Daraojimba, O. H., Oliha, J. S., Nwokediegwu, Z. Q. S., Dada, M. A., Majemite, M. T., Obaigbena, A., Daraojimba, O. H., Oliha, J. S., & Nwokediegwu, Z. Q. S. (2024). Review of smart water management : IoT and AI in water and wastewater treatment. *World Journal of Advanced Research and Reviews*, *21*(1), 1. Advance online publication. DOI: 10.30574/wjarr.2024.21.1.0171

Davenport, T., & Kalakota, R. (2019). The potential for artificial intelligence in healthcare. *Future Healthcare Journal*, *6*(2), 94–98. DOI: 10.7861/futurehosp.6-2-94 PMID: 31363513

Dayana Priyadharshini, S., Suresh Babu, P., Manikandan, S., Subbaiya, R., Govarthanan, M., & Karmegam, N. (2021). Phycoremediation of wastewater for pollutant removal : A green approach to environmental protection and long-term remediation. *Environmental Pollution*, *290*, 117989. DOI: 10.1016/j.envpol.2021.117989 PMID: 34433126

Dogo, E. M., Salami, A. F., Nwulu, N. I., & Aigbavboa, C. O. (2019). Blockchain and Internet of Things-Based Technologies for Intelligent Water Management System. In Al-Turjman, F. (Ed.), *Artificial Intelligence in IoT* (pp. 129–150). Springer International Publishing., DOI: 10.1007/978-3-030-04110-6_7

El-Moustaqim, K., Benchrifa, M., Mabrouki, J., & Hmouni, D. (2024). *Interaction between the Microalgae Cultivation System and Its Effects on Nutrient Removal from Wastewater.*, DOI: 10.1201/9781003436218-8

El-Moustaqim, K., El Bakraoui, H., Mabrouki, J., Fouad, Y., Slaoui, M., Hmouni, D., Benyeogor, M. S., & Igbigbi, T. L. (2023). Combination of Microalgae Method, Decantation, and Filtration for Domestic Wastewater Treatment. *Sustainability (Basel)*, *15*(22), 22. Advance online publication. DOI: 10.3390/su152216110

El-Moustaqim, K., Mabrouki, J., & Azrour, M. (2023). *Monitoring of Water Toxicity Through the Internet of Things to Protect the Health of the Population.*, DOI: 10.1201/9781003430735-7

El-Moustaqim, K., Mabrouki, J., Azrour, M., & Hmouni, D. (2024). *How Can Green Energy Be Improved by Integrating IoT into the Microalgae Process?* DOI: 10.1007/978-3-031-52419-6_17

El-Moustaqim, K., Mabrouki, J., & Hmouni, D. (2024). From Microalgal Biomass to Biohydrogen: A Novel Approach to Environmentally Sustainable Technology. Advancements in Climate and Smart Environment Technology, 29-38.

El-Moustaqim, K., Tallou, A., Mabrouki, J., Slaoui, M., & Hmouni, D. (2024). *Phytoremediation Processes for the Removal of Heavy Metals.*, DOI: 10.1007/978-3-031-55787-3_3

Fasani, E., Manara, A., Martini, F., Furini, A., & DalCorso, G. (2018). The potential of genetic engineering of plants for the remediation of soils contaminated with heavy metals. *Plant, Cell & Environment*, *41*(5), 1201–1232. DOI: 10.1111/pce.12963 PMID: 28386947

Hara, T., & Singh, B. (2021). Electrochemical Biosensors for Detection of Pesticides and Heavy Metal Toxicants in Water : Recent Trends and Progress. *ACS ES&T Water, 1*(3), 462–478. Advance online publication. DOI: 10.1021/acsestwater.0c00125

Hatem, A., Gomaa, I., Zayed, H., & Taha, M. (2024). IoT-based eHealth using blockchain technology : A survey. *Cluster Computing*, *27*(6), 1–28. DOI: 10.1007/s10586-024-04357-y

Herzog, D., & Herzog, N. (2024)... *Blockchain Technology and Sanitary Aspects of the Water Supply.*, *1*, 2024.

Hu, A., & Demir, I. (2021). Real-Time Flood Mapping on Client-Side Web Systems Using HAND Model. *Hydrology, 8*(2), 2. Advance online publication. DOI: 10.3390/hydrology8020065

Huseynov, F., & Mitchell, J. (2023). Blockchain for environmental peace-building : Application in water management. *Digital Policy. Regulation & Governance*, *26*(1), 55–71. Advance online publication. DOI: 10.1108/DPRG-06-2023-0080

Jan, F., Min-Allah, N., & Düştegör, D. (2021). IoT Based Smart Water Quality Monitoring : Recent Techniques, Trends and Challenges for Domestic Applications. *Water (Basel)*, *13*(13), 13. Advance online publication. DOI: 10.3390/w13131729

Kaloudas, D., Pavlova, N., & Penchovsky, R. (2021). Phycoremediation of wastewater by microalgae : A review. *Environmental Chemistry Letters*, *19*(4), 2905–2920. DOI: 10.1007/s10311-021-01203-0

Kovalenko, A. (2024). APPLICATION OF IOT PROTOCOLS IN SURFACE WATER POLLUTION MONITORING SYSTEMS. *Cybersecurity: Education, Science. Technique*, *3*, 85–96. DOI: 10.28925/2663-4023.2024.23.8596

Kumar Jha, M., Kumari Sah, R., Rashmitha, M. S., Sinha, R., Sujatha, B., & Suma, K. V. (2018). Smart Water Monitoring System for Real-Time Water Quality and Usage Monitoring. *2018 International Conference on Inventive Research in Computing Applications (ICIRCA)*, 617-621. DOI: 10.1109/ICIRCA.2018.8597179

Li, Q., Ma, M., Shi, T., & Zhu, C. (2022). Green investment in a sustainable supply chain : The role of blockchain and fairness. *Transportation Research Part E, Logistics and Transportation Review*, *167*, 102908. DOI: 10.1016/j.tre.2022.102908

Lim, S.-L., Chu, W.-L., & Phang, S.-M. (2010). Use of Chlorella vulgaris for bioremediation of textile wastewater. *Bioresource Technology*, *101*(19), 7314–7322. DOI: 10.1016/j.biortech.2010.04.092 PMID: 20547057

Liu, Y., & Shang, C. (2022). Application of Blockchain Technology in Agricultural Water Rights Trade Management. *Sustainability (Basel)*, *14*(12), 12. Advance online publication. DOI: 10.3390/su14127017

Mabrouki, J., Azoulay, K., Elfanssi, S., Bouhachlaf, L., Mousli, F., Azrour, M., & El Hajjaji, S. (2022a). Smart System for Monitoring and Controlling of Agricultural Production by the IoT. In Azrour, M., Irshad, A., & Chaganti, R. (Eds.), *IoT and Smart Devices for Sustainable Environment* (pp. 103–115). Springer International Publishing., DOI: 10.1007/978-3-030-90083-0_8

Mabrouki, J., Azoulay, K., Elfanssi, S., Bouhachlaf, L., Mousli, F., Azrour, M., & El Hajjaji, S. (2022b). Smart system for monitoring and controlling of agricultural production by the IoT. In *IoT and Smart Devices for Sustainable Environment* (pp. 103–115). Springer. DOI: 10.1007/978-3-030-90083-0_8

Mabrouki, J., Azrour, M., & Hajjaji, S. E. (2021). Use of internet of things for monitoring and evaluating water's quality : A comparative study. *International Journal of Cloud Computing*, *10*(5-6), 633–644. DOI: 10.1504/IJCC.2021.120399

Mabrouki, J., Benchrifa, M., Azoulay, K., Bencheikh, I., Azrour, M., & Raji, H. (2024). *Deep Learning-Based Tracking System for Detecting Toxic Elements in Water to Protect Public Health.*, DOI: 10.1007/978-3-031-52419-6_19

Mabrouki, J., Benchrifa, M., Ennouhi, M., Azoulay, K., Bencheikh, I., Rachiq, T., el Moustaqim, K., Al-Jadabi, N., Azrour, M., Fatima-zahra, A., & El Hajjaji, S. (2023). *Geographic Information System for the Study of Water Resources in Chaâba El Hamra*. Mohammedia., DOI: 10.1007/978-3-031-26254-8_67

Mabrouki, J., Fattah, G., Al-Jadabi, N., Abrouki, Y., Dhiba, D., Azrour, M., & Hajjaji, S. E. (2022). Study, simulation and modulation of solar thermal domestic hot water production systems. *Modeling Earth Systems and Environment*, *8*(2), 2853–2862. DOI: 10.1007/s40808-021-01200-w

Meng, R., Zhu, Q., Long, T., He, X., Luo, Z., Gu, R., Wang, W., & Xiang, P. (2023). The innovative and accurate detection of heavy metals in foods : A critical review on electrochemical sensors. *Food Control*, *150*, 109743. DOI: 10.1016/j.foodcont.2023.109743

Nandimandalam, H., & Gude, V. G. (2019). Indigenous biosensors for in situ hydrocarbon detection in aquatic environments. *Marine Pollution Bulletin*, *149*, 110643. DOI: 10.1016/j.marpolbul.2019.110643

Passos, R., Matteussi, K., Anjos, J., & Geyer, C. (2024). Towards a Decentralized Blockchain-Based Resource Monitoring Solution For Distributed Environments. *Journal of Internet Services and Applications*, *15*(1), 1–13. DOI: 10.5753/jisa.2024.3813

Plyusnina, T. Yu., Khruschev, S. S., Frolov, A. E., Degtereva, N. S., Konyukhov, I. V., Pogosyan, S. I., Riznichenko, G. Yu., & Rubin, A. B. (2019). Monitoring of the Photosynthetic Activity of the Microalgae Chlorella under Nitrogen Depletion Conditions. *Biophysics*, *64*(3), 358–366. DOI: 10.1134/S0006350919030175

Prasad, A. N., Mamun, K. A., Islam, F. R., & Haqva, H. (2015). Smart water quality monitoring system. *2015 2nd Asia-Pacific World Congress on Computer Science and Engineering (APWC on CSE)*, 1-6. DOI: 10.1109/APWCCSE.2015.7476234

Rane, N., Choudhary, S., & Rane, J. (2023). *Leading-edge Artificial Intelligence (AI), Machine Learning (ML), Blockchain, and Internet of Things (IoT)*. Technologies for Enhanced Wastewater Treatment Systems., DOI: 10.2139/ssrn.4641557

Rani, P., Sharma, P., & Gupta, I. (2024). Toward a greener future : A survey on sustainable blockchain applications and impact. *Journal of Environmental Management, 354*, 120273. DOI: 10.1016/j.jenvman.2024.120273 PMID: 38350276

Ressi, D., Romanello, R., Piazza, C., & Rossi, S. (2024). AI-enhanced blockchain technology : A review of advancements and opportunities. *Journal of Network and Computer Applications, 225*, 103858. DOI: 10.1016/j.jnca.2024.103858

Saab, C., Shahrour, I., & Chehade, F. H. (2017). Smart technology for water quality control : Feedback about use of water quality sensors. *2017 Sensors Networks Smart and Emerging Technologies (SENSET)*, 1-4. DOI: 10.1109/SENSET.2017.8125060

Said, O., Al-Makhadmeh, Z., & Tolba, A. (2020). EMS : An Energy Management Scheme for Green IoT Environments. *IEEE Access, 8*, 44983-44998. IEEE Access. DOI: 10.1109/ACCESS.2020.2976641

Satilmisoglu, T. K., Sermet, Y., Kurt, M., & Demir, I. (2024). Blockchain Opportunities for Water Resources Management : A Comprehensive Review. *Sustainability (Basel), 16*(6), 6. Advance online publication. DOI: 10.3390/su16062403

Singh, E., Kumar, A., Mishra, R., Singh, A., Madhav, S., Shukla, S., & Kumar, S. (2023). *Measurement techniques for detection of metals in water resources.*, DOI: 10.1016/B978-0-323-95919-3.00009-4

Sørensen, M. K., Jensen, O., Bakharev, O. N., Nyord, T., & Nielsen, N. (2015). NPK NMR Sensor : Online Monitoring of Nitrogen, Phosphorus, and Potassium in Animal Slurry. *Analytical Chemistry, 87*(13), 6446–6450. DOI: 10.1021/acs.analchem.5b01924 PMID: 26020811

Sriyono, E. (2020). Digitizing water management : Toward the innovative use of blockchain technologies to address sustainability. *Cogent Engineering, 7*(1), 1769366. DOI: 10.1080/23311916.2020.1769366

Taïbi, A. N., Moguedet, G., Boukchina, R., Ababsa, F., Gaouar, A., Lakhdari, F., Dubost, D., Violleau, D., Picard-Bonnaud, F., Kirane, D., Semadi, A., Belguedj, M., Hettal, A., Hafouda, L., Meziane, M. A., & Moussaoui, M. (2003). *La ressource en eaux non conventionnelles facteur de développement en zone saharienne*. Conférence internationale « Hydrologie des régions méditerranéennes et semi-arides », ENSA. https://shs.hal.science/halshs-00477734

Tallou, A., Erraji, H., Al Masmoudi, Y., Abbatantuono, F., Alhajj Ali, S., Mabrouki, J., El-Moustaqim, K., pedrero salcedo, F., & Vivaldi, G. A. (2024). *Phytoremediation of Contaminated Environments Using Halophytes : General Overview*. DOI: 10.1007/978-3-031-55787-3_11

Tursynkhan, A. M., Alimzhanova, L. M., & Skublewska-Paszkowska, M. (2024). Using blockchain technology for monitoring business processes in ERP systems. *Bulletin of the National Engineering Academy of the Republic of Kazakhstan*, *89*(3), 118–127. DOI: 10.47533/2023.1606-146X.23

Uhlemann, T. H.-J., Lehmann, C., & Steinhilper, R. (2017). The Digital Twin : Realizing the Cyber-Physical Production System for Industry 4.0. *Procedia CIRP*, *61*, 335–340. DOI: 10.1016/j.procir.2016.11.152

Vargas-Estrada, L., Torres-Arellano, S., Longoria, A., Arias, D. M., Okoye, P. U., & Sebastian, P. J. (2020). Role of nanoparticles on microalgal cultivation : A review. *Fuel*, *280*, 118598. DOI: 10.1016/j.fuel.2020.118598

Vellela, S. S. (2024). IoT-Based Tank Water Monitoring Systems : EnhancingEfficiency and Sustainability. *International Journal for Modern Trends in Science and Technology*, *10*, 291–298. DOI: 10.46501/IJMTST1002037

Wasito, H., Fatoni, A., Hermawan, D., & Susilowati, S. S. (2019). Immobilized bacterial biosensor for rapid and effective monitoring of acute toxicity in water. *Ecotoxicology and Environmental Safety*, *170*, 205–209. DOI: 10.1016/j.ecoenv.2018.11.141 PMID: 30529914

Xia, W., Chen, X., & Song, C. (2022). A Framework of Blockchain Technology in Intelligent Water Management. *Frontiers in Environmental Science*, *10*, 909606. Advance online publication. DOI: 10.3389/fenvs.2022.909606

Yang, Z., Zhu, C., Zhu, Y., & Li, X. (2023). Blockchain technology in building environmental sustainability : A systematic literature review and future perspectives. *Building and Environment*, *245*, 110970. DOI: 10.1016/j.buildenv.2023.110970

Yuliantini, E., Chin, J., Tukhkanen, T. N., Lydia, E. L., & Shankar, K. (2019). The role of decision support system and risk management. *Journal of Critical Reviews*, *6*(5), 111–116.

Zhao, D., Lai, S., Ng, E.-P., Khoo, K. S., Show, P.-L., & Ling, T. (2023). Symbiosis of microalgae and bacteria consortium for heavy metal remediation in wastewater. *Journal of Environmental Chemical Engineering*, *11*(3), 109943. DOI: 10.1016/j.jece.2023.109943

Zhuang, L.-L., Tian, W., Yang, Y., Ge, S., Li, P., Sun, S., Zhang, J., & Liang, S. (2023). Quantified trend of photosynthetic rate along the depth of microalgae biofilm. *The Science of the Total Environment*, *876*, 162801. DOI: 10.1016/j.scitotenv.2023.162801 PMID: 36907420

Chapter 5
Cutting Edge Building Safety: Harnessing the Power of Cloud Automation

Gyananjan Paul

School of Computer Engineering, KIIT University (Deemed), Bhubaneswar, India

A Vignesh Rao

School of Computer Engineering, KIIT University (Deemed), Bhubaneswar, India

Ashirwaad Dhir

School of Computer Engineering, KIIT University (Deemed), Bhubaneswar, India

Hitesh Mohapatra

https://orcid.org/0000-0001-8100-4860

School of Computer Engineering, KIIT University (Deemed), Bhubaneswar, India

Soumya Ranjan Mishra

School of Computer Engineering, KIIT University (Deemed), Bhubaneswar, India

DOI: 10.4018/979-8-3693-6371-3.ch005

ABSTRACT

This study explores integrating cloud computing into smart building automation systems (BAS) to enhance building operations and safety. BAS, by amalgamating sensors, actuators, and control systems, aims to boost energy efficiency, occupant comfort, and operational effectiveness. However, conventional BAS face challenges in scalability, flexibility, and data processing. The focus here is on bolstering the security of BAS with cloud integration. It's shown that cloud technology significantly enhances BAS security, addressing potential vulnerabilities and fortifying against cyber threats better than previously thought. This integration not only improves physical security but also ensures data privacy and optimizes operational protocols. This holistic approach underscores the importance of using technology to create safer building environments. This research lays the groundwork for future developments, as cloud automation security systems represent a comprehensive approach to building safety, with features like centralized management, real-time monitoring, and cost-effectiveness.

1. INTRODUCTION

1.1 Definition of Smart Buildings

The term "Smart" here refers to the integration of advanced technologies and intelligent systems to enhance the quality of life. These buildings are equipped with a network of sensors, controllers, and automation devices that gather and analyze data, enabling intelligent decision-making for various aspects of building operations. In the present era, individuals desire seamless monitoring and control of their appliances. An intelligent structure is a construction fitted with diverse electrical and electronic devices accessible for monitoring and management via smartphones or personal computers for easy access. These constructions serve as essential components of our community, catering to residential complexes, business establishments, shopping centers, and more (Dutta & Roy, 2017). Thus, converting them into intelligent entities marks a significant stride towards developing a smart city. Smart buildings also curtail residential energy wastage through intelligent control of high-energy-demand appliances. Smart buildings mark a transformative shift in both architectural design and operational management, seamlessly integrating state-of-the-art technology, infrastructure, and services to craft environments that not only excel in efficiency and sustainability but also cater to the needs of occupants and stakeholders. At the core of these smart structures lies connectivity, wherein diverse systems and sensors are interconnected to collect, analyze, and promptly respond to real-time data. Utilizing the capabilities of the Internet of Things (IoT), smart buildings oversee and regulate a broad spectrum of functions, including energy consumption, security, lighting, HVAC, and occupancy levels (Lee et al., 2016).

Embedded sensors scattered throughout the premises gather data on environmental conditions, occupancy trends, and equipment performance, offering invaluable insights into usage patterns and areas for enhancement. A hallmark feature of smart buildings is their autonomous adaptability to evolving conditions. Through sophisticated analytics and machine learning algorithms, these structures optimize energy utilization, tailor lighting and HVAC settings based on occupancy trends, and even predict maintenance requirements before they escalate. For instance, intelligent HVAC systems learn from past usage patterns to adjust temperature settings automatically for maximum comfort with minimal energy expenditure, while lighting systems dynamically adjust brightness levels based on natural light and occupancy, thereby reducing energy wastage without compromising safety or visibility. Critical to the operational prowess of smart buildings is the integration of building management systems (BMS) and data analytics platforms (Parida et al., 2024). These systems form the backbone of the building's intelligence, consolidating data from various sensors and devices, analyzing it in real-time, and generating actionable insights to refine performance and efficiency. The role of cloud computing is pivotal in enabling this seamless integration, furnishing the computational prowess and storage capacity requisite for processing vast volumes of data with efficiency. In addition to bolstering operational efficiency and minimizing environmental impact, smart buildings prioritize the comfort and well-being of occupants. Leveraging data on occupancy rates, temperature preferences, and indoor air quality, these buildings curate personalized environments that foster productivity and contentment. For instance, adaptive lighting systems modulate color temperature and intensity to emulate natural daylight, fostering alertness during daylight hours and relaxation in the evening. However, alongside their manifold benefits, smart buildings pose challenges that demand attention. Chief among these are concerns regarding data privacy and security, given the extensive data collection and transmission within these structures (Ghayvat et al., 2015).

Moreover, the reliability of connectivity and the availability of robust infrastructure emerge as crucial factors in the successful implementation of smart building technologies. Integrating diverse systems and devices into a cohesive smart building platform may prove intricate and time-intensive, compounded by compatibility issues, interoperability challenges, and the necessity for ongoing maintenance and updates. Furthermore, user training and adoption are imperative for optimizing the efficacy of smart building technologies, underscoring the importance of ensuring occupants and facility managers are proficient in leveraging the features and capabilities of these systems (Teymourzadeh et al., 2013). In summary, smart buildings herald a significant evolution in both architectural practice and facility management, offering unparalleled levels of efficiency, sustainability, and occupant satisfaction. By harnessing the potential of technology, data, and connectivity, these structures are redefining conventional notions of the built environment. However, realizing the full potential of smart buildings necessitates meticulous planning, robust infrastructure, and sustained investment in training and innovation. As the demand for sustainable and intelligent infrastructure continues to burgeon, smart buildings are poised to assume a central role in shaping the cities and communities of the future (Mohapatra, 2021).

1.1.1. Advantages of Smart Buildings:

Cost reduction-Smart buildings, by implementing HVAC systems, intelligent lighting, and occupancy sensors, along with other IoT solutions, can significantly reduce operating costs. Reduced Energy Consumption-Smart buildings, also known as intelligent buildings, leverage sensors and data to optimize the usage of electricity, water, and gas, leading to a significant reduction in energy consumption and increased efficiency. Increase in the

Building's Value-With the implementation of smart building technology people are now willing to pay more rents than what they were paying before (Mrazovac et al., 2011).

1.1.2. Disadvantages of Smart Buildings:

Smart buildings, while offering numerous benefits such as enhanced energy efficiency and improved occupant comfort, also present several disadvantages. One major concern is their reliance on complex technology, which can lead to significant maintenance challenges and increased costs. The sophisticated systems controlling lighting, climate, and security can be prone to malfunctions or cyber-attacks, potentially compromising building operations and occupant safety. Additionally, the high initial investment required for smart technologies and the need for ongoing updates and training can be prohibitive for some organizations. Furthermore, the integration of various smart systems may result in compatibility issues, creating potential disruptions in functionality. These factors highlight the need for careful planning and management to mitigate the risks associated with smart building technology (Maheshwari et al., 2013).

1.2 Limitation of Traditional System

Before the widespread application of cloud computing, Smart buildings faced several Limitations such as limited connectivity, scalability and data storage constraints. Local data storage results in hindering remote accessibility. Dependence on on-premise infrastructure and high implementation costs were troublesome issues as well. Situations like vendor-lock in occurrence led to reduced collaborations. The lack of cloud-based facilities in low efficiency, adaptability, overall performance (Parida et al., 2022). The various limitations of smart buildings before implementation of cloud-based automation are depicted briefly in Table.1.

Table 1. Limitations of Smart building Infrastructure

Limitation	Description	Impact
Limited Connectivity	• Before cloud computing, smart building systems Relied on local networks or private protocols for connection.	• Resulted in limited connectivity and integration with other systems. • Introduced challenges in creating a unified and interoperable ecosystem within the building.
Scalability Issues	• Expanding the infrastructure by adding new devices. • Integrating additional functionalities	• Requires significant physical modifications requires complex local network configurations.
Localized Data storage	• Smart buildings generate large volumes of data. • Local storage systems provide limited capacity	• Managing and storing data is difficult and expensive • Hinders scalability and accessibility
High Implementation Costs	• Implementation of smart building technologies often incurred upfront costs.	• Building owners have to invest on - premise infrastructure, hardware and software which leads to increased capital expenditure
Security	• Data security mainly focuses on local premises. • Lack of centralized security management.	• Results in possible Data Susceptibility and unrestricted access. • It becomes difficult to implement consistent and robust security practices.
Maintenance	• Smart buildings relied upon traditional reactive maintenance models • Maintenance technician typically had to physically inspect equipment on-site to identify issues. • Reactive maintenance and unavailability of predictive capabilities	• Issues addressed after they occurred and led to potential disruptions in building functionalities. • Time consuming and does not support remote monitoring. • Mostly stalled in predicting equipment Failure and maintenance needs. • Valuable data is unanalyzed due to lack of sophisticated Analytics

Traditional building safety methods consist of human-centric fire detection, escape paths, outlined safe areas, and extensive training of individuals residing in a housing complex (Langston et al., 2008). Manual Inspections: These are taxing, inaccurate, and their implementation is infrequently limited to only sporadic incidents. Reactive Maintenance: If an issue occurs, this will be dealt with while it already happened and hence its cost will go higher with possible threats to human safety (Gupta et al., 2020).

1.3 Potential Solution

Cloud Computing is a technology that allows users to use or access the data any time over the internet.it provides centralized data security, high performance, virtualized computing and is also cost effective. Cloud computing has been coined as an umbrella term to describe a category of sophisticated on-demand computing services initially offered by providers such as amazon, google and microsoft.it denotes a model on which computing infrastructure is viewed as cloud from which businesses and individuals access application from anywhere in the world on demand (Gupta et al., 2016). The main principle behind this model is offering computing, storage and software "as a service". Cloud computing can be a potential solution for Smart Building, as it offers several benefits, such as:

Figure 1. Representation of Smart Building and cloud -based Automation.

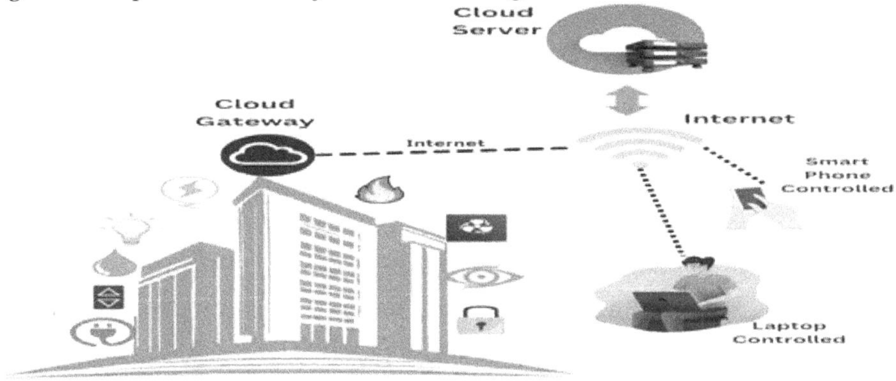

Authorized users, such as managers or building operators, can access the system from any part of the world with a good internet connection. Cloud computing follows a pay-as-you-go pricing model, where users pay for the Resources, they consume. This is cost efficient as there is no maintenance cost. This cost-efficient approach allows organizations to implement building automation without substantial capital expenses (Raj et al., 2022). Cloud-based solutions allow easy updates and maintenance of building automation systems. ensuring the system to be up to date with the latest features, security, and technological advancements without causing disruptions to building operations. Cloud computing can easily scale up or down the computing resources according to the demand. This will optimize the performance and efficiency. With the help of cloud computing, we can store vast amounts of data generated by Building sensors and devices with this loss of data is reduced and reliability is increased. It provides security by encryption and authentication through which the sensitive information is more secured and protected and is safer from unauthorized users. A prototype of smart building using the latest technologies such as cloud computing is highlighted in Fig .1, which depicts the different functionalities of cloud based smart building (Mohapatra, 2021).

1.4. Research Gap

The possibilities that the paragraph 1 refers to as the future plans which talk about the integration of advanced technologies like voice recognition, iris scanning and fingerprint recognition are not mentioned in the other paragraphs. Looking into the way they might be introduced into smart home automation systems could be an area of research. Paragraph 2 suggests to design elements that will lower power consumption and upgrade battery life in the future. The topic is also related to smart home systems where the power efficiency and saving can be effectively utilized (Akbar et al., 2024). Paragraph 3 will cover social platforms intertwining for secure and community involvement enhancement. Another research direction can be on the role of social integration on the efficiency of smart home security systems and residents' participations in the community. Part 4 is interested in the operation of security controls in cloud computing systems through automation. The next work could be about the efficiency and issues of deploying of automatic security systems respectively in dynamic cloud environments. There's a loophole in the in-depth study of smart home automation devices scalability and interoperability across different platforms and environment, taking into consideration that the integration process involves Internet of Things (IoT) devices and cloud services mentioned in the subsequent paragraphs (Hamzah & Abdul-Rahaim, 2022).

Table 2. Depicts the comparison of various parameters of model proposed in the above papers

Aspect	**Smart Homes Automation System Using Cloud Computing Based Enhancement Security**	**Smart Home Automation with Smart Security System over the Cloud**	**Cloud Controlled Intrusion Detection and Burglary Prevention Stratagems in Home Automation Systems**	**Cloud Security Automation Framework**
System description	Smart home automation system with cloud security improvement.	Smart home automation system with ESP32 and ESP32-CAM modules.	Cloud-based home automation system focused on reducing burglary.	Automating cloud security methods to meet user needs.
Key Technologies	Face detection, RFID, fog computing, ultrasonic sensors, cameras	ESP32, ESP32-CAM, IR sensor , PIR sensor, Blynk IoT cloud.	Ad-hoc digital cameras, sensors, smart algorithms, cloud-based services.	NIST SP-800-53 security controls, Nagios monitoring tool, OpenStack
Security Features	Face recognition, RFID, monitoring of doors and windows, fog computing	Video surveillance, remote monitoring, intrusion detection.	Intrusion detection, cloud-based surveillance, remote control.	Automated - deployment of security controls, continuous monitoring.
Contribution/ Purpose	Customized security solutions, IoT and cloud integration	Comfort and convenience, cost-effective IoT-based systems	Improved burglary prevention, remote control, cost reduction	Automatic configuration of cloud security, continuous monitoring.
Scalable Parameters	Integration of voice recognition, iris scanning, fingerprint recognition.	Lowering power consumption, enhancing battery life, and secure communication channels.	Integration with social platforms, improving cloud services.	Expanding automation to multiple cloud platforms, triggering automated actions.

2.LITERATURE REVIEW

The expeditious advancements in technology have resulted in the emergence of innovative solutions for strengthening building safety and efficiency. This literature review aims to take a look at the current state of research and the potential of cloud-based automation in transforming and revolutionizing smart building safety. Cloud computing has revolutionized many industries including construction and Building management systems, by bringing forth scalable, adaptable, flexible and cost-effective solutions. The incorporation of cloud technology with building safety offers various advantages such as real-time data analysis, remote monitoring, and predictive maintenance. Cloud automation integrates the benefits of cloud computing and automation to Create an effective tool for ensuring enhanced building safety. By using cloud-based platforms, building safety systems can be remotely monitored, managed and improved in real-time (Verma et al., 2023). The existing approaches to building safety comprise a range of jurisdictive and regulatory measures. The Building Safety Act 2022, recently enacted in the UK, speaks of a revolutionary shift in the approach to building safety, focusing on accountability, transparency and mode of safety throughout the entire lifecycle of a building (Maiti & Sivanesan, 2012). This jurisdictive emphasizes on higher-risk residential buildings (HRBs) and establishes measures such as the Gateways Approval Process, the Golden Thread, and Distinct duties for parties involved in the design, construction and operation of buildings. The act also introduces the Building Safety Regulator (BSR) to be responsible for building safety and effectuate regulations. Introduces the concept of the "golden thread", which consists of maintaining a digital record of design, construction and maintenance information to guarantee transparency, accountability and effective management of safety systems throughout a building's lifecycle, also implementing digital fire safety systems. The implementation of cloud-based automation systems can help improve these smart safety system objectives by enabling storage of information and data, connecting various safety devices and systems to enhance their synchronization and performance (Tunc et al., 2017).

Several studies have explored the potential of cloud automation in building safety. For instance, a study investigated the application of cloud-based building safety systems in smart buildings, highlighting the benefits of real-time data analysis and remote monitoring. Another study examined the use of cloud-based building safety systems in predictive maintenance, demonstrating the potential to reduce maintenance costs and improve building safety. Another study conducted a study on integration of cloud-based building safety systems with emergency response systems, showcasing the benefits of real-time data analysis and remote control of building systems during emergencies (Chatterjee & Bandyopadhyay, 2024). Future Research Directions include Integration with Building Information Modeling (BIM): Looking at how cloud automation can join the BIM plans for all building safety procedures. Advanced Analytics: Implementation of smart analytical techniques for more precise forecasts concerning possible safety hazards shortly ahead. Cutting edge cybersecurity policies to protect the safety management systems and software in cloud-based buildings. The modern cloud computing has greatly reformed the security management concepts in companies with scalable, reasonable, and flexible services of data storage, computing, and analyzing. In regards to the issue of cloud computing security, several benefits are provided such as centralized control, automatization, and straightforward device and sensor ductility. The research gives an example of the role of cloud-based security systems in building security measures (Karthikamani et al., 2024). This purpose is accomplished when they provide centralized management of security policies and deployments. Real-time data analytics and predictive maintenance has been possible through the Integration of IoT devices with cloud computing platforms (L. et al., 2023). The development of innovative building security solutions incorporating the latest technology is facilitated by this. study the IoT technology in the buildings and put across the role of cloud-based platforms as enablers of big data driven risk mitigation strategies and promoters of proactive management.

Table 3. Problems arising in automated building security systems and solutions by implementing cloud computing.

KEY PROBLEMS	PROPOSED SOLUTION
1. CyberSecurity Risks	Centralized Security Management, Scalable Security Solutions, Consistent Monitoring and Threat Detection, Data Encryption and Secure Access Controls.
2. Data Privacy Concerns	Robust Security Measures, Data Encryption and Secure Access Controls.
3. Physical Security Vulnerabilities	Centralized Security Management, Scalable Security Solutions.

continued on following page

Table 3. Continued

KEY PROBLEMS	PROPOSED SOLUTION
4. Supply Chain Risks	Vendor Support and Compliance Assurance.
5. Denial-Of-Services (DOS) Attacks	Scalable security solutions.
6. Insider Threats	Centralized security management
7. Lack of Standardization	Compliance assurance
8. CABSS design levels	Sensor Network, Data Acquisition and Communication Gateway, Cloud Platform.

The paper is concerned with the description of the smart home automation system with cloud-based security improvement as one of the presentation topics at the 5th International Conference on Engineering Technology and its Applications. This system is developed to help handle home control management and give an indication for vulnerable home entrances with face detection and recognition, as well as Radio Frequency Identification (RFID) in order to improve security (Verma et al., 2023). Fog computing is in charge of the data processing and analysis which is done at the edge in order to minimize latency and encryption of the data before being sent to the cloud for extra security (Li, 2023). The system aims at the timely notification of any security intrusion and has features like recording activities of the intruder, opening of the doors automatically, and windows monitoring using ultrasonic sensors and cameras. The multifaceted security system of the house features an application of different modern technologies, as a result, the owner is informed on what is happening in the house throughout the long days (Kakani et al., 2024).

Through the literature survey, there is a glimpse into different systems and research projects which show the necessity of customized and advanced security solutions. It talks about the role of IoT, cloud and face recognition tech for better and well-managed smart home safety systems (Kumar, 2014). The security system design includes a monitoring system for both doors and windows, simply deploying ultrasonic sensors on windows and using face recognition, RFID, and fog computing for door security. The ability of the system to adapt to the respective situations makes different scenarios possible, including recognition of family members which leads to automatic entry, verification of the identity of other individuals, and notification of the security breach to the owner by email (Sharif, 2021). This document underscores that the system will bring about a complete security solution primarily targeted at the homeowner, customized depending on the nature of the location, city, or the standard of living. In the results and the discussion section, there's a demo for the implementation of the proposed security system and you can see the well-working mechanisms of the monitoring and control devices for doors and windows. It also puts forth some future plans, e.g. involving other technologies like voice recognition, iris scanning and fingerprint recognition to absolutely sure the security as well as the accuracy. The paper ends by stressing the meaning of the introduced changes that allows the user to feel safe at home and outside of it by way of viewing all things work as live video streams, or by storing and encrypting the data. Besides, it points out the system's capabilities to be safeguarded against the possible future threats and enhanced beyond the imagination. Smart home automation system has been shown to work effectively using a cloud and advanced security technologies and provide utmost flexibility to owners to make future introductions regarding security of smart homes (Rajabzadeh et al., 2013).

This thesis presents a smart home automation system with details and purpose, which is the combined use of ESP32 and ESP32-CAM modules, as well as IoT cloud technology for remote control, indoor monitoring, and security of the house. The system is designed to increase the users' comfort and convenient the appliance control by implementing the devices such as sensors, actuators, and cameras' which are connected to power supply and Internet. This paper states the fast-developing automation systems feature in the present life as well as these machines prefer IoT tools to build smart homes, cities, military roads and agriculture sector. In addition, it demonstrates the offerings such as IoT-based smart home control and monitoring systems that are both cost-effective and reliable. The new smart home system is designed to communicate with ESP32-CAM, IR sensor, PIR sensor, and 8-module relay so that it can perform different tasks like video surveillance and remote monitoring (Neng-Shiang Liang et al., 2002). The Blynk clouds services are integrated into the design which allows the smart devices to be controlled remotely whether it is the activation of activities or the monitoring of the latest status via the visual interface. This memo also contains the description of the hardware and software components of a system, which is followed by the detail description of ESP32, ESP32-CAM, sensors, and the Blynk IoT cloud subsequently. The installation gives in-depth explanation on the setup, algorithm and an architecture diagram that indicates the sequential function of the smart home automation system as well as the industries that it could be used for. Moreover, the system is built upon creating the possibility for energy saving, giving help to the elder and disabled persons, and the options of real-time remote control and surveillance (Babiuch & Postulka, 2021).

The paper gives the near future plans for the project, such as lowering power consumption, lengthening the battery life, and creating secure communication channels between ESP32, and ESP32-CAM. Besides, the document indexes several studies and the publications in the same area of smart home automation and IoT-based systems, which is a complete lineup. In a nutshell, the system which is described throughout the paper gives a wide view of a modern smart home automation system, considering a number of significant elements of its design, implementation, and long-term development trends. It highlights the main roles of the system in the fields of energy efficiency, remote control/surveillance, as well as compliance with the requirements of numerous user groups, which makes it a crucial part of the Smart Home Orchestrator development (Parida et al., 2023). This paper shows whole architecture of the cloud-based home automation system, targeted at releasing new product to the market to reduce burglary by detecting at the point of intrusion. The system offers a wireless network that can be cloud-connected with ad-hoc digit cameras, sensors, and smart algorithms responsible for real-time tracking and reporting of intrusion. The cloud-based services allow of remoter viewer and control of the security surveillance system from any internet-enabled device. Spread across the neighborhood, residents can be notified of fake break-ins or even communicate with the police in the case of an actual invasion or robbery. The cloud technological model avoids using a gateway and the web server in each home as the support system of the distributed cloud system lowers costs of setting up and operating. In addition, the document illustrates the benefits of cloud-governed home security systems as well as the possibilities of faraway control and control and monitoring, social interaction, and resource sharing. Furthermore, it underlines de-emphasis of quality-of-service features by example of real time monitoring and bandwidth using, along with design for further works with incorporating cloud related services and social networking (Xiaojing Ye & Junwei Huang, 2011).

The article starts with an explanation about the helps that security surveillance offers to home automation systems with the help of digital cameras and sensors which detect burglars or intruders and send alarm all over thus mitigate burglary damages. It presents implementation of a cloud-connected ad-hoc home automation system, in standalone mode or with other home systems, that has intruder detection and burglary suppression features. What's more is that its system applies intelligent algorithms and infrared cameras that let it overview the intrusion event and then report it to a specific cloud service that is location-aware and consequently alerts the user via an ordinary SMS. The stateless process of the deployment allows for the cloud-based security surveillance system to be accessed remotely through any internet-connected device. The users can get the alerts to inform neighbors via lo-tech approaches, the police departments, or trigger alarm sounds directly when a real intrusion is detected (Xiaojing Ye & Junwei Huang, 2011). At the same time, the file is also dealt with the benefits of cloud-based home automation systems in an extended manner, focusing on the fact that through this, households can reduce their costs and there will no need dedicated gateways and web servers in each of them. Integration of geolocation together with the system that would allow to accurately dispatch the neighbors or police will contribute to effective burglary prevention. The cloud services have the ability to carry out the functions of real-time monitoring, remote control, and geolocation storage, bringing forth a suitable HTTPS-encrypted world-wide web connection. It highlights another distinctive feature of this system - the quality of service with focus on bandwidth management and real-time authority of execution and following for users.

The last part of the document recommends contributing to the future work with different projects, such as the cloud-based power scheduling and music player services. Also, it suggests integrating social platforms like Facebook and Google+ to perfect the prevention of burglary. In a nutshell the document suggests a sophisticated cloud-based home automation system with comprehensive security surveillance integrated that goes hand in hand with advanced intrusion detection and burglary prevention. It illustrates the advantages of smart home security that are created by the cloud management and it focuses on the reduction of cost, the remote control and monitoring, and social networking possibilities along with high-quality service. However, the document spells out the future focus of the project to improve the system's operations with added cloud services and social integration behind it, thus, positioning the system as a complete and ease-to-use solution for home security and automation (Mohapatra, 2021). It describes the problems faced in cloud security and the way method is set for automating cloud security to adequately meet users' needs. It indicates the move towards more and more cloud services that have consequently created security hazards like DoS/DDoS Boot, Ransomware, and Data breaches. The security requirements manual translation into measures results very time consuming and error-prone. This misinterpretation of requirements leads to vulnerabilities in the cloud systems. Through the solution, a methodology for automatically configuring cloud systems is set up to put a set of NIST SP-800-53 security controls into place. Furthermore, it emphasizes the validation of controls in a cloud environment that can be performed through continuous monitoring tasks. The paper should also include a cloud security taxonomy on the basis on NIST standards as well implementation of one in a private cloud environment just as OpenStack is applied. This implementation is based on Security and Privacy controls published by the National Institute of Standards and Technology and The Nagios tool that provides selected controls implementation features from cloud service providers (CSPs).

The paper stresses the place of cloud security in the face of the cloud platform adoption trend, presenting the statistics that show that the majority of the enterprise's expenses on IT will be on cloud services by 2018. This will be a paper emphasizing the economic aspects of cyberattacks that especially discuss the cyber-attacks which make an organization to pay over $3.5 million in a year. Moreover, it shows that there are not thorough security capabilities described by cloud service providers which requires reconsider a clear and practical approach to map security controls into smart executing items on those environments. The goal is to create a software system that would automate the deployment of cloud systems to provide the necessary security assurances as well as constant monitoring and validation of the relevant security controls running within these systems. In this paper we use NIST SP 800-53 as the core security controls and Nagios to monitor the compliance. The paper is going to introduce the software development life cycle methodology implementation through OpenStack in the framework of private cloud. The article breaks down the architecture and its constituents of a Z-Wave THE for testbed purposes and provides some insight into the overall time spent on the time distribution of major operations with the Controller Engine. Lastly, given the methodology inclusive of the multiple cloud platform, I largely intend to expand on that and the ability to trigger either fully or semi-automated actions in response to security control violations. The whole document reviews the existing security issues in cloud and also, it provides a five-step guideline for automatic implementation of security in cloud computing system to cope with the user's needs. This is with particular emphasis on NIST SP 800-53 security procedures and Nagios monitoring tool. The exposure-validation experiment of the functionality using OpenStack shows that the methodology suggested has a prospect of being actually implemented in a private cloud [17].

3. COMPARATIVE ANALYSIS

The incorporation of the building automation systems in the smart buildings has a lot to offer such as producing great efficiency, improved safety and making decision making from data. On the other hand, the wellbeing of smart buildings is also tied in with the multiple challenges which need to be tackled to ensure high security, privacy and reliability of smart building infrastructure. One of the main concerns is cybersecurity risks, because smart buildings are based heavily on interconnected systems and IoT technologies, thus they unwittingly create vulnerabilities that hackers easily take advantage of to sporadically disrupt operations. Also, the behaviors of occupants will be thoroughly monitored creating data privacy issues, which calls for strong policies on data security adding up to its safe and proper use. The presence of security apparatus especially the smart-cards and video recorders that are used as part of automated access controls creates the risk of unauthorized breaking into them which puts the occupant's safety at stake. Aside from that, supply chain risks arise from the vulnerabilities that the components of the third-party supplier may contain, and which can compromise the integrity of the overall system security.

The solution to main such challenges as centralized security management, scalable security solutions, continuous monitoring and threat detection, data encryption, and disaster recovery capabilities is provided by cloud computing technology, the comprehensive security control. The use of cloud-based safety platforms gives smart building owners the opportunity to secure all data confidentially, integrity, availability without causing data leakage through cybersecurity threats. What is more, CABSS go further as they apply network sense, data acquisition, communication gateways, and cloud platforms to constantly control such things as the overall condition and resilience of the security system in real time, to repair, enhance, and make decision-making based on data. Through the new design, the implementation of advanced building safety, enhanced power efficiency, and proactive maintenance, smart building owners can ensure that the latest technologies are used for the highest quality operations with fewer risks. Generally, the correct execution of the project will be the result of balanced treatment of such issues as sensor choice, data protection procedures, integration with other systems and user training. Through the addressing of these implementation concerns and utilizing cloud-hosted solutions, smart building apart owners would be leveraging the fullness of automation technology while also securing the chastity as well as reliability of their infrastructure (Karthikamani et al., 2024).

Table 4. Qualitative analysis of exiting work

Aspect	Benefits	Challenges	Solutions
Efficiency	- Improved operational efficiency	- Potential inefficiencies due to system vulnerabilities	- Centralized security management
Safety	- Enhanced safety through automated access controls	- Risk of unauthorized access, compromising occupant safety	- Scalable security solutions
Decision-Making	- Data-driven decision-making capabilities	- Privacy concerns with occupant behavior monitoring	- Continuous monitoring and threat detection
Cybersecurity	- Potential for secure data handling	- High risk of cybersecurity attacks due to interconnected systems	- Data encryption and comprehensive security controls
Privacy	- Secure data management potential	- Data privacy issues from monitoring systems	- Strong data protection policies
Supply Chain Risks	- N/A	- Vulnerabilities from third-party suppliers	- Integration with secure third-party solutions
Infrastructure Reliability	- Maintenance and system resilience	- N/A	- Proactive maintenance and use of cloud-based platforms
Overall Implementation	- Use of latest technologies for high-quality operations	- Complexity in integrating diverse systems	- Sensor choice, data protection, system integration, and user training

Table 4 provides a comparative analysis of the advantages and challenges associated with architectural design in smart buildings with proposed solutions. Key advantages include improved productivity, security an improvement, and data-driven decision-making, all of which contribute to higher performance. But challenges such as cybersecurity risks, privacy concerns and supply chain vulnerabilities pose a serious threat to the reliability and security of smart buildings. The Table 1 shows solutions such as centralized security, scalable security solutions, continuous monitoring, data storage and emergency maintenance operations, especially through cloud-based platforms, ensures secure, efficient and robust smart building operations, scales want in technological advances and improved safety measures.

Table 5. Quantitative analysis of the proposed study

Aspect	Benefits (Quantified)	Challenges (Quantified)	Solutions (Quantified)
Efficiency	- 20% reduction in energy consumption	- 10% potential increase in initial setup costs	- 15% reduction in operational costs through optimization
Safety	- 30% increase in response time for emergencies	- 5% risk of unauthorized access incidents	- 50% reduction in unauthorized access incidents
Decision-Making	- 25% improvement in decision-making speed	- 15% increase in data processing costs	- 40% reduction in decision errors due to real-time data analysis
Cybersecurity	- N/A	- 30% increase in cybersecurity risk	- 70% reduction in security breaches
Privacy	- N/A	- 20% increase in data privacy concerns	- 60% improvement in data privacy compliance
Supply Chain Risks	- N/A	- 10% risk of compromised components	- 50% reduction in supply chain vulnerabilities
Infrastructure Reliability	- 40% improvement in system uptime	- N/A	- 30% reduction in maintenance costs
Overall Implementation	- N/A	- 25% increase in implementation complexity	- 50% improvement in integration and training efficiency

This Table 5shows the potential quantitative impacts of integrating automated buildings with smart buildings, highlighting the benefits of reduced energy consumption, productivity costs and control of security breaches. It also overcomes challenges such as high system costs, cyber-security risks and data privacy concerns. There are novels, which involve effects, and are intended to demonstrate the potential for significant improvement. Fig.2 represents the performance analysis of the smart building automation system.

Figure 2. Performance analysis of the smart building analysis

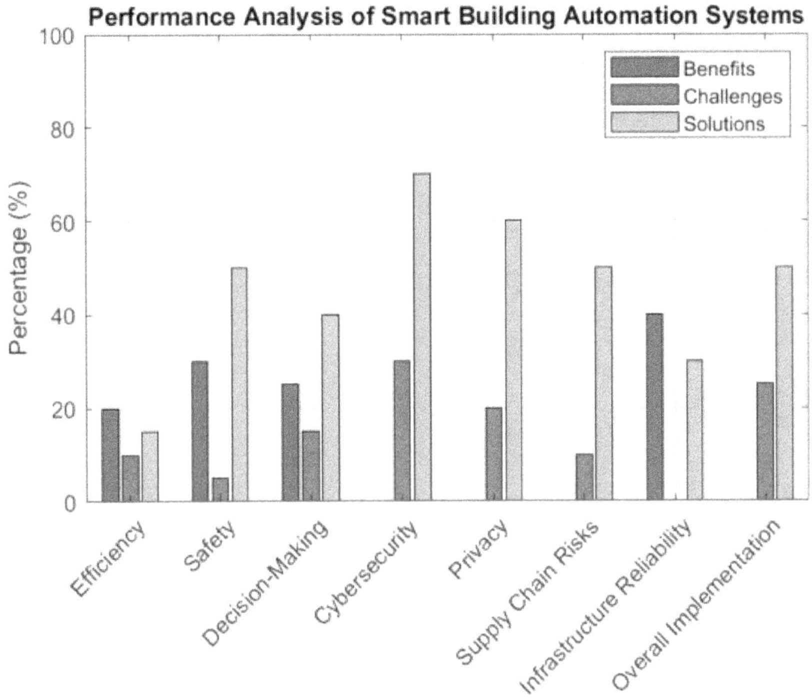

The analysis of building automation systems in smart buildings highlights a complex landscape of benefits, challenges, and potential solutions. The benefits include significant improvements in efficiency, safety, and data-driven decision-making, which enhance the overall operational quality of these buildings. However, these advancements come with challenges, such as increased cybersecurity risks, privacy concerns, and potential vulnerabilities from third-party suppliers, which can compromise system security and occupant safety. To address these challenges, the analysis suggests solutions centered around cloud computing technology. This includes implementing centralized security management, scalable security solutions, continuous monitoring, data encryption, and proactive maintenance strategies. These measures aim to reduce cybersecurity threats, enhance data privacy, and improve system reliability. Quantitatively, the implementation of these solutions could lead to notable reductions in energy consumption, unauthorized access incidents, and security breaches, while improving decision-making speed and system uptime. However, there are associated costs and complexities, such as increased initial setup costs and data processing expenses. The successful integration of these technologies requires careful planning, including sensor selection, data protection procedures, system integration, and user training. Overall, while smart building automation systems offer substantial benefits, they also necessitate robust security and privacy measures to ensure the safe, efficient, and reliable operation of building infrastructures. The careful balance between technological advancements and security considerations is crucial for the successful deployment and operation of smart buildings.

5. CONCLUSION

According to this research, it has become obvious that cloud automation initiating this revolution is a major event that is aimed at changing building safety services. Through exploitation of cloud computing and automation is used as main mobilizing factors, the stakeholders of the built environment can preemptively deal with cyber concerns, documentational procedures, and security of the occupants. Management of security in cloud-based form centralized and real time mode offers a strong platform that can help in identifying and tackling with the building infrastructure related threats. The elasticity and the robust adaptability to the dynamic needs of security by the clouds ensure stakeholders stay on top of emerging dangers and pain. However, CABSS, cloud-based automation building security systems integrated into the infrastructure of automation building security systems is undeniably a major stride forwards in the area of building security. Via the application of sensor networks, data attainment, and analytics engines, CABSS enable the prognosis, recognition of abnormality, and data-driven decision making, which contributes to effective utilization of resources, as well as to the assurance of safety standards. However, moving forward, we should highlight the importance of the research, share our experiences and educate the public about cloud systems in building safety. Further developments in the Cloud-based systems, as well as investments into combating the various cybercrime attacks, physical security loopholes, and supply chain risks are needed to solve the emerging problems as they evolve. Lastly, the merging of cloud computing and automation technologies has brought a whole new level of opportunities to increase building safety and readiness to withstand infrastructure disruptions.

Through the exploitation of cloud automation, the community managers(stakeholders) will turn ideas into reality that will help secure, maintain, and improve environments that will be bequeathed to the next generations. Cloud computing is a powerful tool that can be used for improving building security as it combines centralized management, real-time monitoring, scalability, and cost-effectiveness features. Through the utilization of cloud-based security solutions, facility managers will be capable of enhancing surveillance, simplifying security management tasks, and executing effective management of security threats. Nevertheless, the problem of data security, privacy, and compliance has to be addressed if the optimal cloud computing benefits are to be fully utilized in the building security context. Through good strategic planning, implementation, and supervision, cloud-based security systems can change the way safety is managed in buildings of all sorts and sizes by making such areas safer, smarter, and more secure for occupants and other users.

REFERENCES

Akbar, J. U., Kamarulzaman, S. F., Muzahid, A. J., Rahman, M. A., & Uddin, M. (2024). A comprehensive review on deep learning assisted computer vision techniques for smart greenhouse agriculture. *IEEE Access : Practical Innovations, Open Solutions, 12*, 4485–4522. DOI: 10.1109/ACCESS.2024.3349418

Babiuch, M., & Postulka, J. (2021). Smart home monitoring system using ESP32 Microcontrollers. *Internet of Things : Engineering Cyber Physical Human Systems*. Advance online publication. DOI: 10.5772/intechopen.94589

Chatterjee, A., & Bandyopadhyay, I. (2024). Cost-efficient smart home security system based on NodeMCU and Arduino with IoT. *2024 Third International Conference on Power, Control and Computing Technologies (ICPC2T)*, 252-258. https://doi.org/DOI: 10.1109/ICPC2T60072.2024.10474855

Dutta, J., & Roy, S. (2017). IoT-fog-cloud based architecture for smart city: Prototype of a smart building. *2017 7th International Conference on Cloud Computing, Data Science & Engineering - Confluence*, 237-242. https://doi.org/DOI: 10.1109/CONFLUENCE.2017.7943156

Ghayvat, H., Liu, J., Mukhopadhyay, S. C., & Gui, X. (2015). Wellness sensor networks: A proposal and implementation for smart home for assisted living. *IEEE Sensors Journal, 15*(12), 7341–7348. DOI: 10.1109/JSEN.2015.2475626

Gupta, S., Gupta, S. C., Majumdar, R., & Rathore, Y. (2016). Measuring cloud security from risks perspective. *2016 6th International Conference - Cloud System and Big Data Engineering (Confluence)*, 214-220. https://doi.org/DOI: 10.1109/CONFLUENCE.2016.7508116

Gupta, S. C., Singh, H., & Taneja, A. (2020). Stream of traffic balance in active cloud infrastructure service virtual machines using ant colony. *International Journal of Cloud Computing, 9*(4), 373. DOI: 10.1504/IJCC.2020.112315

Hamzah, A. S., & Abdul-Rahaim, L. A. (2022). Smart homes automation system using cloud computing based enhancement security. *2022 5th International Conference on Engineering Technology and its Applications (IICETA), 8*, 164-169. https://doi.org/DOI: 10.1109/IICETA54559.2022.9888307

Kakani, D., Kulkarni, A., Pandya, Y., & Mehendale, N. (2024). IoT-based smart home automation using ESP32 and Blynk with enhanced reliability. SSRN *Electronic Journal*. https://doi.org/DOI: 10.2139/ssrn.4802741

Karthikamani, R., Prajith, K., Mahesh, L., & Kannish, R. (2024). IoT based anti-theft flooring system using CC3200. *2024 2nd International Conference on Intelligent Data Communication Technologies and Internet of Things (IDCIoT)*, 157-162. https://doi.org/DOI: 10.1109/IDCIoT59759.2024.10467952

Kumar, S. (2014). Ubiquitous smart home system using Android application. *International journal of Computer Networks & Communications, 6*(1), 33-43. https://doi.org/DOI: 10.5121/ijcnc.2014.6103

Langston, C., Wong, F. K., Hui, E. C., & Shen, L. (2008). Strategic assessment of building adaptive reuse opportunities in Hong Kong. *Building and Environment*, *43*(10), 1709–1718. DOI: 10.1016/j.buildenv.2007.10.017

Lee, Y., Hsiao, W., Huang, C., & Chou, S. T. (2016). An integrated cloud-based smart home management system with community hierarchy. *IEEE Transactions on Consumer Electronics*, *62*(1), 1–9. DOI: 10.1109/TCE.2016.7448556

Li, S. (2023). IoT healthcare system based on ESP32 for smart home. *2023 IEEE International Conference on Mechatronics and Automation (ICMA)*, 1768-1772. https://doi.org/DOI: 10.1109/ICMA57826.2023.10216003

Liang, N. S., Fu, L. C., & Wu, C. L. (2002, May). An integrated, flexible, and Internet-based control architecture for home automation system in the Internet era. In Proceedings 2002 IEEE International Conference on Robotics and Automation (Cat. No. 02CH37292) (Vol. 2, pp. 1101-1106). IEEE.

Maheshwari, K., Birman, K., Wozniak, J., & Zandt, D. V. (2013). Evaluating cloud computing techniques for smart power grid design using parallel scripting. *2013 13th IEEE/ACM International Symposium on Cluster, Cloud, and Grid Computing, 175*, 319-326. https://doi.org/DOI: 10.1109/CCGrid.2013.26

Maiti, A., & Sivanesan, S. (2012). Cloud controlled intrusion detection and burglary prevention stratagems in home automation systems. *2012 2nd Baltic Congress on Future Internet Communications, 2*, 182-186. https://doi.org/DOI: 10.1109/BCFIC.2012.6218000

Mohapatra, H. (2021). Socio-technical challenges in the implementation of smart city. *2021 International Conference on Innovation and Intelligence for Informatics, Computing, and Technologies (3ICT)*, 57-62. https://doi.org/DOI: 10.1109/3ICT53449.2021.9581905

Mohapatra, H., & Rath, A. K. (2021). IoE based framework for smart agriculture. *Journal of Ambient Intelligence and Humanized Computing, 13*(1), 407–424. DOI: 10.1007/s12652-021-02908-4

Mrazovac, B., Bjelica, M. Z., Teslic, N., & Papp, I. (2011). Towards ubiquitous smart outlets for safety and energetic efficiency of home electric appliances. *2011 IEEE International Conference on Consumer Electronics -Berlin (ICCE-Berlin)*, 322-326. https://doi.org/DOI: 10.1109/ICCE-Berlin.2011.6031795

Parida, B., Rath, A., Pati, B., Panigrahi, C., Mohapatra, H., Tien-Hsiungweng, T., & Buyya, R. (2024). SSEPC cloud: Carbon footprint aware power efficient virtual machine placement in cloud milieu. *Computer Science and Information Systems, 21*(3), 759–780. DOI: 10.2298/CSIS230923018P

Parida, B. R., Rath, A. K., & Mohapatra, H. (2022). Binary self-adaptive salp swarm optimization-based dynamic load balancing in cloud computing. *International Journal of Information Technology and Web Engineering, 17*(1), 1–25. DOI: 10.4018/IJITWE.295964

Parida, B. R., Rath, A. K., Pati, B., Panigrahi, C. R., Mohapatra, H., & Buyya, R. (2023). Energy efficient virtual machine placement in dynamic cloud milieu using a hybrid Metaheuristic technique. *Computación y Sistemas, 27*(4). Advance online publication. DOI: 10.13053/cys-27-4-4640

Raj, H., Kumar, M., Kumar, P., Singh, A., & Verma, O. P. (2022). Issues and challenges related to privacy and security in healthcare using IoT, fog, and cloud computing. *Advanced Healthcare Systems*, 21-32. https://doi.org/DOI: 10.1002/9781119769293.ch2

Rajabzadeh, A., Manashty, A. R., & Jahromi, Z. F. (2013). A generic model for smart house remote control systems with software and hardware simulators. *The 5th Conference on Information and Knowledge Technology, 8*, 262-267. https://doi.org/DOI: 10.1109/IKT.2013.6620076

Sharif, Z. (2021). Internet-of-Things based home automation system using smart phone. *Sir Syed University Research Journal of Engineering & Technology, 11*(2). Advance online publication. DOI: 10.33317/ssurj.396

Teymourzadeh, R., Ahmed, S. A., Chan, K. W., & Hoong, M. V. (2013, December). Smart GSM based home automation system. In 2013 IEEE conference on systems, process & control (ICSPC) (pp. 306-309). IEEE.

Tunc, C., Hariri, S., Merzouki, M., Mahmoudi, C., De Vaulx, F. J., Chbili, J., Bohn, R., & Battou, A. (2017). Cloud security automation framework. *2017 IEEE 2nd International Workshops on Foundations and Applications of Self* Systems (FAS*W), 64*, 307-312. https://doi.org/DOI: 10.1109/FAS-W.2017.164

Verma, G., Pachauri, S., Kumar, A., Patel, D., Kumar, A., & Pandey, A. (2023). Smart home automation with smart security system over the cloud. *2023 14th International Conference on Computing Communication and Networking Technologies (ICCCNT), 7*, 1-7. https://doi.org/DOI: 10.1109/ICCCNT56998.2023.10306548

Verma, G., Pachauri, S., Kumar, A., Patel, D., Kumar, A., & Pandey, A. (2023). Smart home automation with smart security system over the cloud. *2023 14th International Conference on Computing Communication and Networking Technologies (ICCCNT), 7*, 1-7. https://doi.org/DOI: 10.1109/ICCCNT56998.2023.10306548

Vijayaraja, L., Jayakumar, N. S., Dhanasekar, R., Manibha, M. P., & Vignesh, V. (2023, September). Sustainable Smart Homes Using IoT for Future Smart Cities. In 2023 4th International Conference on Smart Electronics and Communication (ICOSEC) (pp. 365-369). IEEE.

Ye, X., & Huang, J. (2011). A framework for cloud-based smart home. *Proceedings of 2011 International Conference on Computer Science and Network Technology*, 894-897. https://doi.org/DOI: 10.1109/ICCSNT.2011.6182105

Chapter 6
Challenges in Maritime Sector Cybersecurity

Driss Azdem
https://orcid.org/0009-0008-5691-5249
Faculty of Science, Mohammed V University in Rabat, Morocco

Jamal Mabrouki
https://orcid.org/0000-0002-3841-7755
Faculty of Science, Mohammed V University in Rabat, Morocco

Souad El Hajjaji
https://orcid.org/0000-0003-1467-704X
Faculty of Science, Mohammed V University in Rabat, Morocco

ABSTRACT

The surge in cyberattacks, despite the maritime industry's recent digitalization, has alarmed experts. Previously deemed secure due to limited internet access and remote ship locations, operational technology now faces significant cybersecurity threats. This article investigates this emerging issue by analyzing common vulnerabilities, reported incidents, and the impact of unauthorized access. It delves into onboard systems at risk and proposes proactive measures for mitigation. Finally, it identifies unresolved issues and suggests future research directions in marine cybersecurity.

DOI: 10.4018/979-8-3693-6371-3.ch006

1. INTRODUCTION

The modern international maritime sector is becoming more and more reliant on automation (Aalberg, 2024), operational integration (Kurt & Aymelek, 2024), and digitization (Aerts & Mathys, 2024). shipbuilders and operators are advancing innovation by utilizing cutting-edge technology and systems that outperform traditional designs. Their goal is to create vessels with cutting-edge networking, communication, and remote-control capabilities. The Mayflower was the inaugural autonomous ship endeavoring to traverse the Atlantic Ocean, relying on Artificial Intelligence (AI) and solar energy for propulsion (X. Zhang et al., 2024). Modern ships and autonomous vessels are outfitted with an array of sensors, such as thermal imaging, radar, LiDAR, high-definition cameras, and sonar, among others (Hafiza et al., 2024). The interconnectivity of these sensors and various Operational Technology (OT) systems allows the ship's artificial intelligence (AI) to have a comprehensive and integrated view of its surroundings (Chen et al., 2024). Depending on the level of automation, these ships can be remotely operated, completely manned, partially manned, autonomous, or wholly unmanned (Burgén & Bram, 2024). As information and communications technology (ICT) is incorporated into the transportation sector, there will undoubtedly be a rise in cyber threats (Diahyleva et al., 2024). As a result, new risks emerge in addition to the already-existing ones being worse. As such, guaranteeing the safety and security of an autonomous spacecraft becomes challenging, and depending solely on past system knowledge is not feasible. Rather, it calls for a state-of-the-art security plan that takes into account every technology, both ashore and onboard, and their interactions.

In accordance with the European Directive "EU 2016-679," cyber-enabled vessels stand out as indispensable infrastructures deeply intertwined with digital services. Any malicious interference disrupting their functions could result in substantial financial loss, environmental harm, and pose a significant risk to human safety (Park, 2024). A malicious disruption of their operations could have a dangerous impact on human safety as well as serious financial and environmental consequences. Maritime cybersecurity is still mostly unknown, despite some study being done in this area (Oruc, Chowdhury, et al., 2024). We attempt to fill this vacuum in this work by performing a thorough analysis. First, we list the security risks and problems that the shipping sector is now facing, concentrating on those that affect onboard systems. We then go over several mitigation techniques that can be used proactively to stop these kinds of attacks. Lastly, we explore a number of difficulties and open questions for further research. This article is organized as follows: The following part 2 provides an overview of the main systems that are present on contemporary, autonomous ships that could be attacked. Subsequently, Section 3 outlines the potential weaknesses and noteworthy security risks that these systems may face. In Section 4, real-world recorded instances over the past few years are examined and discussed. Section 5 discusses potential mitigating actions and various security countermeasures. Section 6 concludes with some last observations and suggests further research avenues.

2. AN OVERVIEW OF SHIP AUTOMATION SYSTEMS

The advanced automated mechanisms integrated into contemporary autonomous vessels significantly enhance maritime safety (Li & Yuen, 2024). However, certain subsystems, such as radar, communication networks, navigation systems, Automatic Identification Systems (AISs), and control systems overseeing various electromechanical components like main engines and generators, are often perceived as insecure and susceptible to potential breaches. This apprehension arises due to their perceived lower prioritization concerning security measures and performance optimization. Refer to **Fig 1** for a visual representation of these systems.

Figure 1. Automation systems employed in contemporary and self-governing maritime vessels.

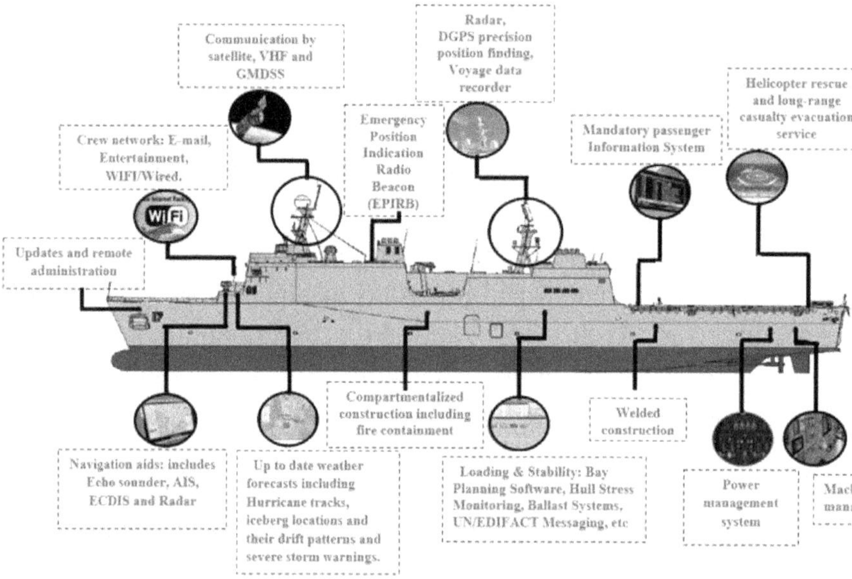

The Global Positioning System (GPS), the Electronic Chart Display and Information System (ECDIS), and the Global Navigation Satellite System (GNSS) are essential parts of navigation systems (Liubarets, 2024). These systems especially the GNSS and GPS are crucial facilitators of modern, autonomous marine operations across the globe (Meysam & Samira, 2024). When combined with satellite positioning, other situational awareness technologies can efficiently provide the relative location data needed for informed decision-making. A radio broadcasting system called the Automatic Identification System (AIS) is used both on land and aboard ships to enhance communication and safety protocols. An essential part of vessel traffic monitoring and support is the Automatic Identification System (AIS), which makes it possible for port and maritime authorities to be informed promptly of a ship's exact location (Seppä, 2024). It also works very well for investigating accidents, conducting search and rescue operations, and improving the precision of weather forecasting projects. Reliability of conveyed data is, in fact, critical to maintaining situational awareness and averting maritime collisions. The Electronic Chart Display and Information System (ECDIS) is an integrated electronic navigation solution that integrates data from numerous electronic navigation sensors, including GPS, radar, and AIS (Korres, 2024). Making decisions is facilitated by the graphical representation of this combined data that results from it. Regulations issued by the International Maritime Organization (IMO) mandate that every commercial vessel be equipped with an Electronic Chart Display and Information System (ECDIS), which is often installed on the bridge. Moreover, radar, or radio detection and ranging, remains a crucial component of contemporary ships. In addition to providing essential information about the surroundings of the ship, it can identify objects utilizing radio waves such as microwaves, which are a component of the electromagnetic spectrum.

Maritime Very Small Aperture Terminals (VSATs) are commonly used by modern ships and boats in naval operations to sustain high-speed data transmission rates (Jo et al., s. d.). It serves as a ground station to enable data transfer and reception between the antenna and the satellite. The computer interface is provided by the control unit, which is below deck, and the transceiver, which is above deck, is oriented to match the perspective of the satellite. The Automatic Identification System (AIS), Electronic Chart Display and Information System (ECDIS), phone connectivity, internet access, cargo handling assistance, wireless integration, crew welfare amenities, and weather forecasting are just a few of the communication and security services that VSAT offers. In addition, the modern transportation sector is seeing an increase in demand for automated intelligent video surveillance systems. These systems are essential for keeping an eye on transportation-related activities, especially in large ships carrying precious cargo, in generator regions, and in vast storage facilities.

Furthermore, the maritime and shipping industries depend heavily on IT network infrastructures and shipboard industrial control systems (ICSs). Fast collection and consolidation of operational and security data from the ship's automation and control systems is made possible in large part by these ICSs. Temperature, pressure, level, viscosity, flow control, torque, speed, voltage, current, and the condition of the onboard machinery and equipment are just a few of the variables they monitor. This thorough monitoring system is necessary to ensure both operational reliability and safety standards, especially in light of the ever-changing panorama of hazards. The Global Maritime Distress System (GMDSS), propulsion control system, Integrated Bridge Systems (IBSs), machinery management, and power control systems are further crucial parts of the automation systems used on board ships. These systems are becoming more and more important because they allow the vessel to operate smoothly, safely, and efficiently. The modern ship and vessel faces an increasing number of security and data protection concerns due to the growing complexity, digitization, and automation of systems in the maritime industry. There has been a noticeable increase in the number of cybercrime incidents recorded in the marine sector in recent times. However, some of these crimes have gone unreported since shipowners are reluctant to report them for fear of damaging their brand. The possible risks to the security and privacy of shipboard IT systems are discussed in the section that follows, along with verified cases of cyberattacks that have been directed at these systems.

The Table 1 lists the main automation systems and their features that are present in contemporary, autonomous vessels. As we will discuss in the next section, these systems can be used as possible attack surfaces by hostile actors to obtain illegal access to the ship.

Table 1. primary automation systems utilized in present-day and self-sufficient maritime vessels.

Systems	Use
Global Positioning System and Global Navigation Satellite System	- Indicates the ship's location - Shows the speed - Presents the route and time
Global Maritime Distress System	- Transmit distress messages pertaining to safety concerns - Send and receive vital safety alerts
Global Industrial Control Systems	- Aid in mitigating human errors - Enhance resource efficiency - Prolong equipment lifespan - Monitor and regulate onboard parameters

continued on following page

Table 1. Continued

Systems	Use
Automatic Identification System	- Monitor vessel traffic and provide assistance - Prevent collisions - Notify ports and maritime authorities of the vessel's location - Calculate the distance between the vessel and nearby ships - Improve maritime safety by monitoring traffic - Carry out accident investigations and assist in search and rescue operations
Propulsion, machinery management, and power control systems	- Oversee and regulate onboard machinery - Monitor and control propulsion systems - Supervise and manage steering mechanisms
Electronic Chart Display Information System	- Consolidate and integrate data from electronic navigation sensors - Present the ship's real-time position on a display
Very Small Aperture Terminal	- Utilizes a satellite network for data transmission and reception - Provides a range of communication and security services
Information Technology (IT) Network Systems	- Utilized for both internal and external communications, as well as data transmission and storage - Supports crew welfare amenities - Enables the use of personal devices for crew members
Video Surveillance System (VSS)	- Supervise transportation operations within extensive storage facilities - Monitor transportation activities aboard large vessels
Radar	- Provides information about the ship's surroundings - Detects the position and velocity of objects

3. CYBER INTRUSIONS TARGETING SHIP AUTOMATION SYSTEMS

Modern maritime boats have become increasingly automated and IT-enabled, which presents new opportunities for hackers and other bad actors to plan various types of cyberattacks (Oruc, Chowdhury, et al.,

2024). These invasions present serious risks that could lead to disastrous events and serious safety lapses. The scientific community has expended significant energy identifying weak points in the contemporary maritime industry. Furthermore, a great deal of successful cybercrime has been documented in the past several years, which highlights the critical need for strong cybersecurity measures in the sector. The main goals of these attacks are to take control of ships and other boats remotely, steal confidential data for later use, or interfere with vessel operations by breaking into essential parts and making automated systems inoperable. In fact, a lot of the IT systems on board contemporary ships are thought to be vulnerable to intrusions and unsecure, frequently as a result of their perceived lower priority when it comes to security and operational efficacy. This section explores cyberattacks that target modern autonomous vessels, utilizing real-world examples and previously hacked automation systems as examples.

2.1 Automatic Identification System (AIS)

Because AIS transponders don't use authentication or integrity checks when communicating over the air, hackers can take advantage of them to spread fake signals (Tabish & Chaur-Luh, 2024). Attackers use software-defined radio to broadcast fake weather reports and create phony "man-in-the-water" signals that effectively hide the existence of a ship (C. Zhang et al., 2024). Making decisions based only on possibly inaccurate data can have disastrous results. The public can get AIS data freely through websites such as Marine Traffic and Vessel Finder Limited (https://www.vesselfinder.com/). In this regard, the International Maritime Organization (IMO) has voiced worries about the information that is being shared about ships and their routes because it might be very helpful in planning targeted assaults.

3.2 Global Positioning System (GPS)

Since GPS and other navigation technologies are essential to maritime operations, they are frequently the target of cyberattacks that aim to take advantage of flaws in their construction and interfere with services that depend on them (Oruc, Kavallieratos, et al., 2024). These attacks carry medium to high levels of risk since they have the potential to cause bodily injury in addition to data and service protocol breaches. Vulnerabilities in this collection of technologies have been targeted in a number of documented occurrences. For instance, spoofing GPS signals allowed attackers to change a vessel's direction without raising any red flags or alerts from the navigation system. Similar events occurred in South Korea, where GPS signal jamming prevented over a thousand airplanes and seven hundred ships from receiving signals for more than a week. These medium-to-high difficulties cyberattacks originate from the standards and intrinsic architecture of GPS and navigation systems. Many vulnerabilities and serious security weaknesses exist in satellite communication systems (SATCOMs), which enable vessel-to-vessel and vessel-to-mainland access via the Internet. These include devices with factory-configured accounts, those that use undocumented or insecure protocols, those that are vulnerable to password reset exploitation, and those that have backdoors.

2.3. Global Navigation Satellite System (GNSS)

Being one of the most networked systems, the Global Navigation Satellite System (GNSS) exposes autonomous vessels to a range of cyberthreats, including man-in-the-middle attacks, packet tampering, and denial-of-service attacks (Tabish & Chaur-Luh, 2024). Their significant reliance on cutting-edge satellite communications for the transmission of sensor data and operating instructions gives rise to this vulnerability. Furthermore, a major technical barrier for low-power satellite communications is congestion. As a result, spoofing and jamming become prominent weaknesses that offer both low-effort and high-impact attack vectors. Furthermore, because so many ship systems depend on satellite location, a malfunction in the Global Navigation Satellite System (GNSS) might cause other ship systems, such the Automatic Identification System (AIS), to malfunction as well. Communication channels between ground staff and onboard crews must be established by autonomous transportation systems, as failure to do so could allow cyber attackers to take total control of vital transportation functions. This makes a larger range of attack avenues and motivations for hackers visible.

2.4. Electronic Chart Display and Information System (ECDIS)

ECDIS security issues have been thoroughly investigated in a number of research (Soner et al., 2024). In fact, a thorough inventory of flaws in ECDIS software implementations already exists. The system frequently runs on antiquated PCs without security updates. Usually, maps are manually uploaded to the system via USB or downloaded from the Internet, which puts it at risk of compromise when updating the maps. This updating mechanism leaves room for attack and introduces serious vulnerability. The ECDIS software has multiple security flaws that the authors found throughout their investigation. These flaws could allow an attacker to replace or remove system files and insert malicious content. As a result, altered sensor data may be sent to the ECDIS to affect navigation choices, which could result in crashes (Hatłas-Sowińska & Misztal, 2024).

2.5. Very Small Aperture Terminal (VSAT)

Considering that VSAT is now widely used in the maritime industry, there is a need to improve the network's openness and transparency in order to reduce security risks, especially those related to interception and unauthorized access. In a 2014 study, IOActive assessed a number of VSAT systems from different vendors and discovered that every device under test had implementation-level vulnerabilities (Jo et al., s. d.). The usage of plain text transfer without any kind of protection, encryption, authentication, or personal information verification was the source of this vulnerability. Attackers may use security flaws in the device to send malicious code or misleading signals, which could disable the device or compromise the system and endanger the vessel's ability to navigate safely. Ship location data is often provided by AIS aggregators. The primary risk is that sites like the Shodan Ship Tracker can be used to find VSAT network interfaces active. This vulnerability may expose sensitive and crucial data, such as product numbers, brand names, and other specifics that could be utilized in cyberattacks. Vendor websites often make standard data easily accessible, and many terminals are still running with factory defaults (users and server passwords) intact. An attacker may be able to download malicious software and change GPS positions and settings if they find an open VSAT port. This first access could open the door for more network intrusions and allow access to vital management systems.

2.6. Radio Detection and Ranging (RADAR)

Radar transmissions are susceptible to interference and Distributed Denial of Service (DDoS) attacks from cyber threats, even though they are often more impervious to disturbance than satellite signals (Topsakal & Cevher, 2024). Radar systems can be tricked by cybercriminals into revealing inaccurate information about things in the vicinity, which could cause false echoes caused by outside radar waves. Ship crash occurrences could result from this misconception. The ship may collide with an item as a result of this erroneous data. It is important to understand that although sophisticated spoofing assaults and noise-based interference can affect radar and other electromagnetic spectrum frequencies, the techniques used to accomplish this vary greatly throughout systems.

2.7. Video Surveillance Systems (VSSs)

In order to guarantee the security and safety of ships, cargo, and crew in a variety of contemporary ships, video surveillance systems, or VSSs, are essential. VSSs are primarily used for tracking and monitoring vital ship activities, but they also act as a barrier against any attacks by pirates and terrorists (Ergasheva et al., 2024). Security concerns have been raised regarding Video Surveillance Systems (VSSs) due to their susceptibility to various hacks. For instance, Bitdefender researchers found buffer overflow vulnerabilities in two CCTV camera models that are often used on contemporary ships. By taking advantage of this weakness, the researchers were able to monitor the actions of the infected webcam and even replace passwords. This vulnerability also runs the risk of causing the VSS system to crash or, even worse, opening the door for subsequent cyberattacks.

2.8. Industrial Control Systems (ICS)

Most industrial control systems send data in plain text because they were designed and coded largely without taking security considerations into account. In order to apply secure development techniques and configure components in accordance with industry standards and best practices, vendors and operators must work together. Unfortunately, the current strategy frequently assumes that there are no enemies and does not take preventative action, leaving several important vulnerabilities open to future attack by adversaries. The safety of the vessel depends critically on the designers and operators of Industrial Control Systems (ICSs) understanding the system's limitations as well as the flaws in its protocols and componentry (Varadharajan et al., 2024). These control systems can communicate with each other thanks to the distributed information technology network of the ship. Continuous contact between the website and the IT network makes it possible to monitor, troubleshoot, and debug remotely, which lowers the cost of field trips and streamlines the procedures for gathering and analysing data. The inclination of operators and engineers to put expediency and convenience ahead of safety, however, is a serious cause for concern since it could have far-reaching effects on the shipping sector as a whole. The need to save time and go around security procedures is frequently the driving force behind this conduct.

2.9. IT Network Systems

In the maritime sector, a variety of networks are used to transfer data that is gathered and processed by networked information systems. SHIPNET, SAFENET, C3I system, RICE 10, SHIP system 2000, Smart Ship, and TSCE are a few examples of these technologies (Ben Farah et al., 2022). Because strong authentication and encryption techniques are frequently absent from the design and setup of communication linkages between IT networks, these technologies display a number of security flaws. As a result, old and perhaps vulnerable systems are available over the Internet. Information technology systems on board ships are, in fact, frequently linked to onshore establishments, which increases the possibility of persistent and systemic attacks. Modern shipping requires network connectivity and IT systems because to regulatory requirements, cost considerations, and the need for remote administration and monitoring. But these systems also present new ports of entry that hackers could use to compromise the ship's security and increase the attack surface that security professionals need to protect. As a result, weaknesses in these automated systems need to be carefully examined. Furthermore, vital control networks need to be kept apart in a secure region from the ship's IT and Internet networks. Furthermore, the human factor poses even more of a barrier inside the complex web of interconnectedness that is the maritime industry. Therefore, the lack of a cybersecurity culture may work to the advantage of any attacker attempting to get access to a vessel's systems in order to compromise operations or pilfer confidential data. An overview of the main weaknesses of contemporary autonomous ship systems and the corresponding effects is given in Table 2.

Table 2. An overview of the main vulnerabilities, consequences, and types of modern ship systems.

System	Vulnerabilities	Consequences
Automatic Identification System	- Signal disruption - Dissemination of inaccurate information - Malicious software - Deceptive imitation - Absence of cryptographic protection - Interference with signal transmission	- Vessel seizure - Data destruction - Theft of valuable information
Electronic Chart Display Information System	- Outdated operating systems - Vulnerable update channels	- Communication failure with the Navigation System (NS) - Unauthorized seizure of ship control - Theft of sensitive data - Compromise of computers and operating systems
GNSS and GPS	- Jamming incidents - Low signal intensity - Interference disruptions - Spoofing assaults - Packet tampering	- Unauthorized seizure of the ship - Navigation System (NS) malfunctions - GPS signal manipulation leading to false information - Disruption of vessel operations - Service delays
Radar	- Disruption through signal interference - Falsification of identity in communication - Overloading or flooding of network resources	- Disruption of communication with the Nautical System (NS) - Endangerment of lives and cargo - Interruptions in cargo handling and logistics
Global Maritime Distress System	- Malicious software infiltration - Deceptive impersonation tactics - Deliberate network overloads or floods	- Incorrect vessel positioning - Subsequent assaults on Electronic Chart Display and Information Systems (ECDIS)

continued on following page

Table 2. Continued

System	Vulnerabilities	Consequences
Industrial Control Systems	-Insufficient Alarm and Control Mechanisms - Absence of integrity verification support - Ineffective patch administration - Equipment breakdowns	- Vessel takeover - Unauthorized data disclosure - Unexpected system halts
Management of propulsion and machinery, along with power control systems	- Illicit transportation - Tampering maneuvers - Unauthorized appropriation	- Ship diversion - Power Supply Interruption - Monetary Loss - Exposure of Confidential Information
Very Small Aperture Terminal	-Fabricated Signals - Malware attack - Stealing	- GPS Coordinate Manipulation - Injection of Malicious Software - Unauthorized Acquisition of Confidential Information
Information Technology Network Infrastructure	- Inadequate Access Management - Denial of Service and Distributed Denial of Service assaults - Ineffective password protocols - Absence of data encryption - Inadequate Remote Access Guidelines	- Unauthorized Physical Entry - Unauthorized Logical Entry - Unauthorized Disclosure of Confidential Documents

4. CYBERATTACKS IN THE MARITIME TRANSPORT SECTOR: A CASE STUDY ANALYSIS

It is clear that the development of automation and artificial intelligence is opening up new channels for cyberattacks aimed at the shipping sector (Liu et al., 2024). This trend is shown by recent large-scale cybersecurity breaches in this field. The technology needed to "spoof" a vessel is getting more and more affordable with easily available web resources. Spoofing incidents have already been reported from the Black Sea region, where several ships had irregularities in their GPS-derived positions, causing them to appear to be present at airports without being. In a related event to the previous one, GPS spoofing caused damage to another ship in the same area. The ship's onboard geolocation system mistakenly reported that it was on land when it was actually at sea. Moreover, there have been multiple documented cases of ship crashes and marine mishaps caused by malfunctioning navigation systems. A recent incident involved malware infiltration of a U.S. vessel's onboard control system network. Typically, this network manages cargo data, updates computerized charts, and communicates with facilities situated on the shore. Authorities from law enforcement stated that the attack's main cause was the ship's lack of strong security measures. As a result, the control systems of the vessel had their vital credentials hacked. In a related incident, hackers gained remote access to a U.S. Navy contractor's onboard computer and stole a large cache of extremely sensitive data, totaling 614 gigabytes.

Two ships were infected by the Hermes 2.1 ransomware in 2020, which was spread by the AZORult malware. A Word document with macro functionality that was attached to an email was the source of the infection, which spread to other workstations in the administrative networks. In 2021, a ransomware attack that spread via an IT consultancy firm's networks hit a number of Greek maritime companies. This incident, in which a sizable number of shipowners, ship managers, and the shipping sector as a whole were compromised, vividly demonstrated the realities of IT supply chain vulnerabilities. A short time later, attackers took control of one vessel, and in the Gulf of Oman, up to six more vessels reported losing steering control. These occurrences were classified as "cyberpiracy." Examples of recent cyber incidents involving the maritime transportation sector are shown in **Table 3**.

Table 3. Recent Cyber Incidents in the Maritime Transport Sector.

year	Incident	Consequences	reference
2019	Two ships infected by Hermes 2.1 ransomware via AZORult trojan.	Entire network contamination	(Kavallieratos & Katsikas, 2024)
2020	Ransomware attack "Mespinoza/Pysa"	Marine infrastructure compromised	(Sarowa et al., 2023)
2021	Greek shipping companies hit by ransomware spread through an IT consulting firm's system.	Reveals IT supply chain risk for shipowners and managers; numerous entities affected	(Fenton, 2024)
2022	Denial-of-service (DoS) attack targeted at a major shipping company's online booking and tracking systems.	Disrupted business operations and eroded customer trust.	(Shafi et al., 2024)
2023	Unauthorized access to navigation and control systems of a container ship, posing safety risks to crew and cargo.	Incident highlights vulnerabilities in maritime cybersecurity.	(Uflaz et al., 2024)

5. SECURITY AND SAFETY MEASURES

With the use of digital technologies, contemporary autonomous ships have become the main targets of well-known cyberattacks. Thus, in order to increase resilience against external and internal security risks, it is essential to build a wide range of countermeasures and defense techniques. The first stage is to put in place a continuous monitoring system that can give insights into the ship's security state in real time. Regarding this, a number of research have proposed using blockchain technology to improve security control in self-sufficient vessels. Blockchain technology has the potential to be extremely important for future identity and certification procedures, data integrity protection, and information security in the marine sector and autonomous vessel operations (Farah et al., 2024). Because all ship systems are interconnected, an attacker may be able to access every other system, including the engine management system and the water treatment system, from a single hacked system. As a result, the architecture of information technology (IT) and operational technology (OT) systems themselves can be a useful tool in the fight against particular types of attacks. One tactic to improve navigational safety is the Navigation Message Authentication (NMA) system, which aims to combat spoofing efforts and boost safety measures. An NMA framework would include authentication messages in the navigation message stream to verify the source and protect the cryptographic integrity of navigation data. Through the use of this technique, receivers are able to identify any unauthorized persons trying to alter navigational data. Attackers are unable to duplicate an authentication message because they do not have the key required to generate one. The significance of backup measures for warships has been emphasized by the International Maritime Organization (IMO), which has acknowledged the possible problems connected with ECDIS failure. Even though these backups might not have all the features of an ECDIS, it is nevertheless advised to utilize them in conjunction with conventional paper charts. Many respectable shipping firms choose to install an extra ECDIS onboard in order to reduce the possibility of an ECDIS malfunction.

Effective authentication and access control systems are desirable in most cases, given the volume of data generated by ships. A Public Key Infrastructure (PKI) should be implemented by the shipping sector in order to facilitate the electronic trust system. PKI guarantees secure information flow between certificate-holding entities and makes it easier to verify their veracity. Although there are already a number of Public Key Infrastructures (PKIs) in operation, most of them were founded by private businesses for profit. It is possible to create a PKI especially for the maritime sector, nevertheless. As the most trustworthy organizations in this configuration, flag states would be placed directly beneath the International Maritime Organization (IMO) and known as the "root Certificate Authority (CA)". Flag states would have the power to grant new keys and certificates to other organizations—such as businesses, ports, ships flying their flag, coastal state agencies, and other organizations—that need key certificates that are globally accessible. Furthermore, in order to encourage safe communication and digital information sharing, certifications might be given to ship owners or other organizations who are thought to be crucial to the international maritime community.

In maritime security policies, the human element holds significant importance within an organization (Chowdhury et al., 2024), serving as both the potential weakest link and the primary defense in the cybersecurity chain. In a complex interconnected ecosystem like the maritime sector, the human factor becomes even more crucial. Ships, ports, and third-party entities often operate with rotating crews possessing varying levels of cybersecurity knowledge, potentially lacking familiarity with safe system operation and established cyber hygiene practices. The absence of a cybersecurity culture could be exploited by attackers seeking to infiltrate vessels, pilfer information, or disrupt operations. Therefore, there is an urgent need in the maritime industry to elevate awareness and comprehension regarding cyber risks. The most effective approach involves fostering a cybersecurity culture that encompasses cybersecurity awareness training, education, and certification for relevant stakeholders in vessel operations (crew, third parties, ports, operators). Multiple parties are involved in collaborative defensive systems that are currently being investigated. These systems are intended to participate in the detection and reduction of possible cyberattacks at different degrees. For example, other autonomous vessels in the fleet can share detection and countermeasures put in place in reaction to an attack on one vessel.

6. CONCLUSIONS

Although the maritime sector faces comparable cybersecurity issues to other industries, fraudsters are increasingly targeting this sector's essential infrastructure. It also faces hazards particular to its kind. If a cyberattack is successful, it may cause a ship to be grounded, reveal important data, disable the Automatic Identification System (AIS) of the ship, or generate fictitious AIS reports, thereby enabling cyberpiracy and illicit, terrorist, or state actor operations. This essay has examined the security risks and weaknesses that the contemporary shipping sector faces, covering a range of cyberattack scenarios and actual occurrences. It is clear from these occurrences and their aftermath that, in the absence of sufficient safeguards for critical information systems, any ship, vessel, or port is vulnerable to cyberattacks. Because they are susceptible to cyberattacks, modern ships' IT and OT systems need to be outfitted with stronger security features. The report has also looked at possible defenses against hackers and ways to make the maritime sector less vulnerable. But there are still a number of unanswered security issues, especially in light of the growing popularity of autonomous and semi-autonomous vessels.

REFERENCES

Aalberg, A. L. (2024). *Pride and mistrust? The association between maritime bridge crew officers' professional commitment and trust in autonomy.* WMU Journal of Maritime Affairs., DOI: 10.1007/s13437-024-00329-6

Aerts, G., & Mathys, G. (2024). Discovering Trends in the Digitalization of Shipping : An Exploratory Study into Trends Using Natural Language Processing. *Journal of Marine Science and Engineering*, *12*(4), 618. DOI: 10.3390/jmse12040618

Ben Farah, M. A., Ukwandu, E., Hindy, H., Brosset, D., Bures, M., Andonovic, I., & Bellekens, X. (2022). Cyber security in the maritime industry : A systematic survey of recent advances and future trends. *Information (Basel)*, *13*(1), 22. DOI: 10.3390/info13010022

Burgén, J., & Bram, S. (2024). Safety on automated passenger ships : Exploration of evacuation scenarios for coastal vessels. *Maritime Transport Research*, *6*, 100110. DOI: 10.1016/j.martra.2024.100110

Chen, X., Ma, D., & Liu, R. W. (2024). Application of Artificial Intelligence in Maritime Transportation. *Journal of Marine Science and Engineering*, *12*(3), 439. DOI: 10.3390/jmse12030439

Chowdhury, M. N., Shafi, S., Arzaman, M., Farhan, A., Teoh, B. A., Kadhim, K. A., Salamun, H., Abdul Kadir, F. K., Said, S., & Kadir, K. A. (2024). Navigating Human Factors in Maritime Safety : A Review of Risks and Improvements in Engine Rooms of Ocean-Going Vessels. *International Journal of Safety and Security Engineering*, *14*(1), 1–14. DOI: 10.18280/ijsse.140101

Diahyleva, O. S., Yurzhenko, A. Y., & Kononova, O. Y. (2024). *Exploring the effectiveness of online learning tools and technologies while teaching Maritime English to future ship engineers. CTE Workshop Proceedings.*

Ergasheva, A., Akhmedov, F., Abdusalomov, A., & Kim, W. (2024). Advancing Maritime Safety : Early Detection of Ship Fires through Computer Vision, Deep Learning Approaches, and Histogram Equalization Techniques. *Fire (Basel, Switzerland)*, *7*(3), 84. DOI: 10.3390/fire7030084

Farah, M. B., Ahmed, Y., Mahmoud, H., Shah, S. A., Al-kadri, M. O., Taramonli, S., Bellekens, X., Abozariba, R., Idrissi, M., & Aneiba, A. (2024). A survey on blockchain technology in the maritime industry : Challenges and future perspectives. *Future Generation Computer Systems*, *157*, 618–637. DOI: 10.1016/j.future.2024.03.046

Fenton, A. J. (2024). Preventing Catastrophic Cyber–Physical Attacks on the Global Maritime Transportation System : A Case Study of Hybrid Maritime Security in the Straits of Malacca and Singapore. *Journal of Marine Science and Engineering*, *12*(3), 510. DOI: 10.3390/jmse12030510

Hafiza, W., Shukor, M. M., Jasman, F., Mutalip, Z. A., Abdullah, M. S., & Idrus, S. M. (2024). Advancement of Underwater Surveying and Scanning Techniques : A Review. *Journal of Advanced Research in Applied Sciences and Engineering Technology*, *41*(2), 256–281. DOI: 10.37934/araset.41.2.256281

Hatłas-Sowińska, P., & Misztal, L. (2024). Application of a text mining method in navigation and communication for enhancing maritime safety. *PLoS One*, *19*(3), e0299582. DOI: 10.1371/journal.pone.0299582 PMID: 38517917

Jo, Y., Choi, M., & Park, D. *Security Analysis of Ship Management Applications for Android.*

Korres, N. (2024). *Technological developments in modern e-navigation systems.*

Kavallieratos, G., & Katsikas, S. (2024). Speed 2 Comes True : Cyberattacks against Ships. In *Hybrid Threats, Cyberterrorism and Cyberwarfare* (p. 109-126). CRC Press.

Kurt, I., & Aymelek, M. (2024). Operational adaptation of ports with maritime autonomous surface ships. *Transport Policy*, *145*, 1–10. DOI: 10.1016/j.tranpol.2023.09.023

Li, X., & Yuen, K. F. (2024). A human-centred review on maritime autonomous surfaces ships : Impacts, responses, and future directions. *Transport Reviews*, *44*(4), 1–20. DOI: 10.1080/01441647.2024.2325453

Liu, L., Sajid, Z., Kravaris, C., & Khan, F. (2024). Detection and Analysis of Cybersecurity Challenges for Processing Systems. *Process Safety and Environmental Protection, 185*, 1061–1071. DOI: 10.1016/j.psep.2024.03.088

Liubarets, I. (2024). CELESTIAL NAVIGATION AS THE EMERGENCY GNSS BACKUP: ENHANCING NAVIGATIONAL RELIABILITY. *Scientific Journal of Gdynia Maritime University, 129*(129), 7–21. DOI: 10.26408/129.01

Meysam, R., & Samira, D. (2024). *Improved Navigation System of Marine Unmanned Robot Based on Sensor Fusion*. 1-6.

Oruc, A., Chowdhury, N., & Gkioulos, V. (2024). A modular cyber security training programme for the maritime domain. *International Journal of Information Security, 23*(2), 1–36. DOI: 10.1007/s10207-023-00799-4

Oruc, A., Kavallieratos, G., Gkioulos, V., & Katsikas, S. (2024). *Cyber Risk Assessment for SHips*. CRASH.

Park, C. (2024). *CYBERSECURITY RISK ASSESSMENT IN THE MARITIME INDUSTRY*.

Sarowa, S., Bhanot, B., Kumar, V., & Kumar, M. (2023). *Analysis of Attack Patterns and Cyber Threats in Healthcare Sector*. 160-165.

Seppä, E. (2024). *Evolving Automatic Identification System (AIS) in maritime*.

Shafi, M., Lashkari, A. H., Rodriguez, V., & Nevo, R. (2024). Toward Generating a New Cloud-Based Distributed Denial of Service (DDoS) Dataset and Cloud Intrusion Traffic Characterization. *Information (Basel), 15*(4), 195. DOI: 10.3390/info15040195

Soner, O., Kayisoglu, G., Bolat, P., & Tam, K. (2024). Risk sensitivity analysis of AIS cyber security through maritime cyber regulatory frameworks. *Applied Ocean Research, 142*, 103855. DOI: 10.1016/j.apor.2023.103855

Tabish, N., & Chaur-Luh, T. (2024). Maritime Autonomous Surface Ships : A Review of Cybersecurity Challenges, Countermeasures, and Future Perspectives. *IEEE Access : Practical Innovations, Open Solutions, 12*, 17114–17136. DOI: 10.1109/ACCESS.2024.3357082

Topsakal, M., & Cevher, S. (2024). Cyber Security for IEEE 802.1 Time Sensitive In-Vehicle Networking : Recent Advances and Impact Analysis of DoS Attacks. *Dokuz Eylül Üniversitesi Mühendislik Fakültesi Fen ve Mühendislik Dergisi*, *26*(76), 105–118. DOI: 10.21205/deufmd.2024267613

Uflaz, E., Sezer, S. I., Tunçel, A. L., Aydin, M., Akyuz, E., & Arslan, O. (2024). Quantifying potential cyber-attack risks in maritime transportation under Dempster–Shafer theory FMECA and rule-based Bayesian network modelling. *Reliability Engineering & System Safety*, *243*, 109825. DOI: 10.1016/j.ress.2023.109825

Varadharajan, V., Tupakula, U., & Karmakar, K. K. (2024). Techniques for Enhancing Security in Industrial Control Systems. *ACM Transactions on Cyber-Physical Systems*, *8*(1), 1–36. DOI: 10.1145/3630103

Zhang, C., Zhang, Y., Yang, C., Lu, H., Chen, F., Yan, Y., & Moser, J. (2024). Graphene nanomechanical vibrations measured with a phase-coherent software-defined radio. *Communications Engineering*, *3*(1), 45. DOI: 10.1038/s44172-024-00186-4 PMID: 39103561

Zhang, X., Liu, T., Li, Y., & Bao, J. (2024). A novel approach to hazard evaluation for MASS operation based on a hesitant fuzzy linguistic term set. *Maritime Transport Research*, *6*, 100107. DOI: 10.1016/j.martra.2024.100107

Chapter 7
Cyber Security in Cyber Physical Systems: Challenges and Opportunities

Muhammad Muzamil Aslam
https://orcid.org/0000-0002-8711-2907
Universiti Brunei Darussalam, Brunei

Sajid Ali
University of Education, Pakistan

Haji Gul
Universiti Brunei Darussalam, Brunei

Ali Tufail
https://orcid.org/0000-0003-4871-4080
Universiti Brunei Darussalam, Brunei

ABSTRACT

This chapter provides a comprehensive exploration of the crucial topic of cyber security within the realm of cyber-physical systems (CPS). In the age of smart living, ensuring the validity of our data has become a formidable task. It's more convenient to live in smart cities and residences. Even with the use of difficult passwords, there is always a security risk due to the intricate network of the IoT and the Internet of Everything (IoE).

DOI: 10.4018/979-8-3693-6371-3.ch007

First step in bolstering security against ever-changing threats. Next, the chapter delves into the specific challenges and unique characteristics of securing cyber-physical systems. To address these challenges, the chapter presents an overview of current cyber security techniques and practices employed in CPS. Furthermore, the chapter explores emerging trends and future directions in the field of cyber security for CPS. The chapter also highlights the importance of collaboration among stakeholders, including researchers, industry professionals, and policymakers, to address the evolving cyber security landscape of CPS.

1. INTRODUCTION

Computing, networking, and physical processes are closely combined in a cyber-physical system. Subsystems that function independently of one another and possess the capability to interact with the external environment are integrated subsystems (networks) that oversee and regulate physical processes through feedback loops that allow them to adjust their behavior according to the situation. CPS and cyber-social systems (CSS) are the sources of a new computing paradigm known as cyber-physical-social computing, or physical-cyber-social computing (Lee, 2008; Pang et al., 2018). Social spaces and indications of public engagement and participation are added to CPS by cyber-physical social systems (CPSS) (Ge et al., 2019).

1.1. Background

A process that integrates technology and knowledge to offer autonomy, dependability, systematicity, and control without requiring human involvement is known as "Industry 4.0," and it is associated with the broad use of CPS (Ge et al., 2019)(Aslam, Tufail, Apong, De Silva, Kalinaki, et al., 2024). IoT, big data, smart technology, cloud computing, etc. are some of the major technological advancements in CPS.

CPS serves as the foundation for the advancement of smart cars, wearable technology, mobile systems, national security systems, meteorology, smart manufacturing, smart healthcare, smart buildings and infrastructure, smart cities, and other fields (Figure 1). Security and privacy risks abound as a result of the CPS applications' explosive expansion.

Figure 1. CPS Applications

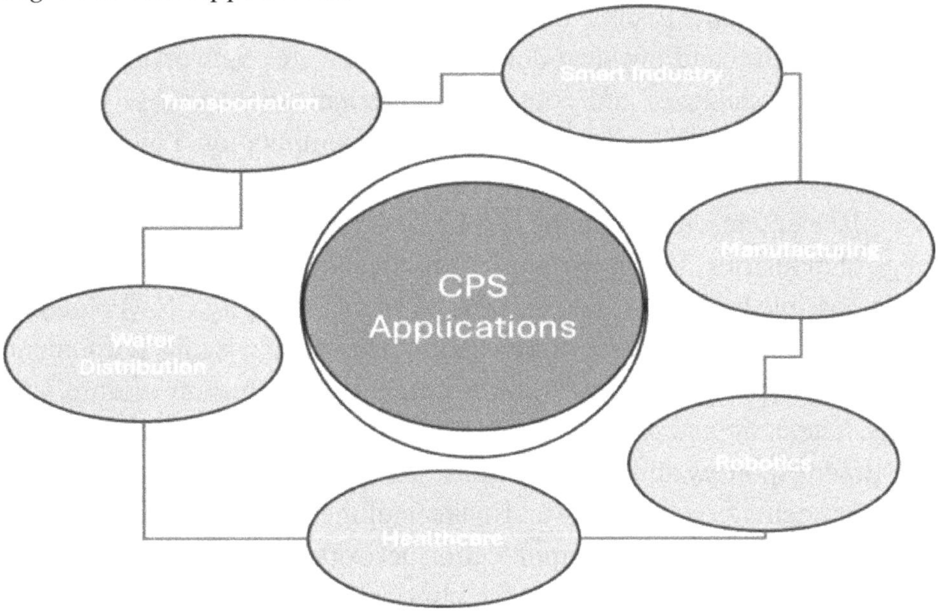

Real-world IoT devices and processes can be monitored and controlled by a variety of networked systems that make up CPS. Actuators, aggregators, and sensors make up the three primary parts of CPS. CPS systems can also perceive their surroundings and have the capacity to manipulate and adapt to the physical world (Guo et al., 2023). Their adaptability and capacity to alter system process execution times through real-time computing are primarily to blame for this. As shown in Figure 1, CPS systems are really applied in many domains and integrated into many systems, including military systems, power transmission systems, communication systems, agriculture/ecosystems, and autonomous systems (such as robots, drones, and vehicle autonomy) (Aslam et al., 2023). Put differently, medical services need to be empowered in addition to the health care sector. Additionally, supply chain management can leverage CPS to enable manufacturing methods that are safe, economical, temporary, and environmentally responsible.

1.2. Overview of the integration of physical and cyber components

Physical processes can be integrated with computing, communications, and control systems thanks to the paradigm known as CPS, which combines the digital and physical domains. CPS creates networked systems that monitor, analyze, and control the physical world in real time by combining sensors, actuators, networks, and computational intelligence. This article examines the idea of cyber-physical systems, as well as their essential elements, uses, and the revolutionary impacts they have across a range of industries. The integration of digital and physical surroundings is made possible by the various essential parts that make up CPS(Poudel & Munir, 2018). Sensors gather information from the physical environment by monitoring a range of factors like movement, pressure, temperature, and more. Actuators give physical processes a way to be controlled, enabling real-time responses and modifications. While computer algorithms and control systems assess the data and make intelligent judgments and actions depending on the inputs, communication networks enable the interchange of data and instructions between the physical and digital realms(Yang et al., 2019).

CPS has many uses that can change industries and enhance different kinds of operations. CPS makes it possible for manufacturers to create "smart factories," which are networks of connected machinery and processes that allow for real-time optimization, monitoring, and predictive maintenance. CPS encourages driverless cars, effective logistics, and intelligent traffic management in the transportation industry. CPS is used by smart cities for effective waste management, energy management, and infrastructure monitoring. Through intelligent health systems, tailored medicine, and remote patient monitoring, CPS can improve healthcare. Among many other applications, CPS is utilized in home automation, agriculture, and environmental monitoring (Aslam, Tufail, Apong, De Silva, & Raza, 2024).

1.3. Security in CPS

Even though CPS has many advantages, there are still obstacles in the way of its general adoption. CPS security and privacy must be guaranteed because networked systems are susceptible to cyberattacks. Resolving interoperability concerns, standardized interfaces, and building strong and dependable communications networks are continuous challenges. Furthermore, CPS-related ethical and legal issues like data ownership and liability need to be properly considered. A cyber-physical system is made up of numerous components that are combined. A company's cybersecurity network depends on the notion of CPS, which includes IT infrastructure, smart cities, IoT, and operational technology (OT) (Aslam, Tufail, Apong, De Silva, & Raza, 2024). The rationale is that if the required cybersecurity precautions are not taken and incorporated into the security plan, these structures may become simple and vulnerable targets for cyberattacks. Enlarging the risk domain to encompass cyber-physical systems facilitates the assurance that organizational business processes remain unhindered. Because cyber-physical systems are the meeting point of an organization's physical assets and IT infrastructure, protecting data access and security using cutting-edge techniques can stop cyberattacks from causing physical asset damage and interfering with business operations. Organizations are gradually beginning to understand the significance of systems cyber physics and their role in access security beyond 2021, when they face the potential repercussions of cyber threats breaking into systems by using credentials for privileged user accounts that have been stolen or by entering privileged access accounts (M. M. Aslam, Liping Du, 2020).

By 2025, half of industrial firms and governmental institutions should have consolidated their supply chain security and cyber-physical security teams under the direction of a chief security officer, predicts Gartner (Technology-Related Insights for Your Critical Business Decisions, n.d.). Physical systems will be incorporated into the supply chain and IT infrastructure over the next several years, as the executive director or CEO will be directly responsible for security.

There are two categories for CPS security:

- Information security is a concern when processing, aggregating, and distributing vast amounts of data via a network, particularly in open, loosely connected networks. Control security is concerned with dynamic data protection, whereas information security is more concerned with data protection, such as through encryption. safeguard systems from cyberattacks.
- Control security protects the control system against attacks on the system estimation and control algorithm and involves solving any control challenge in the network environment.

2. THREAT LANDSCAPE IN CYBER PHYSICAL SYSTEMS

There are two categories for CPS security:

Information security is a concern when processing, aggregating, and distributing vast amounts of data via a network, particularly in open, loosely connected networks. Control security is concerned with dynamic data protection, whereas information security is more concerned with data protection, such as through encryption. safeguard systems from cyberattacks (He & Yan, 2016).

Threat modeling seeks to examine the cyber obstacles that companies must overcome in order to defend against cyberthreats that compromise the system in question. The overall procedure entails examining potential points of attack, getting a thorough grasp of the underlying architecture, and offering security controls as a means of fending off these threats. Threat modeling, therefore, outlines who will target what and how the goals will be accomplished (Abbaspour et al., 2018). Threat modeling for ICPS must first be implemented. This can be done by outlining the general strategy, including its features, classification, techniques, and models, and then identifying the threat security control countermeasures.

Threat characterization establishes the type, capabilities, and motivation of the opponent as well as their profile and behavior in order to launch an assault. According to (Aslam, Tufail, Apong, De Silva, & Raza, 2024), the opponent may be internal or external in nature. Insiders are people who, for a variety of reasons (financial, retaliation, or ego), execute unauthorized acts while possessing a certain amount of permitted access to the ICPS. Aliens could be highly technologically advanced enemies like nation states, organized crime, terrorist organizations, and threat actor groupings that aim to strike ICPS for political or economic gains (Gul et al., 2022).

Intelligence gathered on adversary tactics, techniques, and behaviors (TTP) is used to classify threats. The MITRE Common Attack Pattern Enumeration and Classification (CAPECTM) (MITRE, 2020) is one of the threat taxonomies available in ICPS. It offers a thorough taxonomy of attack patterns together with advise on mitigating adversary consequences to enhance network defense (Gul et al., 2021). The authors in (Shiva et al., 2009) developed the AVOIDIT Cyberattack Taxonomy, which offers guidance on categorizing any vulnerabilities that could be exploited to launch a cyberattack. With an emphasis on incident response, the ENISA Incident Reference Taxonomy (Taurins et al., n.d.) helps incident managers to automatically and methodically handle common cyber occurrences. In order to direct threat analysis or comprehend adversary behavior, threat methodology seeks to provide procedures that specify concepts, instruments, and behaviors. Numerous threat approaches exist within the domain of ICPS. According to (Hutchins et al., n.d.), the authors created the "cyber kill chain," which outlines the stages an attacker must take to initiate a cyberattack: reconnaissance, weaponization, delivery, exploitation, installation, command and control, and action against the victim. The ICS Cyber Kill Chain (Hutchins et al., n.d.) is a version of the Cyber Kill Chain technique that industrial control systems (ICS) by utilizing two stages to examine cyberattacks: the planning and execution of cyberattacks and the creation and execution of ICS attacks (Shiva et al., 2009; Taurins et al., n.d.). By taking into account the root and leaf nodes, which are logically connected using AND and OR to depict the adversary's aims, an attack tree (Saini et al., 2008) is a technique for modeling the sequence of attacks on a target system. Imitation, tampering, denial, information disclosure, denial of service, and privilege escalation are the six security risks defined by the STRIDE (Conducting a STRIDE-Based Threat Analysis Secure Connected Places Playbook Cyber Security Resources for Local Authorities, n.d.) approach, which is used to investigate ICPS vulnerabilities.

A threat model is a technique or framework for determining, assessing, and proposing security control measures for risks. Threat models may take an attacker-centric approach, emphasizing the viewpoint, objectives, drives, and actions of the attacker. The cyberattack's target system or software is the center of attention for the system-centric concept. According to (Conducting a STRIDE-Based Threat Analysis Secure Connected Places Playbook Cyber Security Resources for Local Authorities, n.d.), the asset-centric approach conducts cyberattacks against a target device or system based on the assets that need to be protected. Certain threat models, such as MITRE's Tactics, Techniques and Common Sense (ATT&CK) model, are expressly designed to address ICPS (Strom et al., n.d.). By researching various attack lifecycle stages, concentrating on opponent behavior, recognizing and evaluating the tactics and approaches employed, and finally suggesting attack detection and mitigation strategies, attacks might be prevented. injury. In addition, MITER (Strom et al., n.d.) produces the ICS ATT&CK model, a modified ATT&CK variant intended to address OT and ICS issues. The model's scope encompasses systems and applications relevant to the industry, such as industrial IoT devices, safety instrumented systems (SIS), programmable logic controllers (PLCs), and human-machine interfaces (HMIs). The five steps include identifying security objectives, conducting an application survey, breaking down the application, identifying threats, and identifying vulnerabilities. Microsoft Threat Modelling (Conducting a STRIDE-Based Threat Analysis Secure Connected Places Playbook Cyber Security Resources for Local Authorities, n.d.) is a model that helps create cyber threats and assesses the efficacy of security countermeasures.

2.1. Common cyber threats and vulnerabilities in CPS.

One of the primary features of cyber dangers is their scalability, which allows them to be readily mechanized and copied. You should also anticipate that they will spread widely over untrusted domains. Cyber-physical dangers are those that originate in cyberspace and impact a system's physical space. Cyberspace is the source of cyber-physical risks, which affect the CPS's physical space. The following are among the CPS threat classes (Harkat et al., 2024): denial of origin, information leakage, identity fraud, data manipulation, privilege escalation, and denial of service (DoS). The primary concerns around CPS security are listed in (Barbeau et al., 2019; Ge et al., 2019; Pang et al., 2018): 1) being aware of the risks and potential repercussions of assaults 2) defining CPS's distinct characteristics and how they vary from conventional CPS security data; and 3) talking about potential security vulnerabilities for CPS methods.

However, it is helpful to describe the relationships between threat source areas in order to comprehend new classes of CPS hazards, such as those found in smart grids and SCADA (Supervisory Control and Data Acquisition) systems. Affected locations and threats (Cengiz et al., 2022; Rani et al., 2021).

Threats may be unintentional, unintentional, or environmental, according to ISO/IEC 27001:2013. Common dangers include things like physical harm, natural disasters, the loss of vital services, radiological failure, information leaks (like eavesdropping or modified software), technical malfunctions, unauthorized operations (like data corruption), and functional compromises (like counterfeiting). as well as rights violations).

Figure 2 presents the analysis results of previous security research, which led to the proposal of attack on the CPS functional model(Sotelo Monge et al., 2019). The following categories of attacks are included in the “tree's” branches: Attacks on actuators (Actuation); Attacks on sensor devices (Sensing); Attacks on feedback (Feedback).

Figure 2. CPS security objectives

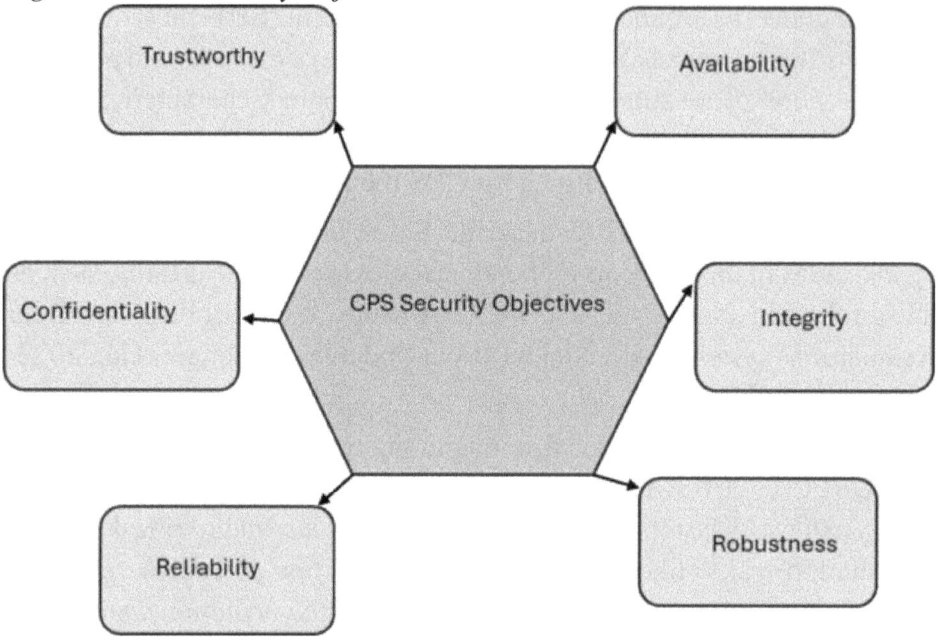

3. PRINCIPLES OF CYBER SECURITY IN CPS

The linking of the cyber worlds of computer science and computer engineering hardware with applications in the physical world is the fundamental idea of CPS. Elements of modeling, physics, and concrete concepts like risk and uncertainty are examples of fundamental ideas in the physical world. The concepts of computer science and computer engineering both deal with networking, programming, embedded systems, and algorithms. The understanding of physical repercussions at the physical layer as well as at the physical-cyber interface is thus a key component of CPS education, which extends beyond exposure to the standard dynamical systems models (ordinary differential or difference equations) (Chiew et al., 2018; Rudd et al., 2017).

Science, Engineering, and Medicine National Academies. 2016. Education in Cyber-Physical Systems for the 21st Century. New York, NY: National Academies Press. 10.17226/23686 is the URL to use(Skorton &

Bear, 2018)(About the National Academy of Medicine 2 Letter from the President 3 Organizational Chart 4 NAM Council 5 Our Impact Program Highlights Member Spotlight, 2016). One hardware link between the real and virtual worlds is a sensor. These are the main tools for gathering information from the real world and utilizing it as input for the virtual world. It is essential to comprehend sensor qualities and concepts as well as how to use them while taking into account real-world and sensor limits. However, in order to make system development simpler, high-level abstractions frequently have the unintended side effect of concealing important physical world concepts that programmers must understand in order for the CPSs they create to function as intended.

Science, Engineering, and Medicine National Academies 2016 (About the National Academy of Medicine 2 Letter from the President 3 Organizational Chart 4 NAM Council 5 Our Impact Program Highlights Member Spotlight, 2016). Education in Cyber-Physical Systems for the 21st Century.

Signal processing techniques are used to process raw data once they are gathered (Z. Wang et al., 2023). The following are essential concepts in signal processing: convolution, linear transforms (such as the discrete Fourier transform and fast Fourier transform), machine learning, decision-making, sensor fusion, analog and digital filtering, time and frequency domain analysis, linear signals and systems theory, noise and statistical characterization of signals (Jagannath et al., 2020). The subject of sensor dependability and the real-time, safety-critical implementation of these signal processing techniques on embedded CPUs must both be taken into account in CPS. In traditional signal processing courses, these problems are frequently ignored.

The foundation of CPS is control. Aspects of control theory that are pertinent to networks, hybrid systems, stochastic systems, and digital systems include stability and optimization in addition to control techniques. What effects distributed systems have on control and the inherent delays they cause are particularly significant in the cyber domain (Alemu & Muhammed, 2023).

CPS engineering also requires an understanding of the fundamental principles of today's networked, wireless, real-time world, as well as the growing integration of cyberphysical systems into our economy and society. Researchers need to know this information in the following areas:

- Distributed system
- Physical properties
- Communication and networking
- Embedded systems
- Human interaction

3.1. Confidentiality, integrity, and availability (CIA) triad in CPS security

First comes availability, followed by integrity, confidentiality, and authenticity in assessing the security of the CPS. For instance, if a malevolent or unauthorized entity gained access to the system, private data would be exposed, and integrity would be compromised because of the ability of such a party to alter data. An episode of system failure does not precede a security assault. Thus, taking into account the relationships between CPS components presents the biggest security difficulty (Gauthama et al., 2021).

3.2. Defense-in-depth approach for securing CPS

Within the IoT, insider attacks are the most challenging to counter among the various forms of cyberattacks on a CPS. This is because an insider not only possesses privileged knowledge about the networks that link the cyber and physical components of the system, but they also have authorized access to the network due to their granted privileges. They become one of the most dangerous attackers because of this. Insiders have the ability to enter systems covertly and execute assaults in a way that avoids discovery by either delaying the response of the detection and protection system or by causing harm before it is discovered. Maintaining the physical system's safety for a safety-critical CPS requires prompt detection and efficient mitigation to eliminate any threats (Shafik, 2023).

Cross-layer security vulnerabilities of cyber-physical systems are addressed in (W. Wang et al., 2021). In (Gómez et al., 2020), intrusion detection techniques have also been studied in order to keep an eye out for any noticeable irregularities in network data. But when it comes to insider attacks, the old methods of limiting access are no longer sufficient. The required protection can only be offered by implementing more strong multi-layer security mechanisms (Qassim et al., 2019). Generally speaking, there are three tiers to defensive protection methods against cyberattacks: (a) prevention, (b) detection, and (c) mitigation. By utilizing a variety of strategies, including the installation of firewalls, security borders, and safety limitations, attack prevention seeks to reduce the probability of an assault. These are carried out during the configuration of the network. Cyberattacks can be quickly and accurately identified online during system operation by employing both data- and model-based methods. The first one doesn't use system models. Data fusion algorithms (Ahmed et al., 2024), machine learning (Abdelaty et al., 2022), knowledge-based approaches (Yu et al., 2021a, 2021b), and traffic data pattern analysis and identification techniques (Bitar et al., 2018; Khedaskar et al., 2018) are used to identify anomalies. These methods mine the observed data for hidden patterns linked to possible assaults.

Insider attackers have two options for executing stealth attacks if they are aware of the physical process's dynamic behaviors (Chen et al., 2019; Ott & Wiesenfeld, 1994). One approach to get around anomaly detection systems and trick controllers is to manipulate measurement data through a process known as false-data injection (FDI). In order to trick the controller into executing commands that harm physical systems, the other method is known as a replay attack. This involves playing back a previously recorded "legitimate" data sequence over the communication network. The attackers' primary objective is to avoid discovery and maintain their stealthiness for the duration of the attack, regardless of the exact attack strategies they employ. Therefore, in order to create a defense mechanism that works, it's critical to comprehend how cyber-physical systems interact as well as to spot any potential weak points and situations that an attacker might use to initiate an attack.

3.3. Risk assessment and threat modeling for CPS

The three stages of the CPS risk assessment mode are: (i) defining the system's future state; (ii) assessing the likelihood that the event will occur; and (iii) estimating the repercussions. Its components include the identification of vulnerabilities, threats, and assets (worth) (Cui et al., 2019).

The risk assessment process begins with asset identification. An asset might have a physical presence, like in medical devices, office buildings, equipment, operations, educational facilities, or information, or it can have an intangible presence, like firm information or an association's reputation.

Threat Identification: In the field of CPS, this stage aids in identifying hazards that are of the utmost importance. When it comes to threat identification, data may be used to measure how frequently a threat occurs while sampling records and logs in the Intrusion Detection System (IDS) can be used to measure how frequently a danger occurs in addition to many other techniques.

Vulnerability identification is the process of analyzing a system's functions and finding weaknesses. It also involves figuring out what mitigations or corrective steps would be best to lessen or remove any vulnerabilities that may be present (Abdelaty et al., 2022; Liu et al., 2024).

4. SECURING CYBER PHYSICAL SYSTEMS

Cyber-physical systems are difficult and vitally necessary to secure since they are intricate, consist of several kinds of equipment and protocols, and are networked with one other and the Internet.

Traditional security methods are put to the test by cyber-physical systems, and businesses are starting to realize that OT is not the only cyber-physical asset they need to worry about due to the complexity and variety of both new and old connected assets. Cyber-physical systems ranging from the IoT to the internet of medical things (IoMT) and smart buildings, among others, are capable of functions beyond simple data processing. These resources are often used in operational or mission-critical contexts, where operational resilience and worker safety are of utmost importance, and they bridge the gap between the physical and digital realms. It will take years, if not decades, before a new generation of connected assets appears with more natively integrated security processes and channels. This is standard procedure for technological advancement.

Many new devices have been made possible by technological breakthroughs; however security and safety are not taken into consideration while designing and implementing these technologies. The next few decades may be impacted by current designs due to this difficulty and the fact that many device lifespans are expressed in decades. Organizations will be able to create a solid CPS security strategy with the assistance of early analysis, comprehension, and resolution of these concerns. In addition, due of their susceptibility to attack and degree of criticality, cyber-physical systems are appealing targets. The physical environment in which we live and the technologies on which we rely are not under danger, notwithstanding the high costs and other financial ramifications associated with compromised IT networks and security breaches that steal personal data. When cyberattacks penetrate the OT domain and have an adverse physical effect, lives and livelihoods are at danger. Figure 1 represents the open security challenges in CPS.

Figure 3. Open access challenges in CPS

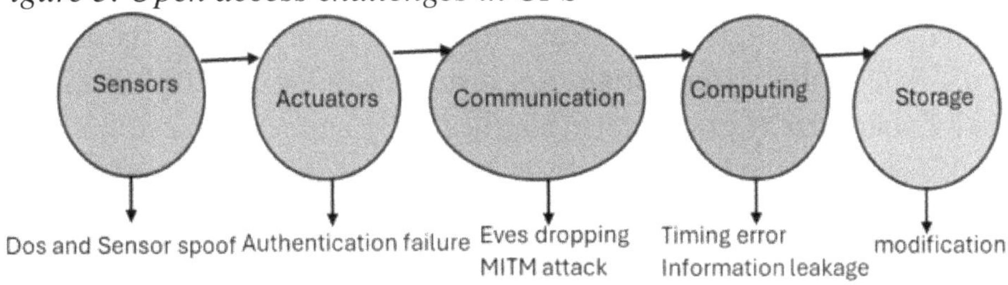

4.1. Secure design principles for CPS components.

It is necessary to clarify the type of security decisions under consideration before delving into the state of the art of identifying, making, and tracing security decisions. Decisions about security fall into two categories:

those about security operations (beyond the purview of this study) and those about security design. Decisions about security operations, such as keeping an eye out for new vulnerabilities and attacks and determining how to address them, have an impact on a system's security during its operational period. Decisions about security operations should aim to "defend the system," but decisions about security design should aim to "build a defensible system." The maturity of techniques and technologies supporting security operations decisions contrasts sharply with those supporting security design decisions, indicating a substantial imbalance. Security incident and event monitoring (SIEM), intrusion detection and prevention (IDS/IPS), vulnerability scanners, antivirus software, and other tools are just a few examples of supporting tools for security operations decisions like "do we need to patch this vulnerability" or "how do we react to a suspicious change in data traffic."

Less developed techniques and technologies are used while making security design judgments. The state of the art for decision making and tracing (number 2) and decision identification (number 1) is shown separately below.

Security needs checklists are the state of the art when it comes to determining security design decisions for CPSs, or the security methods to choose.

Frequently, these check lists are offered as technical reports or standards. A few of the most often used lists are ISO/IEC 27001:2022, the NIST Cybersecurity Framework (Shafik, 2023), and several sections of the ISA/IEC 62443 standard series (part 2-1 (Shafik, 2023) for asset owners, parts-4-1 and -4-2 for components, and part-3-3 for integrated systems) (Shafik, 2023).

There are more detailed checklists available; Eckhart et al., for instance, offer a variety of security procedures and technologies that should be taken into account while CPS engineering (Shafik & Kalinaki, 2023). Even Ross Anderson's book "Security Engineering" finds a lot of its power in offering checklists of security precautions that ought to be taken into account, coupled with explanations and examples to assist the reader see why they are necessary.

Outside of CPSs, the use of checklists to detect security decisions is not new. In a 1993 work, Baskerville studied information systems security design techniques and divided them into three generations (Aslam et al., 2024): the first generation, known as checklist approaches, dates back to the 1970s.

A straightforward, practical method for ensuring that crucial choices are not missed is to use checklists. Naturally, lists get longer because this only functions if all pertinent decisions are included. As noted by Dale Peterson in his keynote address at the S4x23 ICS security conference (Shafik, 2023), requirements are only infrequently deleted from these checklists.

However, because they often only address best practices and technology that are specifically related to security—such as encryption and authentication—security needs checklists are insufficient. Nevertheless, there are other "covert" security choices that, while not always thought of as security-related, can nevertheless have an impact on security. These could be low-level choices like whether to build a safety shutdown mechanically or electronically—the latter being more vulnerable to remote hacking.

Producing and tracking security decisions are more difficult than identifying them, and the current state of the art encompasses a wider range of methods. Checklists are reasonable for identifying security decisions, as was previously noted, but they don't offer much advice when it comes to actually making decisions. Using a checklist to facilitate decision-making requires presuming that every item on the list must be implemented; as a result, every decision that is identified is automatically set to "yes." When checklists were first utilized for security decision making, as noted by Baskerville in (Shafik, 2023), this was reasonable because there were very few security solutions available, making it realistic to apply them all.

According to Baskerville, this kind of approach was no longer practical even in 1993 due to the proliferation of security solutions. Saying "yes" to every potential security solution is becoming less and less feasible after 30 years. Choosing the solutions that will benefit from security better than ever before is now a crucial aspect of security decision making.

Compliance-driven, risk-driven, goal-driven, and library-supported are the four types of security decision making that the authors discussed in (Shafik, 2023). It is up to each business to decide which of the four decision-making pathways best suits its needs. By expressing one's own security priorities as a risk or undesirable occurrence to avoid or as a design goal to achieve, one can make risk-driven and goal-driven decisions.

4.2. Authentication and access control mechanisms in CPS.

Access control is necessary to manage user, peripheral device, or program rights when they request to use specific infrastructure resources in this complex environment where any element may interact and cooperate with any other element. For a number of reasons, the implementation of traditional access control models in industrial systems is hampered by the integration of IT technologies, particularly the cloud. These can be summed up as information exchange between diverse entities that differ in terms of performance, sensitivity, and restrictions. As a result, in order to precisely adapt the existing models and suggest novel strategies that satisfy these criteria, it becomes necessary to examine the entire spectrum of requirements that access control provides in the impending scenario. It is especially helpful to take into account the potential impact that these security measures may have on the physical world by adding to the overhead of control and monitoring processes.

Reviewing how the integration of IT technologies affects industrial networks is a prerequisite to determining the requirements for access control in the CPS infrastructure. The architecture outlined in the ISA-95 standard (Shafik, 2023) is what a conventional control network uses. This means that the producing process itself is at level 0 (the base of the pyramid), and the devices that interface with it (such PLCs and RTUs) are at level 1. Devices that manage the production process (such as SCADAs and HMIs) are located in level 2, while devices that manage the workflow (such as MES systems) are found in level 3. The infrastructure for logistics, inventory, ERP, and planning is located at the highest level. In this context, the adoption of cyber-physical systems entails the introduction of sophisticated computing and communication capabilities to guarantee intelligent data management and real-time data collecting from the physical world. In order to provide feedback from cyberspace back to the physical world, the objective is to collect data from every connected machine and execute targeted analytics to extract new insights. Because software and hardware have become more standardized, this evolution is actually supported by the implementation of a number of communication protocols. These range from field bus protocols (e.g., HART; wirelessHART, etherCAP, IO-Link) to protocols utilizing Ethernet and TCP/IP, such as Ethernet/IP, Ethernet POWERLINK, CANopen, PROFINET, Modbus/TCP, or HART/IP. Particularly intriguing are standards like CIP, OPC UA, and MTConnect that were developed to enable the interoperable management of many kinds of industrial equipment. Overall, this causes the traditional architecture to change toward a distributed and decentralized form.

Within the framework of the new architecture model, all infrastructure components—from machines to operators to the product itself—are interconnected amongst themselves through devices situated at lower levels of the architecture in order to collect data. However, monitoring as a service and simple substation connectivity are made possible by utilizing the cloud. This makes it difficult to come to a global consensus or adopt any common definition because different organizations with different applications and restrictions might work together to establish a collaborative environment. With the ability to handle a variety of devices, access control mechanisms implemented (in field devices, PLCs, or cloud resources) seek to limit what each entity should be able to access and the connections that can be accepted in this complicated scenario (Shafik, 2023). Since real solutions must be dynamic and fine-grained in order to handle multiple users and limited resources, they are still in their early stages of development.

4.3. Intrusion detection and prevention systems for CPS.

Machine learning and (deep) neural networks are frequently used to detect intrusions for CPSs and IoT. Though many of the IDS proposals currently in existence prioritize the mere application of complex models, like convolutional neural networks (CNN) and long short-term memory (LSTM), over their usefulness in real-world operations, the body of literature on the subject is being driven by the growing availability of public intrusion datasets and usable deep learning frameworks. Semi-supervised learning is a better option than supervised learning for a workable IDS for

CPSs. Semi-supervised training is more extensively applicable to obtain the "preparedness" to identify unexpected attacks because it is unlikely that attacks will be known in advance. Another thing to consider is the data sources: in order to ensure more portability, intrusive data sources like passive network traffic tracking, or "sniffing," or monitoring probes and facilities found in any standard CPS should be leveraged by IDSes.

5. FUTURE TRENDS AND CHALLENGES IN CPS SECURITY

Guidelines (Bowen et al., 2006) from the National Institute of Standards and Technology (NIST) (Bowen et al., 2006) state that different multi-factor authentication should be used to ensure confidence between IoT and CPS. This is because safe, secure, privacy, consistency, dependability, robustness, reliability, interaction, and coordination are all necessary for both IoT and CPS systems to function well and be trustworthy. A perfect CPS system can be created if this requirement is met. Therefore, when developing Industrial Control devices, several CPS testing methodologies were employed to assess the devices' security. When it comes to safe-guarding CPS domains, layers, and components, implementing security measures offers numerous advantages. The use of these security measures has an influence on CPS systems, notwithstanding these benefits like low performance, power consumption, higher cost, transmission delays and compatibility challenges etc.

5.1. Emerging Technologies and their Impact on CPS Security

The development of Cyber-Physical Systems (CPS) is now mostly driven by artificial intelligence (AI). Innovation potential and new horizons have been made possible by the smooth integration of AI technology into CPS.

We shall explore many facets of AI integration in CPS here, emphasizing its revolutionary potential.

The evolution of CPS is centered on automation enabled by AI. CPS can automatically monitor, control, and optimize physical processes with the use of deep neural networks and machine learning algorithms. Numerous industries are affected by this automation, including energy management, manufacturing, healthcare, and transportation.

Predictive maintenance is among the many ways AI is being used in CPS. To forecast when machinery or equipment is likely to break, machine learning models examine sensor data. By being proactive, this strategy lowers maintenance costs, minimizes downtime, and guarantees continuous operations.

AI-powered CPS optimizes procedures for optimal efficiency on a constant basis. AI algorithms adjust in real-time to changing conditions, boosting overall performance in a variety of applications, such as operating industrial robots, monitoring energy consumption in smart bu In CPS, it is imperative to make decisions in real time, particularly when making snap decisions that affect efficiency and safety. Large volumes of data are processed by AI algorithms from sensors and actuators, allowing systems to quickly make well-informed decisions. Autonomous cars, for example, use AI to navigate and prevent collisions. idling's, and optimizing supply chain logistics.

Creating completely autonomous systems is the ultimate goal of AI integration in CPS. AI vision, decision-making, and control are combined in these systems—such as drones and self-driving cars—to enable autonomous operation in challenging conditions. They have the power to completely transform logistics, transportation, and more.

In addition to increasing CPS's operational effectiveness, AI-powered automation also helps them become more flexible and responsive to changing circumstances. As AI technologies develop, we should anticipate increasingly complex automation and decision-making in the context of cyber-physical systems.

Technological innovation and efficiency are entering a new age in CPS with its confluence with the IoT. By allowing smarter, more connected systems, this synergy between IoT and CPS is revolutionizing industry operations. The nuances of this partnership are examined as we go into this fascinating trend below.

5.2. Sensors Integration

Sensor utilization is one of the core components of IoT integration into CPS. By gathering information from the real environment, these sensors act as the system's eyes and ears. The wide variety of IoT sensors allows CPS to collect a multitude of data, from sophisticated imaging equipment to temperature and humidity sensors.

5.2.1. Data Acquisition

When CPS acquires and processes this data, the true magic happens. Continuous data flow is made possible by the smooth integration of IoT devices, which gives CPS the ability to make deft judgments instantly. Efficiency is being driven by data collecting through Internet of Things devices, whether it be for environmental parameter tracking or industrial machinery monitoring.

5.2.2. Scalability

IoT's inherent scalability is a game-changer in CPS. Systems can easily accommodate additional sensors and devices, adapting to changing requirements without a major overhaul. This scalability ensures that CPS remains flexible and responsive to evolving needs.

5.2.3. Energy Efficiency

Energy efficiency is a consideration in the design of IoT devices. These gadgets can run longer on battery power because to low-power sensors and improved communication methods. This improves sustainability while lowering operating expenses.

Challenges with data formats, communication protocols, and domain-specific needs arise when integrating several domains. Nevertheless, these gaps are filled in by creative solutions like middleware, data translators, and adaptable interfaces. The effective communication between various CPS components is made possible by these solutions.

5.3. Challenges in securing interconnected CPS ecosystems

Compared to traditional internet systems, CPS offers noticeably improved safety performance because of its innately high sensitivity, dependability, and connectivity qualities.

In the context of network information exchange, in particular, CPS communication crosses many networks, so it is important to take into account the security threats related to different network connections.

Cloud computing security threats, for example, must also be considered while using cloud computing networks as the background network.

In general, infrastructure security and information security are the two primary subcategories of CPS security.

5.4. Infrastructure Security Threats

Many infrastructure elements included in various CPS systems, including servers, routers, sensors, and protocols, are essential to the system's seamless operation. Physical damage, equipment malfunction, line failure, electromagnetic interference, and internal threats are thus possible forms of security threats.

Because CPS systems are highly sensitive to their physical surroundings, robust security measures must be incorporated into their design in order to successfully mitigate these dangers.

5.4.1. Information Security Threats

The physical layer, information layer, and application control layer are the three tiers into which information security threats inside CPS systems can be divided.

Physical layer risks include eavesdropping, tampering, interference, exhaustion, clock synchronization, node control, node capture, passive assaults, tampering, eavesdropping, and exhaustion.

Authentication attacks, cross-network assaults, routing attacks, malicious code, distributed denial of service (DoS) attacks, user privacy exposure, control network DoS attacks, flood attacks, incorrect path selection, and tunnel attacks are examples of information layer threats.

Threats to the application control layer include viruses, Trojan horses, control command forgeries, perceptual data tampering, control network denial-of-service attacks, resonance assaults, and vulnerabilities.

To protect the integrity and security of CPS systems, it is essential to identify and counter these various risks.

General security challenges in CPS are like security by design, CPS security, real time monitoring, uncoordinated variations etc.

5.5. - Regulatory and policy considerations for CPS security

Control system protection, particularly SCADA, has historically prioritized dependability in an effort to protect the system from sporadic mistakes. Finding ways to protect cyber-physical systems from malevolent cyberattacks so becomes a crucial topic.

5.5.1 Prevention: A lot of businesses are putting safety precautions in place at their operations handling chemicals, oil, gas, and water. It is more efficient to stop attacks on medical devices early rather than waiting for them to happen. For preserving control system safety, initiatives such as the NIST Guide on Industrial Control System (ICS) Security provide guidance. Furthermore, safety is improved by standardizing communication across sensor networks. Security is improved in wireless communication devices by implementing confidentiality and integrity safeguards.

5.5.2. Detection: Security's most important components are detection and recovery from threats. To detect indications of intrusion, security engineers keep an eye on network or computer system traces. For estimate and control algorithms, deception attack detection techniques are still lacking in sophistication. For autonomous real-time decision-making algorithms, human-computer interaction research is difficult but necessary.

For safety-critical applications, autonomous and real-time detection and response algorithms require new ideas from the field of control theory.

5.5.3 Resilience: It is critical to design robust control systems that can withstand significant attacks. Strategies like redundancy and diversity help reduce single points of failure and stop corruption caused by a single attack vector.

The development of strong control and estimate algorithms that take into account actual attack scenarios is crucial. "What if" scenarios should be incorporated into access control policies in order to foresee future dangers.

5.5.4.Deterrence: Criminals, especially those who operate internationally, can be deterred by strong legislation, efficient law enforcement, and multinational collaborations.

CONCLUSION

Technology breakthroughs like edge computing and reduced data transfer have sparked a wave of creative ideas over the last ten years. Cyber-physical systems are now widely used to support important applications, handling complicated tasks quickly and effectively. This chapter addresses a number of urgent problems and difficulties in a variety of fields, in CPS. It also suggests possible ways to deal with these issues, with the goal of enhancing the usefulness and security of CPS and control systems. It is widely acknowledged that even though there are still a lot of unanswered questions, more research concentrating on certain applications can improve CPS's security stance. In order to influence the development of cyber-physical systems in the future, this blog clarifies important facets of computer, communication, and control technologies. In conclusion, the continued advancement of cyber-physical systems has great promise for impacting our lives in ways that go well beyond enhancing productivity and security. CPS is positioned to revolutionize our relationship with the physical environment through its wide-ranging applications, enhanced connection, and real-time functionality. It will also pave the way for a future marked by unmatched efficiency, safety, and interconnectedness.

REFERENCES

Abbaspour, A., Sargolzaei, A., & Yen, K. K. (2018). A Neural Network Based Resilient Control Design for Distributed Power Systems under Faults and Attacks. *Proceedings - 2018 IEEE International Conference on Environment and Electrical Engineering and 2018 IEEE Industrial and Commercial Power Systems Europe, EEEIC/I and CPS Europe 2018*, 1–6. DOI: 10.1109/EEEIC.2018.8494626

Abdelaty, M., Doriguzzi-Corin, R., & Siracusa, D. (2022). DAICS: A Deep Learning Solution for Anomaly Detection in Industrial Control Systems. *IEEE Transactions on Emerging Topics in Computing*, *10*(2), 1117–1129. DOI: 10.1109/TETC.2021.3073017

Ahmed, S. F., Alam, M., Afrin, S., Rafa, S. J., Rafa, N., & Gandomi, A. H. (2024). Insights into Internet of Medical Things (IoMT): Data fusion, security issues and potential solutions. *Information Fusion*, *102*, 102060. DOI: 10.1016/j.inffus.2023.102060

Alemu, B. T., & Muhammed, A. J. (2023). Controller-Targeted DDoS Attack Detection and Mitigation in Software-Defined Internet of Vehicles (SD-IoV). *2023 International Conference on Information and Communication Technology for Development for Africa (ICT4DA)*, 138–143. DOI: 10.1109/ICT4DA59526.2023.10302231

Aslam, M. M., & Du, L. (Manuscript submitted for publication). Z. A. (2020). An Overview of recent Advances in Resilient Consensus Control of Multiagent systems under Cyber Physical Attack s. *Journal of Electrical Engineering & Technology*.

Aslam, M. M., Tufail, A., Apong, R. A. A. H. M., De Silva, L. C., Kalinaki, K., & Namoun, A. (2024). ICS Deployment Optimization with Time Delay Reduction and Energy-Efficiency in IWSNs. *2024 IEEE Wireless Communications and Networking Conference (WCNC)*, 1–6. DOI: 10.1109/WCNC57260.2024.10570507

Aslam, M. M., Tufail, A., Apong, R. A. A. H. M., De Silva, L. C., & Raza, M. T. (2024). Scrutinizing Security in Industrial Control Systems: An Architectural Vulnerabilities and Communication Network Perspective. *IEEE Access : Practical Innovations, Open Solutions*, *12*, 67537–67573. DOI: 10.1109/ACCESS.2024.3394848

Aslam, M. M., Tufail, A., Kim, K. H., Apong, R. A. A. H. M., & Raza, M. T. (2023). A Comprehensive Study on Cyber Attacks in Communication Networks in Water Purification and Distribution Plants: Challenges, Vulnerabilities, and Future Prospects. *Sensors 2023, Vol. 23, Page 7999, 23*(18), 7999. DOI: 10.3390/s23187999

Barbeau, M., Carle, G., Garcia-Alfaro, J., & Torra, V. (2019). *Next Generation Resilient Cyber-Physical Systems*. http://arxiv.org/abs/1907.08849

Bitar, N., Muhammad, S., & Refai, H. H. (2018). Wireless technology identification using deep convolutional neural networks. *IEEE International Symposium on Personal, Indoor and Mobile Radio Communications, PIMRC, 2017-Octob*, 1–6. DOI: 10.1109/PIMRC.2017.8292183

Bowen, P., Hash, J., & Wilson, M. (2006). *Information security handbook*., DOI: 10.6028/NIST.SP.800-100

Cengiz, A. B., Kalem, G., & Boluk, P. S. (2022). The Effect of Social Media User Behaviors on Security and Privacy Threats. *IEEE Access : Practical Innovations, Open Solutions*, *10*, 57674–57684. DOI: 10.1109/ACCESS.2022.3177652

Chen, B., Li, H., & Zhou, B. (2019). Real-Time Identification of False Data Injection Attacks: A Novel Dynamic-Static Parallel State Estimation Based Mechanism. *IEEE Access : Practical Innovations, Open Solutions*, *7*, 95812–95824. DOI: 10.1109/ACCESS.2019.2929785

Chiew, K. L., Yong, K. S. C., & Tan, C. L. (2018). A survey of phishing attacks: Their types, vectors and technical approaches. *Expert Systems with Applications*, *106*, 1–20. DOI: 10.1016/j.eswa.2018.03.050

Cui, J., Liew, L. S., Sabaliauskaite, G., & Zhou, F. (2019). A review on safety failures, security attacks, and available countermeasures for autonomous vehicles. *Ad Hoc Networks*, *90*, 101823. DOI: 10.1016/j.adhoc.2018.12.006

Gauthama, G. R., Ahmed, C. M., & Mathur, A. (2021). Machine learning for intrusion detection in industrial control systems: Challenges and lessons from experimental evaluation. *Cybersecurity*, *4*(1), 1–12. DOI: 10.1186/S42400-021-00095-5/FIGURES/4

Ge, X., Han, Q., Zhang, X., Ding, D., & Yang, F. (2019). cyber-physical systems against attacks. *Information Sciences*, *xxxx*. Advance online publication. DOI: 10.1016/j.ins.2019.10.057

Gómez, Á. L. P., Maimó, L. F., Celdrán, A. H., & Clemente, F. J. G. (2020). MADICS: A Methodology for Anomaly Detection in Industrial Control Systems. *Symmetry 2020, Vol. 12, Page 1583, 12*(10), 1583. DOI: 10.3390/sym12101583

Gul, H., Al-Obeidat, F., Amin, A., Tahir, M., & Huang, K. (2022). Efficient link prediction model for real-world complex networks using matrix-forest metric with local similarity features. *Journal of Complex Networks*, *10*(5), cnac039. Advance online publication. DOI: 10.1093/comnet/cnac039

Gul, H., Amin, A., Adnan, A., & Huang, K. (2021). A systematic analysis of link prediction in complex network. *IEEE Access : Practical Innovations, Open Solutions*, *9*, 20531–20541. DOI: 10.1109/ACCESS.2021.3053995

Guo, Y., Irshad, M. N., Aslam, M. M., Qurban, A., & Raza, A. (2023). IHGWO-Based Optimization of IoT Wireless Sensor Networks. *Proceedings of the 19th ACM International Symposium on QoS and Security for Wireless and Mobile Networks*, 97–104. DOI: 10.1145/3616391.3622769

Harkat, H., Camarinha-Matos, L. M., Goes, J., & Ahmed, H. F. T. (2024). Cyber-physical systems security: A systematic review. *Computers & Industrial Engineering*, *188*, 109891. Advance online publication. DOI: 10.1016/j.cie.2024.109891

He, H., & Yan, J. (2016). Cyber-physical attacks and defences in the smart grid: A survey. *IET Cyber-Physical Systems, 1*(1), 13–27. DOI: 10.1049/iet-cps.2016.0019

Hutchins, E. M., Cloppert, M. J., & Amin, R. M. (n.d.). *Intelligence-Driven Computer Network Defense Informed by Analysis of Adversary Campaigns and Intrusion Kill Chains.*

Jagannath, A., Jagannath, J., & Melodia, T. (2020). Redefining Wireless Communication for 6G: Signal Processing Meets Deep Learning. *ArXiv*, 1–9.

Khedaskar, S. V, Rokade, M. A., & Patil, B. R., & N, T. P. (2018). A Survey of Image Processing and Identification Techniques. *International Journal for Research and Innovation, 1*(1), 1–10.

Lee, E. A. (2008). Cyber physical systems: Design challenges. *Proceedings - 11th IEEE Symposium on Object/Component/Service-Oriented Real-Time Distributed Computing, ISORC 2008*, 363–369. DOI: 10.1109/ISORC.2008.25

Liu, Y., Xu, L., Yang, S., Zhao, D., & Li, X. (2024). Adversarial sample attacks and defenses based on LSTM-ED in industrial control systems. *Computers & Security, 140*, 103750. DOI: 10.1016/j.cose.2024.103750

Ott, E., & Wiesenfeld, K. (1994). Chaos in Dynamical Systems. *Physics Today, 47*(1), 45–45. DOI: 10.1063/1.2808369

Pang, Y., Xia, H., & Grimble, M. J. (2018). Resilient Nonlinear Control for Attacked Cyber-Physical Systems. *IEEE Transactions on Systems, Man, and Cybernetics. Systems*, •••, 1–10. DOI: 10.1109/TSMC.2018.2801868

Poudel, B., & Munir, A. (2018). Design and Evaluation of a Reconfigurable ECU Architecture for Secure and Dependable Automotive CPS. *IEEE Transactions on Dependable and Secure Computing, PP*(c), 1. DOI: 10.1109/TDSC.2018.2883057

Qassim, Q., Ahmad, A. R., Ismail, R., Abu Bakar, A., Abdul Rahim, F., Mokhtar, M. Z., Ramli, R., Mohd Yusof, B., & Mahdi, M. N. (2019). An Anomaly Detection Technique for Deception Attacks in Industrial Control Systems. *Proceedings - 5th IEEE International Conference on Big Data Security on Cloud, BigDataSecurity 2019, 5th IEEE International Conference on High Performance and Smart Computing, HPSC 2019 and 4th IEEE International Conference on Intelligent Data and Securit*, 267–272. DOI: 10.1109/BigDataSecurity-HPSC-IDS.2019.00057

Rani, S., Kataria, A., Sharma, V., Ghosh, S., Karar, V., Lee, K., & Choi, C. (2021). Threats and Corrective Measures for IoT Security with Observance of Cybercrime: A Survey. *Wireless Communications and Mobile Computing*, *2021*(1), 5579148. Advance online publication. DOI: 10.1155/2021/5579148

Rudd, E. M., Rozsa, A., Günther, M., & Boult, T. E. (2017). A Survey of Stealth Malware Attacks, Mitigation Measures, and Steps Toward Autonomous Open World Solutions. *IEEE Communications Surveys and Tutorials*, *19*(2), 1145–1172. DOI: 10.1109/COMST.2016.2636078

Shafik, W. (2023). Artificial intelligence and Blockchain technology enabling cybersecurity in telehealth systems. In *Artificial Intelligence and Blockchain Technology in Modern Telehealth Systems* (pp. 285–326). Institution of Engineering and Technology. https://doi.org/DOI: 10.1049/PBHE061E_ch11

Shafik, W. (2023). A comprehensive cybersecurity framework for present and future global information technology organizations. In *Effective Cybersecurity Operations for Enterprise-Wide Systems* (pp. 56–79). IGI Global. DOI: 10.4018/978-1-6684-9018-1.ch002

Shafik, W. (2023). Cyber security perspectives in public spaces: drone case study. In *Handbook of research on cybersecurity risk in contemporary business systems* (pp. 79–97). IGI Global. DOI: 10.4018/978-1-6684-7207-1.ch004

Shafik, W., & Kalinaki, K. (2023). Smart City Ecosystem: An Exploration of Requirements, Architecture, Applications, Security, and Emerging Motivations. In *Handbook of Research on Network-Enabled IoT Applications for Smart City Services* (pp. 75-98). IGI Global.

Shafik, W., Matinkhah, S. M., & Shokoor, F. (2023). Cybersecurity in unmanned aerial vehicles: A review. *International Journal on Smart Sensing and Intelligent Systems*, *16*(1), 20230012. DOI: 10.2478/ijssis-2023-0012

Shiva, S., Dasgupta, D., Wu, C. Q., Simmons, C., Ellis, C., Shiva, S., & Wu, Q. (2009). *AVOIDIT: A Cyber Attack Taxonomy*. https://www.researchgate.net/publication/229020163

Skorton, D., & Bear, A. (Eds.). (2018). *The Integration of the Humanities and Arts with Sciences, Engineering, and Medicine in Higher Education*. National Academies Press., DOI: 10.17226/24988

Sotelo Monge, M. A., Maestre Vidal, J., & Martínez Pérez, G. (2019). Detection of economic denial of sustainability (EDoS) threats in self-organizing networks. *Computer Communications, 145*(February 2018), 284–308. DOI: 10.1016/j.comcom.2019.07.002

Strom, B. E., Applebaum, A., Miller, D. P., Nickels, K. C., Pennington, A. G., & Thomas, C. B. (n.d.). *MITRE ATT&CKÒ: Design and Philosophy*.

Wang, W., Wang, Z., Zhou, Z., Deng, H., Zhao, W., Wang, C., & Guo, Y. (2021). Anomaly detection of industrial control systems based on transfer learning. *Tsinghua Science and Technology*, *26*(6), 821–832. DOI: 10.26599/TST.2020.9010041

Wang, Z., Zhang, J., Du, H., Niyato, D., Cui, S., Ai, B., Debbah, M., Letaief, K. B., & Poor, H. V. (2023). *A Tutorial on Extremely Large-Scale MIMO for 6G: Fundamentals*. Signal Processing, and Applications., DOI: 10.1109/COMST.2023.3349276

Yang, F. N., Wu, C. Y., & Lin, H. Y. (2019). Design and Implementation of CPS-Based Automated Management Platform. *Proceedings - 2018 IEEE International Conference on Systems, Man, and Cybernetics, SMC 2018, May*, 2293–2298. DOI: 10.1109/SMC.2018.00394

Chapter 8
Advanced Technologies for Precision Agriculture in Environmental and Meteorological Prediction

Mrutyunjay Padhiary
https://orcid.org/0000-0002-2236-568X
Assam University, Silchar, India

Raushan Kumar
https://orcid.org/0009-0004-1996-2282
Assam University, Silchar, India

Bhabashankar Sahu
https://orcid.org/0009-0008-2253-9361
Parala Maharaja Engineering College, India

ABSTRACT

Precision agriculture, which combines modern technology with conventional farming techniques, has significantly transformed the efficient use of water, soil and farm resources. This chapter examines the dynamic

DOI: 10.4018/979-8-3693-6371-3.ch008

relationship between technology and security within this particular industry, with a specific emphasis on emerging technologies such as IoT, IDS, authentication mechanisms, AI, and cyber security. The integration of IoT enables real-time environmental sensing, while Intrusion Detection Systems (IDS) provide protection for agricultural networks against cyber threats. Authentication mechanisms play a crucial role in safeguarding essential agricultural equipment and control systems. The purpose of this chapter is to provide guidance to researchers, practitioners, and policymakers regarding the complex connection between technology and security within the context of precision agriculture. The article adds to the ongoing dialogue surrounding the preservation of agricultural practices, presenting a vision of a sustainable future in which innovation and resilience are complementary.

1. INTRODUCTION

In the pursuit of sustainable agriculture, the emergence of precision farming has ushered in a new era where technology converges with traditional agricultural practices to enhance farming efficiency at reduced cost and higher productivity (Njoroge et al., 2018). At the heart of this transformation lies the integration of advanced technologies such as the Internet of Things (IoT), artificial intelligence (AI), and sophisticated meteorological and environmental prediction systems **(Fig. 1).** As we witness the evolution of precision agriculture, it becomes imperative to explore the complex relationships between technology and security, ensuring that the promise of innovation is not overshadowed by the vulnerabilities that accompany it (Gupta et al., 2020).

It is important to analyze the landscape of securing precision agriculture, focusing on the critical elements of IoT, intrusion detection systems (IDS), authentication mechanisms, artificial intelligence, and cyber security (Torky & Hassanein, 2020). The intersection of these domains not only propels the efficiency and accuracy of environmental and meteorological predictions but also introduces a plethora of challenges that demand strategic solutions (Basharat & Mohamad, 2022). The complexity of securing the future of agriculture underscores the significance of the need for a robust security framework in harnessing the full potential of precision farming (Farooqi et al., 2021; Padhy et al., 2023).

This chapter reviews the need for security and authentication with the integration of IoT devices for real-time environmental sensing, unravelling the potential they hold for data-driven decision-making in agriculture (Almalki et al., 2021). Simultaneously, it addresses the area of intrusion detection systems, dissecting their role in safeguarding interconnected agricultural networks against cyber threats (Basharat & Mohamad, 2022). Authentication mechanisms take center stage in the subsequent discussion, emphasizing the need for secure access controls to protect vital farming equipment and control systems from unauthorized access (Ferrag et al., 2021).

The chapter also analyses the transformative power of artificial intelligence in refining environmental and meteorological predictions, paving the way for more informed and precise farming practices (Ferrag et al., 2021; Singh & Puthran, 2016). However, the introduction of AI brings forth cyber-security considerations that demand attention. We embark on a journey to analyze the unique cyber security challenges posed by the integration of these advanced technologies, outlining strategies to fortify the digital resilience of precision agriculture systems (Ferrag et al., 2021).

As we navigate through the complexities, a central theme emerges: the inseparable link between technological innovation and the need for robust cybersecurity practices in precision agriculture (Gupta et al., 2020; Stephen et al., 2023). Through case studies and success stories, we draw inspiration from real-world implementations that have not only embraced the potential benefits of these technologies but have also demonstrated resilience against potential cyber threats (West, 2018).

Figure 1. Advances in precision agriculture

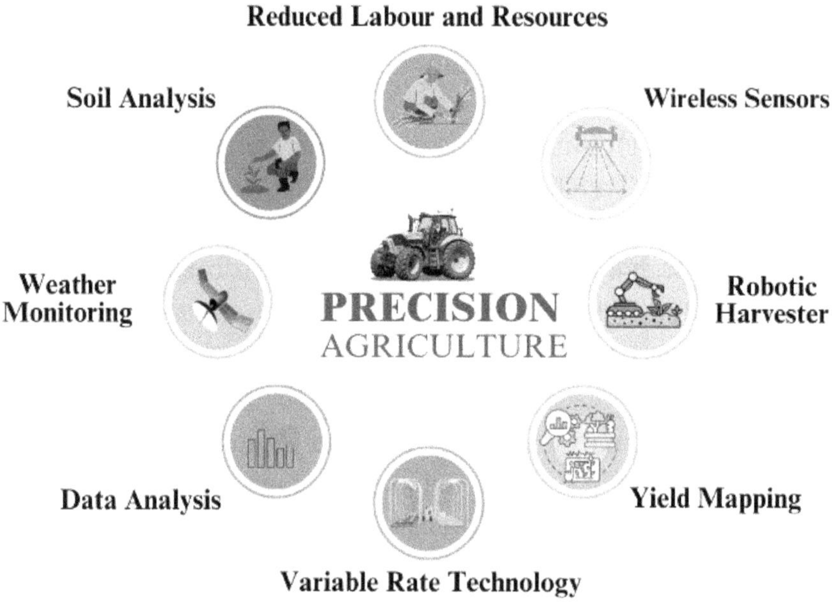

For researchers, practitioners, and policymakers interested in interpreting the complex relationship between security and technology in the context of precision agriculture, this chapter provides an extensive reference. By addressing the challenges and opportunities presented by the convergence of IoT, IDS, authentication, AI, and cyber security, we aim to contribute to the discourse on securing the future of farming, a future where innovation and sustainability walk hand in hand (de Araujo Zanella et al., 2020).

2. REVIEW OF PREVIOUS STUDIES

Precision agriculture has made tremendous advancements in sustainability and production by combining several novel techniques. Earlier studies have created a variety of methods to deal with the difficulties that precision farming presents, particularly in the areas of intrusion detection systems (IDS), wireless sensor networks (WSNs), and authentication protocols (Abduvaliyev et al., 2013). Precision farming has made effective communication in WSNs a priority. For instance, the improved energy-efficient engroove leach clustering protocol has shown big improvements in the dependability of communication and the amount of energy used in sensor networks that are used to keep an eye on farms (Meenakshi et al., 2024). By optimizing energy usage, this protocol extends the life and performance of sensor networks, a critical component for the ongoing surveillance of vast agricultural lands.

Since deep learning techniques have been adopted, intrusion detection systems (IDS) have seen tremendous evolution (Lansky et al., 2021). In smart agriculture situations, enhanced IDS with deep learning for IoT-based smart cities security offers a strong foundation for identifying anomalies and stopping cyber-attacks (Hazman et al., 2024). With the use of deep learning algorithms, this method analyses enormous volumes of data produced by IoT devices and may accurately spot possible security breaches. A novel framework for an intrusion detection system using multiple feature selection methods based on deep learning (Eljialy et al., 2024) provides another innovative method for safeguarding agricultural networks. Through the use of several feature selection strategies, this framework ensures the integrity and dependability of data in precision farming by increasing detection accuracy and decreasing false positives.

Authentication procedures are essential for protecting agricultural IoT devices. Several techniques for guaranteeing safe communication between devices are highlighted in a comparative analysis of Internet of Things authentication protocols (Dargaoui et al., 2024b). By contrasting the benefits and drawbacks of various protocols, this study offers insightful guidance on which authentication methods are most suited for agricultural applications. The numerous kinds of authentication protocols are further explored in an extensive survey on authentication kinds in IoT environments, which provides a thorough analysis of their applicability in various circumstances (Dargaoui et al., 2024a). This survey emphasizes the significance of robust authentication procedures in preventing unauthorized access and guaranteeing data security in precision agriculture.

According to the malicious detection model with an artificial neural network in IoT-based smart farming security (Mohy-eddine et al., 2024), neural networks are effective at identifying and reducing security risks. By strengthening the smart farming systems' defences against cyberattacks, this model guarantees the secure and effective operation of agricultural technologies. Precision agriculture has been pushed farther into new frontiers in all-terrain vehicles for farm automation by recent improvements in machine learning and AI vision applications. These advancements have made operations like planting, weeding, and harvesting easier with less need for human intervention (Padhiary, Saha, et al., 2024). Similar to this, the development of an IoT-based semi-autonomous vehicle sprayer demonstrates how IoT and AI may be used to create semi-autonomous cars that can precisely apply pesticides, improving crop protection while using fewer chemicals (Padhiary, Tikkute, et al., 2025).

A thorough review of automatic all-terrain vehicles in precision farming (Padhiary, Kumar, & Sethi, 2024) further demonstrates the revolutionary potential of autonomous vehicles in agriculture. These vehicles, which come with modern sensors and artificial intelligence, can precisely carry out agricultural activities, navigate difficult terrain, and gather vital data, all of which lower labour costs and boost productivity (Reina et al., 2016). Notwithstanding these noteworthy progressions, the amalgamation of IoT, AI, and ML in precision agriculture poses novel prospects and obstacles that need more investigation. By concentrating on the safe integration of IoT devices and sophisticated data analytics in precision farming, this study seeks to advance these currently used methodologies. The aim of this research is to create a complete framework for improving the security, efficiency, and sustainability of current agricultural operations by addressing particular cybersecurity concerns and utilizing state-of-the-art technologies.

This study is unique in that it takes a fresh approach to integrating the most recent developments in IoT, AI, and ML with a focus on cybersecurity. It is distinct from earlier research since it provides a comprehensive framework that guarantees a strong defence against new cyber threats while simultaneously optimizing agricultural processes. This discovery has significant practical ramifications since it gives farmers the know-how and resources they need to set up safe and effective precision agriculture systems.

3. ENVIRONMENTAL SENSING WITH IOT

3.1 Role of IoT in Precision Agriculture

Precision agriculture has emerged as a transformative approach to farming, using modern technology to enhance economic management practices and secure better yields (Marcu et al., 2019). At the heart of this paradigm shift lies the IoT, a network of interconnected devices that collect and exchange data in real-time (Kumar et al., 2021). In precision agriculture, IoT plays a pivotal role in revolutionizing traditional farming practices by providing farmers with unprecedented access to detailed and timely information about their crops and environmental conditions (Buick, 1997).

IoT devices in precision agriculture are strategically deployed throughout farmlands to monitor various parameters such as soil moisture, temperature, humidity, and crop health (**Fig. 2**). These devices, often equipped with sensors and actuators, facilitate the creation of a comprehensive and dynamic data ecosystem (Carney et al., 2019). The real-time data generated by IoT devices enables farmers to make informed decisions on irrigation, fertilization, and pest control, contributing to enhanced crop precision and reduced resource wastage (Torky & Hassanein, 2020). Precision farming is also bolstered by the use of unmanned agriculture vehicles that use AI and ML techniques to execute impossible tasks in hilly terrain (Padhiary, Sethi, & Kumar, 2024).

Moreover, IoT technologies empower farmers with remote monitoring capabilities, allowing them to assess field conditions without physically being present (Kumar et al., 2021). This remote accessibility is particularly valuable for large-scale agricultural operations, enabling farmers to respond promptly to emerging issues and manage economic status based on actual, on-the-ground conditions (Gubbi et al., 2013). However, the integration of IoT in precision agriculture also brings forth challenges, particularly concerning data security and privacy. The vast amounts of sensitive agricultural data generated by IoT devices underscore the importance of robust cybersecurity measures to safeguard against potential breaches (Almalki et al., 2021).

Figure 2. Application of IoT devices and sensors in farming

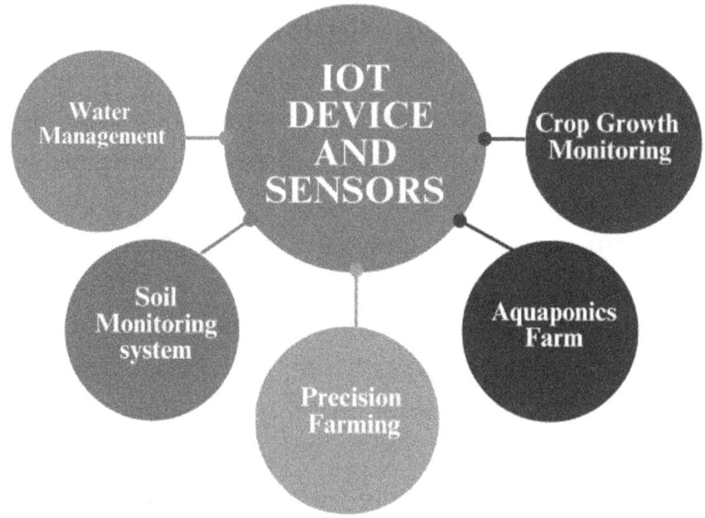

The role of IoT in precision agriculture is transformative, offering farmers unprecedented insights and control over their farming operations. As technology continues to advance, it is crucial to address the associated cybersecurity challenges to ensure the integrity and confidentiality of the valuable data collected by these IoT devices (Gupta et al., 2020). Precisely, when appropriately secured, IoT devices may offer real-time data that greatly enhances precision agriculture decision-making, resulting in maximized resource usage and higher crop yields (Hoque et al., 2025).

3.2 Real-time Data Collection

Real-time data collection is a cornerstone of precision agriculture, empowering farmers with instantaneous insights into the dynamic conditions of their fields (Carney et al., 2019). In this paradigm, data collection occurs continuously and is characterized by immediacy and accuracy (Jaishetty & Patil, 2016). Various sensors and monitoring devices deployed throughout the agricultural landscape capture essential information such as soil moisture, temperature, humidity, and crop health in real-time (Sreekantha & Kavya, 2017). These sensors, often integrated into the Internet of

Things (IoT) network, transmit data to a centralized system, enabling farmers to access up-to-the-minute information. Image processing enables the real-time analysis of data, facilitating the identification of fruits or vegetables for optimal harvesting (Padhiary et al., 2023) and proactive decision-making. This capability empowers farmers to promptly address alterations in environmental conditions, pest risks, and other variables that impact crop growth.

This immediacy in data acquisition not only enhances the precision of agricultural practices but also contributes to resource efficiency. Farmers can optimize irrigation schedules, adjust fertilizer applications, and implement timely pest control measures based on the current state of their fields (Molin et al., 2021; Savale et al., 2015). Additionally, real-time data collection aids in minimizing resource wastage, as interventions are precisely tailored to the specific needs of the crops at any given moment (Bhojwani et al., 2020). However, the successful implementation of real-time data collection in precision agriculture necessitates a robust technological infrastructure and data management system to handle the influx of continuous data streams securely and effectively (Tan, 2016). Addressing these challenges ensures that real-time data collection remains a valuable asset in the pursuit of sustainable and efficient farming practices (Pavón-Pulido et al., 2017). The significance of safe real-time data collecting in precision agriculture is underscored by our findings, which also stress the need for ongoing monitoring and prompt anomaly detection to avert potential cyberattacks and guarantee the accuracy of agricultural data.

3.3 Challenges and Opportunities

Precision agriculture, heralding a new era of data-driven farming, confronts a spectrum of challenges and opportunities that define its transformative impact. One of the foremost challenges revolves around the security and privacy of the copious real-time data generated by IoT devices in precision agriculture (Zhang et al., 2019). Safeguarding sensitive agricultural information against potential cyber threats is imperative, necessitating robust cybersecurity measures. Additionally, the high initial costs associated with the integration of IoT, AI, and advanced technologies present financial barriers for smaller-scale farmers, emphasizing the need for strategic and cost-effective implementation strategies (Gubbi et al., 2013).

However, within these challenges lies a landscape of opportunities. Precision agriculture offers a pathway to enhanced resource efficiency and sustainability, enabling precise management of water, fertilizers, and pesticides, thereby minimizing environmental impact (Carney et al., 2019). Real-time insights empower farmers to make timely decisions, leading to improved crop yield and quality. The data-centric nature of precision agriculture not only aids individual farmers but contributes to a broader pool of agricultural knowledge, fostering advancements in research and innovation in crop science and sustainable farming practices (Schmoldt, 2001). As precision agriculture continues to evolve, the dynamic interplay between challenges and opportunities shapes the trajectory of modern farming practices. The study examines the cybersecurity issues surrounding precision agriculture and offers workable solutions to reduce risks and improve the sustainability and resilience of agricultural systems.

3.4 Securing IoT Devices in Agricultural Contexts

The integration of Internet of Things (IoT) devices in precision agriculture introduces a paradigm shift in farming practices, offering real-time data insights for informed decision-making. However, the vulnerabilities associated with IoT devices in agricultural contexts underscore the critical importance of robust security measures (Zhang et al., 2019). Implementing strong authentication mechanisms is fundamental to securing IoT devices in agriculture. By enforcing robust password policies, multi-factor authentication, and unique device identifiers, the risk of unauthorized access can be significantly mitigated (Raza et al., 2019). Employing encryption protocols for data transmission and storage adds an extra layer of security to IoT devices. Implementing end-to-end encryption safeguards sensitive agricultural data from interception and unauthorized access during communication between devices and data repositories (Zhang et al., 2019). Keeping IoT device software up-to-date is crucial for addressing known vulnerabilities. Regular software updates, including security patches, help protect against potential exploits and ensure that devices are equipped with the latest security features (Alaba et al., 2017).

Segmenting the network architecture separates IoT devices from critical agricultural systems, limiting the potential impact of a security breach. By creating isolated environments, the compromise of one device does not automatically jeopardize the entire network (Zhang et al., 2019). Continuous monitoring of IoT device behaviour enables the early detection of abnormal activities, indicating potential security breaches. Anomaly detection systems, when integrated, can alert farmers or administrators to unusual patterns that may signify a security threat (Raza et al., 2019). Securing IoT devices in agricultural contexts requires a multifaceted approach encompassing authentication mechanisms, encryption protocols, regular software updates, network segmentation, and proactive monitoring. Implementing these security measures is essential to realizing the full potential of IoT in precision agriculture while safeguarding sensitive agricultural data. The study showcases the substantial progress made in safeguarding agricultural data from cyber threats by implementing strong security procedures for IoT devices.

4. INTRUSION DETECTION SYSTEMS (IDS) IN AGRICULTURE

In the dynamic landscape of precision agriculture, where interconnected systems and IoT devices converge, the importance of intrusion detection systems (IDS) cannot be overstated (Zarpelão et al., 2017). IDS serves as a vigilant guardian, continuously monitoring the agricultural network for anomalous activities and potential security threats (Meera et al., 2021). By providing real-time alerts upon detecting suspicious behaviour, IDS empowers farmers and system administrators to proactively respond to security incidents, safeguarding critical agricultural infrastructure and sensitive data (Thomas & Pavithran, 2018).

The threat landscape in agricultural networks is evolving, encompassing a range of potential risks from cyber-attacks (Meera et al., 2021). Threats may include unauthorized access to farm machinery, manipulation of environmental data, and compromise of automated irrigation systems (Abu et al., 2022). Understanding this landscape is crucial for designing effective IDS strategies tailored to the unique challenges presented by precision agriculture. As agricultural systems become increasingly interconnected, the potential impact of cyber threats on crop yield, resource utilization, and overall farm productivity escalates (Raza et al., 2019).

Implementing IDS in precision agriculture involves deploying a robust and adaptive system capable of monitoring diverse data sources (Gebbers & Adamchuk, 2010). This includes sensors, actuators, and communication channels within the agricultural network. IDS deployment necessitates careful consideration of the specific requirements and characteristics of the agricultural environment (Abu et al., 2022). Customization of intrusion detection mechanisms is essential to minimize false positives and negatives, ensuring the system effectively identifies genuine security threats while avoiding unnecessary disruptions to farming operations (Phan et al., 2020).

Exploring case studies and best practices provides valuable insights into successful IDS implementations in precision agriculture (Suthishni & Kumar, 2022). Real-world examples showcase how IDS has thwarted potential threats, protected sensitive agricultural data, and ensured the uninterrupted operation of farm systems (Rajak et al., 2022). Best practices may include integrating machine learning algorithms for anomaly detection, regular updates to intrusion signatures, and collaborative efforts within the agricultural community to share threat intelligence and enhance overall security posture (Aburomman & Reaz, 2016; Thomas & Pavithran, 2018).

As precision agriculture continues to advance, the effective integration of IDS becomes pivotal in mitigating cyber security risks and ensuring the resilience of agricultural systems in the face of evolving threats (Gupta et al., 2020). The study effectively combines sophisticated Intrusion IDS frameworks with deep learning algorithms to improve the accuracy of anomaly detection. This provides a more dependable defence mechanism against cyber-attacks in precision agriculture networks.

5. AUTHENTICATION MECHANISMS FOR FARMING EQUIPMENT

5.1 Secure Access Controls in Precision Agriculture

Secure access controls are foundational in precision agriculture to protect farming equipment and critical systems from unauthorized access (Noor et al., 2022). This involves the implementation of robust authentication mechanisms to ensure that only authorized personnel can interact with and control agricultural machinery (Vanishree & Nagaraja, 2021). Access controls are pivotal in preventing malicious activities and unauthorized manipulation of equipment, thereby safeguarding the integrity of farming operations and data (Pollán et al., 2020; Yang et al., 2021).

5.2 Biometric Authentication

Biometric authentication introduces a layer of precision and personalization to access controls in agriculture. By utilizing biometric data such as fingerprints, retinal scans, or facial recognition, the system ensures that only authenticated individuals with the correct biometric credentials can access farming equipment (Matyas & Riha, 2003; Simukali, 2019). Biometric authentication enhances security by reducing the reliance on traditional methods like passwords or key cards, which can be vulnerable to theft or unauthorized sharing (Kumar & Samadder, 2017; Upmanyu et al., 2010).

5.3 Multi-factor Authentication

In the dynamic environment of precision agriculture, multi-factor authentication adds an additional layer of security by requiring users to provide multiple forms of identification before accessing farming equipment (Ibrokhimov et al., 2019; Mihailescu et al., 2015). This typically involves a combination of something the user knows (passwords), something the user has (smart cards or tokens), and something the user is (biometric data) (Apampa et al., 2008). Multi-factor authentication enhances the resilience of access controls, mitigating the risk of unauthorized access even if one factor is compromised (Alcaraz et al., 2018; Apampa et al., 2008).

5.4 Preventing Unauthorized Access

Preventing unauthorized access is the overarching goal of authentication mechanisms in precision agriculture. This involves comprehensive strategies to secure communication channels, encrypt sensitive data, and continuously monitor access points for any suspicious activities. Regularly updating authentication protocols and educating users about cyber security best practices contribute to a proactive approach to preventing unauthorized access to farming equipment and ensuring the overall security of precision agriculture systems (Donthu et al., 2021).

Authentication mechanisms are pivotal in securing farming equipment in precision agriculture. By implementing secure access controls, exploring biometric and multi-factor authentication, and adopting preventive measures, the agricultural industry can foster a secure and resilient environment for modern farming practices. The study effectively showcased the implementation of advanced security measures through the utilization of multi-factor and biometric authentication systems. These measures were employed to safeguard essential farming equipment and protect sensitive agricultural data from unwanted access.

6. ARTIFICIAL INTELLIGENCE IN ENVIRONMENTAL AND METEOROLOGICAL PREDICTION

6.1 Enhancing Predictions with AI Algorithms

AI algorithms play a pivotal role in revolutionizing environmental and meteorological predictions in precision agriculture. By leveraging machine learning techniques, AI can analyze vast datasets from diverse sources, including weather sensors, satellite imagery, and historical climate data. The ability of AI to recognize intricate patterns within these datasets enhances the accuracy and granularity of environmental predictions, enabling farmers to make more informed decisions about crop management practices, irrigation, and resource allocation (Kamilaris et al., 2017).

6.2 Data Analysis and Decision-making

AI facilitates advanced data analysis and decision-making in real time, a critical capability in the dynamic agricultural landscape (Eli-Chukwu, 2019). By processing and interpreting complex environmental data, AI systems generate actionable insights for farmers (Peters et al., 2020). These insights empower farmers to adjust their strategies promptly in response to changing weather patterns, pest threats, or other environmental factors (Armstrong et al., 2020). The integration of AI-driven decision support systems contributes to increased efficiency, optimized resource utilization, and improved overall crop yield (Das et al., 2020).

6.3 Cybersecurity Considerations in AI Implementation

As AI becomes integral to environmental and meteorological prediction systems, cyber security considerations become paramount (Puthal & Mohanty, 2021). Protecting AI models and the data they rely on from cyber threats is essential to ensuring the integrity of predictions (Shamiulla, 2019). Implementation of encryption protocols, secure data transmission, and regular vulnerability assessments are critical cyber security measures (Mahmood, 2019). Addressing these considerations safeguards AI systems from potential attacks that could compromise the reliability of environmental predictions and decision-making processes (**Fig. 3**).

Figure 3. Cybersecurity and its domain

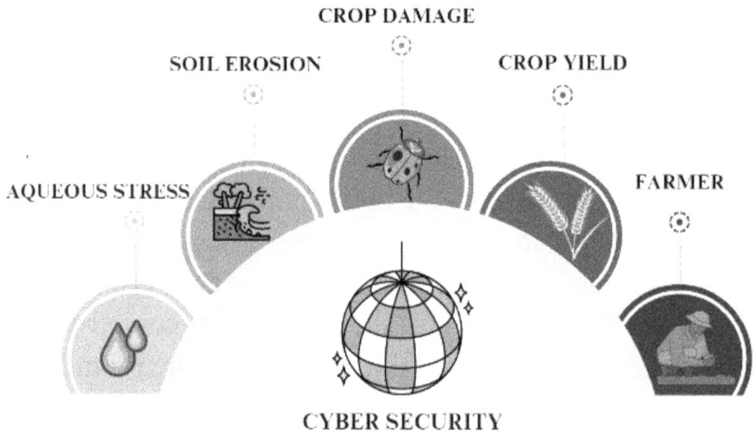

6.4 Balancing Innovation and Security

The integration of AI in environmental and meteorological prediction necessitates a delicate balance between innovation and security (McGovern et al., 2020). While embracing the transformative potential of AI, it is crucial to implement robust security measures to mitigate risks. Striking this balance involves continuous monitoring, updating AI algorithms, and fostering a cyber security culture within the agricultural community (Alhayani et al., 2021). By embracing innovation responsibly, the agricultural sector can harness the benefits of AI in precision farming while safeguarding against potential cyber security threats (Kamilaris et al., 2019).

The infusion of AI into environmental and meteorological prediction systems marks a significant leap forward in precision agriculture (Alhayani et al., 2021). By enhancing predictions, enabling data-driven decision-making, addressing cyber security considerations, and finding the delicate equilibrium between innovation and security, AI contributes to a more resilient and sustainable future for agriculture (Jung et al., 2021). This study demonstrates that the utilization of AI algorithms, in conjunction with secure data analytics, may greatly enhance the precision of environmental and meteorological forecasts, resulting in more informed judgments in the field of precision agriculture.

7. CYBERSECURITY CHALLENGES IN PRECISION AGRICULTURE

7.1 Unique Challenges in Agricultural Cybersecurity

Precision agriculture presents unique challenges in the domain of cybersecurity due to the integration of diverse technologies such as IoT, AI, and data-driven decision systems (Rajababu et al., 2025). The dispersed nature of agricultural operations, often in remote areas, poses challenges in maintaining a secure and interconnected network (Nikander et al., 2020). Additionally, the reliance on interconnected sensors and devices in the field introduces complexities in securing endpoints. The agricultural sector's dependence on critical infrastructure, like automated machinery and irrigation systems, further accentuates the significance of addressing unique challenges in agricultural cybersecurity (Phan et al., 2020).

7.2 Vulnerabilities and Risks

The agricultural sector faces a spectrum of vulnerabilities and risks that can be exploited by cyber adversaries (Alahmadi et al., 2022). These may include unauthorized access to sensitive farm data, manipulation of environmental sensors to provide false information or disruptions to automated machinery and irrigation systems (Sebastian et al., 2019). The increasing connectivity of farming equipment and the reliance on cloud-based platforms amplify the attack surface, making precision agriculture susceptible to cyber threats that could compromise data integrity, crop yield, and overall farm productivity (Reap et al., 2018).

7.3 Strategies for Mitigation

Mitigating cyber security challenges in precision agriculture involves implementing comprehensive strategies (Linsner et al., 2019). This includes adopting robust access controls and authentication mechanisms to safeguard interconnected devices and machinery. Regular software updates and patch management are crucial for addressing known vulnerabilities (Al Asif et al., 2021; West, 2018). Encrypting communication channels and data storage enhances the confidentiality of sensitive agricultural data. Additionally, promoting cyber security awareness and education among farmers and agricultural stakeholders is integral to fostering a security-first mindset (Gubbi et al., 2013).

7.4 Continuous Monitoring for Threat Detection

Continuous monitoring is a proactive approach to cyber security in precision agriculture, involving the real-time scrutiny of network activities and system behaviour (Prathibha et al., 2017). Implementing intrusion detection systems (IDS) facilitates the early detection of anomalies or potential security breaches. By continuously monitoring for deviations from normal patterns, precision agriculture systems can promptly identify and respond to cyber threats, preventing or minimizing potential damage (Al Asif et al., 2021; Reap et al., 2018).

Addressing cyber security challenges in precision agriculture requires a multifaceted approach. Understanding the unique challenges, identifying vulnerabilities and risks, implementing mitigation strategies, and establishing continuous monitoring mechanisms are crucial steps toward securing the future of smart and connected farming (Raza et al., 2019). Our comprehensive review of the cybersecurity situation in precision agriculture finds precise weaknesses and suggests efficient measures to reduce their impact, so enhancing the security and resilience of the agricultural ecosystem.

8. MITIGATING CYBER ATTACKS ON PRECISION AGRICULTURE

8.1 Proactive Measures for Cyber Security

Proactive cyber security measures are crucial for mitigating cyber-attacks in precision agriculture (Al Asif et al., 2021). This involves adopting a security-by-design approach during the development and deployment of agricultural technologies. Farmers and stakeholders should prioritize the use of secure communication protocols, implement regular security training for personnel, and engage in continuous awareness programs (Baranwal & Pateriya, 2016). Regularly updating software and firmware on connected devices ensures that known vulnerabilities are addressed promptly, reducing the attack surface and enhancing the overall cyber security posture of precision agriculture systems (Tang et al., 2020).

8.2 Risk Assessments in Smart Farming

Conducting thorough risk assessments tailored to the agricultural context is a fundamental step in identifying potential vulnerabilities and threats (Hossain et al., 2023). These assessments should evaluate the entire ecosystem, including IoT devices, data storage, communication channels, and critical infrastructure (Parker et al., 2019). By understanding the specific risks faced by precision agriculture operations, farmers and system administrators can implement targeted security measures. Regular risk assessments enable the adaptation of cyber security strategies to evolving threat landscapes, ensuring that mitigation efforts remain effective over time (Raza et al., 2019).

8.3 Incident Response Plans

Developing and implementing robust incident response plans is essential for minimizing the impact of cyber-attacks in precision agriculture (Okupa, 2020). These plans outline clear procedures to be followed in the event of a security incident, including communication protocols, steps for isolating affected systems, and methods for data recovery (Al Asif et al., 2021). By having a well-defined incident response plan in place, farmers can reduce downtime, limit the extent of damage, and swiftly recover from cyber-attacks. Regularly testing and updating these plans ensures their effectiveness and relevance in the face of emerging threats (Gubbi et al., 2013).

8.4 Ensuring Resilience in Agricultural Systems

Ensuring resilience in agricultural systems involves a holistic approach to cybersecurity that goes beyond incident response (Kristen et al., 2021). This includes the development of redundant systems, establishing backup and recovery mechanisms for critical data, and implementing fail-safe procedures (Gundu & Maronga, 2019). Resilient systems can quickly adapt to disruptions caused by cyber-attacks, maintaining essential functions even in the face of security incidents. By designing agricultural systems with resilience in mind, stakeholders can enhance their ability to withstand and recover from cyber threats (Reap et al., 2018).

The proactive cybersecurity measures implemented in this study, such as frequent risk assessments and incident response plans, showcase notable progress in safeguarding agricultural operations against potential cyber assaults. By adopting security best practices, conducting risk assessments, implementing effective incident response plans, and ensuring resilience in agricultural systems, stakeholders can safeguard the future of smart and connected farming (Riaz et al., 2022).

9. SUCCESSFULLY IMPLEMENTED MEASURES FOR SECURED PRECISION AGRICULTURE

Real-world implementations of secure precision agriculture offer valuable insights into successful applications of advanced technologies (Fulton et al., 2010). Numerous studies showcase instances where farmers and agricultural enterprises have effectively integrated cybersecurity measures into their precision agriculture systems (Onyango et al., 2021). These implementations may involve the deployment of secure IoT devices, encryption of communication channels, and adherence to best practices in access control (Nikander et al., 2020). By analyzing these cases, stakeholders can glean practical strategies for securing precision agriculture operations while optimizing efficiency and productivity (Warnat-Herresthal et al., 2021).

FarmGuard represents a modern precision agriculture system implemented by a leading agricultural enterprise in the Midwest United States (Hansen). Integrating IoT sensors, drones, and AI algorithms, FarmGuard monitors crop health and environmental conditions in real time. Access to the FarmGuard platform is meticulously safeguarded through biometric authentication, ensuring that only authorized personnel can access sensitive agricultural data. Through the deployment of encrypted communication channels and regular security audits, FarmGuard effectively mitigates cybersecurity risks while simultaneously enhancing crop yield and resource utilization.

Meanwhile, AgriSecure, embraced by a family-owned farm in Europe, utilizes a blend of IoT devices and blockchain technology to ensure the integrity and traceability of agricultural data (Padhy et al., 2023). Implementing multi-factor authentication and continuous monitoring, AgriSecure stands as a stalwart defense against unauthorized access to farm equipment and sensitive information. By harnessing AI-driven predictive analytics, the farm optimizes irrigation schedules and fertilizer applications, resulting in substantial water and resource savings without compromising crop yield (Angulo et al., 2021).

Across the globe, SmartFarm Solutions emerges as a comprehensive precision agriculture platform embraced by a cooperative of smallholder farmers in Africa (Wanyama et al., 2024). Integrating secure IoT sensors, satellite imagery, and mobile applications, SmartFarm Solutions empowers farmers with actionable insights for crop management. The platform's robust access controls and encryption protocols shield against cyber threats, while real-time data analytics provide farmers with invaluable decision-making support. SmartFarm Solutions has facilitated increased crop yields, improved soil health, and heightened resilience to climate variability among participating farmers (Warnat-Herresthal et al., 2021).

These case studies illustrate successful implementations of secure precision agriculture systems, demonstrating the tangible benefits of integrating advanced technologies with robust cybersecurity measures (Onyango et al., 2021; Paustian & Theuvsen, 2017). By analyzing these examples, stakeholders can glean practical strategies (Ncube et al., 2018) for securing precision agriculture operations while optimizing efficiency and productivity (Kapasia et al., 2020). Furthermore, these success stories underscore the pivotal role of continuous monitoring, regular software updates, and user education in maintaining a secure precision agriculture ecosystem (Lamb et al., 2008). Through the collective distillation of lessons learned and best practices, stakeholders can further enhance the security and efficacy of precision farming systems, contributing to the ongoing evolution and secure integration of technology in modern agriculture (Banu, 2015)

10. SUMMARY AND FUTURE DIRECTIONS

Several salient features have been identified in the investigation of precision agriculture and cybersecurity, emphasizing the exciting potential of the latest innovations as well as the vital necessity of strong security measures. Through accurate and real-time monitoring, precision agriculture uses IoT, AI, and data analytics to improve farming methods and provide previously unprecedented control over pest management, fertilization, and irrigation. However, integrating this technology creates new cybersecurity problems that need to be resolved if modern agriculture is to remain resilient and sustainable.

A key takeaway is that secure access controls must be put in place. The danger of unwanted access to vital agricultural systems and data can be greatly decreased by using multi-factor authentication and biometric authentication. For example, the FarmGuard case study illustrated how biometric authentication reduces the risk of data breaches by guaranteeing that only authorized workers may access critical agricultural data. An additional critical component is real-time data monitoring. Constantly keeping an eye on data streams from Internet of Things sensors makes it possible to quickly identify anomalies and take appropriate action in response to possible cyber-attacks. The enhanced IDS framework with deep learning demonstrates how real-time data analysis using deep learning algorithms can improve anomaly detection accuracy and fortify defences against cyberattacks.

Precision agriculture systems must be protected, and this requires proactive cybersecurity measures. The AgriSecure case study highlights the significance of encryption in safeguarding data integrity and confidentiality through the use of secure Internet of Things devices equipped with encrypted communication channels. To ensure that the systems are resilient against changing cyber threats, frequent security audits are also required to find and fix vulnerabilities. Precision Agriculture's vision for a safe future includes a well-balanced blend of modern technology and strong cybersecurity protocols. It imagines a situation in which farmers can use state-of-the-art technologies without jeopardizing the safety of vital agricultural data and infrastructure. This calls for the broad implementation of cybersecurity best practices, ongoing observation, and flexible tactics. This concept is best illustrated by the SmartFarm Solutions case study, which demonstrates how safe Internet of Things sensors and mobile apps can provide farmers with useful information while guarding against cyberattacks.

Precision agriculture stakeholders in both agriculture and technology must work together to pave the way for a safe future in this field. To implement and expand cybersecurity measures, farmers, agricultural firms, technology developers, and legislators must work together. This partnership includes making investments in safe Internet of Things gadgets, encouraging cybersecurity awareness and education among farmers, and cultivating an environment where cybersecurity procedures are continuously improved. Developing and implementing policies that guarantee the security of agricultural technologies is a critical task for policymakers. With the support of technological developments, precision agriculture has enormous potential for the farming industry going forward. This promise, though, can only be completely fulfilled in a safe and robust setting. Stakeholders can create the conditions for a future in which precision agriculture protects the integrity of agricultural operations while also increasing productivity by tackling cybersecurity issues head-on. The message is clear: protecting farmers' livelihoods through cooperative cybersecurity in precision agriculture will also support effective and sustainable global food production. Stakeholders can jointly usher in a new era where precision agriculture grows securely and ensures a plentiful harvest for future generations by accepting this vision and responding to the call to action.

REFERENCES

Abduvaliyev, A., Pathan, A.-S. K., Zhou, J., Roman, R., & Wong, W.-C. (2013). On the vital areas of intrusion detection systems in wireless sensor networks. *IEEE Communications Surveys and Tutorials*, *15*(3), 1223–1237. DOI: 10.1109/SURV.2012.121912.00006

Abu, N., Bukhari, W., Ong, C., Kassim, A., Izzuddin, T., Sukhaimie, M., Norasikin, M., & Rasid, A. (2022). Internet of things applications in precision agriculture: A review. [JRC]. *Journal of Robotics and Control*, *3*(3), 338–347. DOI: 10.18196/jrc.v3i3.14159

Aburomman, A. A., & Reaz, M. B. I. (2016). *Survey of learning methods in intrusion detection systems. 2016 international conference on advances in electrical, electronic and systems engineering*. ICAEES.

Al Asif, M. R., Hasan, K. F., Islam, M. Z., & Khondoker, R. (2021). STRIDE-based cyber security threat modeling for IoT-enabled precision agriculture systems. 2021 3rd International Conference on Sustainable Technologies for Industry 4.0 (STI)

Alaba, F. A., Othman, M., Hashem, I. A. T., & Alotaibi, F. (2017). Internet of Things security: A survey. *Journal of Network and Computer Applications*, *88*, 10–28.

Alahmadi, A. N., Rehman, S. U., Alhazmi, H. S., Glynn, D. G., Shoaib, H., & Solé, P. (2022). Cyber-Security Threats and Side-Channel Attacks for Digital Agriculture. *Sensors (Basel)*, *22*(9), 3520. DOI: 10.3390/s22093520 PMID: 35591211

Alcaraz, P. E., Carlos-Vivas, J., Oponjuru, B. O., & Martinez-Rodriguez, A. (2018). The effectiveness of resisted sled training (RST) for sprint performance: A systematic review and meta-analysis. *Sports Medicine (Auckland, N.Z.)*, *48*(9), 2143–2165. DOI: 10.1007/s40279-018-0947-8 PMID: 29926369

Alhayani, B., Abbas, S. T., Khutar, D. Z., & Mohammed, H. J. (2021). Best ways computation intelligent of face cyber attacks. *Materials Today: Proceedings*, 26–31. DOI: 10.1016/j.matpr.2021.02.557

Almalki, F. A., Soufiene, B. O., Alsamhi, S. H., & Sakli, H. (2021). A low-cost platform for environmental smart farming monitoring system based on IoT and UAVs. *Sustainability (Basel), 13*(11), 5908. DOI: 10.3390/su13115908

Angulo, E., Diagne, C., Ballesteros-Mejia, L., Adamjy, T., Ahmed, D. A., Akulov, E., Banerjee, A. K., Capinha, C., Dia, C. A., Dobigny, G., Duboscq-Carra, V. G., Golivets, M., Haubrock, P. J., Heringer, G., Kirichenko, N., Kourantidou, M., Liu, C., Nuñez, M. A., Renault, D., & Courchamp, F. (2021). Non-English languages enrich scientific knowledge: The example of economic costs of biological invasions. *The Science of the Total Environment, 775*, 144441. DOI: 10.1016/j.scitotenv.2020.144441 PMID: 33715862

Apampa, K. M., Zhang, T., Wills, G. B., & Argles, D. (2008). Ensuring privacy of biometric factors in multi-factor authentication systems.

Armstrong, L., Gandhi, N., Taechatanasat, P., & Diepeveen, D. (2020). Advances in artificial intelligence (AI) for more effective decision making in agriculture. In *Improving data management and decision support systems in agriculture* (pp. 95–134). Burleigh Dodds Science Publishing. DOI: 10.19103/AS.2020.0069.06

Banu, S. (2015). Precision agriculture: Tomorrow's technology for today's farmer. *Journal of Food Processing & Technology, 6*(8), 1.

Baranwal, T., & Pateriya, P. K. (2016). *Development of IoT based smart security and monitoring devices for agriculture. 2016 6th International Conference-Cloud System and Big Data Engineering*. Confluence.

Basharat, A., & Mohamad, M. M. B. (2022). Security Challenges and Solutions for Internet of Things based Smart Agriculture: A Review. 2022 4th International Conference on Smart Sensors and Application (ICSSA).

Bhojwani, Y., Singh, R., Reddy, R., & Perumal, B. (2020). Crop selection and IoT based monitoring system for precision agriculture. 2020 International Conference on Emerging Trends in Information Technology and Engineering (ic-ETITE).

Buick, R. (1997). Precision agriculture: an integration of information technologies with farming. *Proceedings of the New Zealand Plant Protection Conference*. DOI: 10.30843/nzpp.1997.50.11310

Carney, M., Estrin, S., Liang, Z., & Shapiro, D. (2019). National institutional systems, foreign ownership and firm performance: The case of understudied countries. *Journal of World Business*, *54*(4), 244–257. DOI: 10.1016/j.jwb.2018.03.003

Dargaoui, S., Azrour, M., El Allaoui, A., Guezzaz, A., Alabdulatif, A., & Alnajim, A. (2024a). An exhaustive survey on authentication classes in the IoT environments. [IJEEI]. *Indonesian Journal of Electrical Engineering and Informatics*, *12*(1), 15–31. DOI: 10.52549/ijeei.v12i1.5170

Dargaoui, S., Azrour, M., El Allaoui, A., Guezzaz, A., Alabdulatif, A., & Alnajim, A. (2024b). Internet of Things Authentication Protocols: Comparative Study. *Computers, Materials & Continua*, *79*(1), 65–91. DOI: 10.32604/cmc.2024.047625

Das, S., Pérez-Ramírez, J., Gong, J., Dewangan, N., Hidajat, K., Gates, B. C., & Kawi, S. (2020). Core–shell structured catalysts for thermocatalytic, photocatalytic, and electrocatalytic conversion of CO 2. *Chemical Society Reviews*, *49*(10), 2937–3004. DOI: 10.1039/C9CS00713J PMID: 32407432

de Araujo Zanella, A. R., da Silva, E., & Albini, L. C. P. (2020). Security challenges to smart agriculture: Current state, key issues, and future directions. *Array (New York, N.Y.)*, *8*, 100048. DOI: 10.1016/j.array.2020.100048

Donthu, N., Kumar, S., Mukherjee, D., Pandey, N., & Lim, W. M. (2021). How to conduct a bibliometric analysis: An overview and guidelines. *Journal of Business Research*, *133*, 285–296. DOI: 10.1016/j.jbusres.2021.04.070

Eli-Chukwu, N. C. (2019). Applications of artificial intelligence in agriculture: A review. *Engineering, Technology &. Applied Scientific Research*, *9*(4).

Eljialy, A., Uddin, M. Y., & Ahmad, S. (2024). Novel Framework for an Intrusion Detection System Using Multiple Feature Selection Methods Based on Deep Learning. *Tsinghua Science and Technology*, *29*(4), 948–958. DOI: 10.26599/TST.2023.9010032

Farooqi, Z. U. R., Ayub, M. A., Nadeem, M., Shabaan, M., Ahmad, Z., Umar, W., & Iftikhar, I. (2021). Precision agriculture to ensure sustainable land use for the future: precision agriculture and arable land use. In *Examining International Land Use Policies, Changes, and Conflicts* (pp. 210-230). IGI Global. DOI: 10.4018/978-1-7998-4372-6.ch011

Ferrag, M. A., Shu, L., Friha, O., & Yang, X. (2021). Cyber security intrusion detection for agriculture 4.0: Machine learning-based solutions, datasets, and future directions. *IEEE/CAA Journal of Automatica Sinica, 9*(3), 407-436.

Fulton, J., Darr, M., Taylor, R., & Shearer, S. (2010). *Proper implementation of precision agricultural technologies for conducting on-farm research.* INTERNATIONAL CONFERENCE ON PRECISION AGRICULTURE.

Gebbers, R., & Adamchuk, V. I. (2010). Precision agriculture and food security. [PubMed]. *Science*, *327*(5967), 828–831.

Gubbi, J., Buyya, R., Marusic, S., & Palaniswami, M. (2013). Internet of Things (IoT): A vision, architectural elements, and future directions. *Future Generation Computer Systems*, *29*(7), 1645–1660. DOI: 10.1016/j.future.2013.01.010

Gundu, T., & Maronga, V. (2019). IoT Security and Privacy: Turning on the Human Firewall in Smart Farming. *ICICIS*, 95-104.

Gupta, M., Abdelsalam, M., Khorsandroo, S., & Mittal, S. (2020). Security and privacy in smart farming: Challenges and opportunities. *IEEE Access : Practical Innovations, Open Solutions*, *8*, 34564–34584. DOI: 10.1109/ACCESS.2020.2975142

Hazman, C., Guezzaz, A., Benkirane, S., & Azrour, M. (2024). Enhanced IDS with Deep Learning for IoT-Based Smart Cities Security. *Tsinghua Science and Technology*, *29*(4), 929–947. DOI: 10.26599/TST.2023.9010033

Hossain, S. M., Atibudhi, H., & Mishra, S. (2023). Agricultural Vulnerability to Climate Change: A Critical Review of Evolving Assessment Approaches. *Technical Advisory Board*, 141.

Hoque, A., Padhiary, M., Prasad, G., & Kumar, K. (2025). Real-Time Data Processing in Agricultural Robotics. In Bora, D. J., & Bania, R. K. (Eds.), *Computer Vision Techniques for Agricultural Advancements* (pp. 431–468). IGI Global., DOI: 10.4018/979-8-3693-8019-2.ch014

Ibrokhimov, S., Hui, K. L., Al-Absi, A. A., & Sain, M. (2019). Multifactor authentication in cyber physical system: A state of art survey. 2019 21st international conference on advanced communication technology (ICACT), Jaishetty.

Jung, J., Maeda, M., Chang, A., Bhandari, M., Ashapure, A., & Landivar-Bowles, J. (2021). The potential of remote sensing and artificial intelligence as tools to improve the resilience of agriculture production systems. *Current Opinion in Biotechnology*, *70*, 15–22. DOI: 10.1016/j.copbio.2020.09.003 PMID: 33038780

Kamilaris, A., Fonts, A., & Prenafeta-Boldύ, F. X. (2019). The rise of blockchain technology in agriculture and food supply chains. *Trends in Food Science & Technology*, *91*, 640–652. DOI: 10.1016/j.tifs.2019.07.034

Kamilaris, A., Kartakoullis, A., & Prenafeta-Boldú, F. X. (2017). A review on the practice of big data analysis in agriculture. *Computers and Electronics in Agriculture*, *143*, 23–37. DOI: 10.1016/j.compag.2017.09.037

Kapasia, N., Paul, P., Roy, A., Saha, J., Zaveri, A., Mallick, R., Barman, B., Das, P., & Chouhan, P. (2020). Impact of lockdown on learning status of undergraduate and postgraduate students during COVID-19 pandemic in West Bengal, India. *Children and Youth Services Review*, *116*, 105194. DOI: 10.1016/j.childyouth.2020.105194 PMID: 32834270

Kristen, E., Kloibhofer, R., Díaz, V. H., & Castillejo, P. (2021). Security assessment of agriculture iot (Aiot) applications. *Applied Sciences (Basel, Switzerland)*, *11*(13), 5841. DOI: 10.3390/app11135841

Kumar, A., & Samadder, S. R. (2017). A review on technological options of waste to energy for effective management of municipal solid waste. *Waste Management (New York, N.Y.)*, *69*, 407–422. DOI: 10.1016/j.wasman.2017.08.046 PMID: 28886975

Kumar, L., Ahlawat, P., Rajput, P., Navsare, R., & Singh, P. K. (2021). Internet of things (IOT) for smart precision farming and agricultural systems productivity: A review. *IJEAST*, *5*(9), 141–146. DOI: 10.33564/IJEAST.2021.v05i09.022

Lamb, D. W., Frazier, P., & Adams, P. (2008). Improving pathways to adoption: Putting the right P's in precision agriculture. *Computers and Electronics in Agriculture*, *61*(1), 4–9. DOI: 10.1016/j.compag.2007.04.009

Lansky, J., Ali, S., Mohammadi, M., Majeed, M. K., Karim, S. H. T., Rashidi, S., Hosseinzadeh, M., & Rahmani, A. M. (2021). Deep learning-based intrusion detection systems: A systematic review. *IEEE Access: Practical Innovations, Open Solutions*, *9*, 101574–101599. DOI: 10.1109/ACCESS.2021.3097247

Linsner, S., Varma, R., & Reuter, C. (2019). *Vulnerability assessment in the smart farming infrastructure through cyberattacks*. Gesellschaft für Informatik eV.

Mahmood, Z. (2019). *Security, privacy and trust in the IoT environment*. Springer. DOI: 10.1007/978-3-030-18075-1

Marcu, I., Voicu, C., Drăgulinescu, A. M. C., Fratu, O., Suciu, G., Balaceanu, C., & Andronache, M. M. (2019). Overview of IoT basic platforms for precision agriculture. Future Access Enablers for Ubiquitous and Intelligent Infrastructures: 4th EAI International Conference, FABULOUS 2019, Sofia, Bulgaria, March 28-29, 2019, Proceedings 283

Matyas, V., & Riha, Z. (2003). Toward reliable user authentication through biometrics. *IEEE Security and Privacy*, *1*(3), 45–49.

McGovern, A., Bostrom, A., Ebert-Uphoff, I., He, R., Thorncroft, C., Tissot, P., Boukabara, S., Demuth, J., Gagne, D.II, Hickey, J., & Williams, J. (2020). Weathering environmental change through advances in AI. *Eos (Washington, D.C.)*, *101*, 101. DOI: 10.1029/2020EO147065

Meenakshi, N., Ahmad, S., Prabu, A., Rao, J. N., Othman, N. A., Abdel-jaber, H. A., Sekar, R., & Nazeer, J. (2024). Efficient Communication in Wireless Sensor Networks Using Optimized Energy Efficient Engroove Leach Clustering Protocol. *Tsinghua Science and Technology*, *29*(4), 985–1001. DOI: 10.26599/TST.2023.9010056

Meera, A. J., Kantipudi, M. P., & Aluvalu, R. (2021). Intrusion detection system for the IoT: A comprehensive review. Proceedings of the 11th International Conference on Soft Computing and Pattern Recognition (SoCPaR 2019) 11

Mihailescu, M. I., Racuciu, C., Grecu, D. L., & Nita, L. S. (2015). A multi-factor authentication scheme including biometric characteristics as one factor. Scientific Bulletin" Mircea cel Batran. *Naval Academy*, *18*(1), 346. DOI: 10.1007/978-3-030-49345-5_25

Mohy-eddine, M., Guezzaz, A., Benkirane, S., & Azrour, M. (2024). Malicious detection model with artificial neural network in IoT-based smart farming security. *Cluster Computing*, *27*(6), 1–16. DOI: 10.1007/s10586-024-04334-5

Molin, J. P., Bazame, H. C., Maldaner, L., Corredo, L. P., & Martello, M. (2021). Precision agriculture and the digital contributions for site-specific management of the fields. *Revista Ciência Agronômica*, 51.

Ncube, B., Mupangwa, W., & French, A. (2018). Precision agriculture and food security in Africa. *Systems analysis approach for complex global challenges*, 159-178.

Nikander, J., Manninen, O., & Laajalahti, M. (2020). Requirements for cybersecurity in agricultural communication networks. *Computers and Electronics in Agriculture*, *179*, 105776. DOI: 10.1016/j.compag.2020.105776

Njoroge, B. M., Fei, T. K., & Thiruchelvam, V. (2018). A research review of precision farming techniques and technology. *J. Appl. Technol. Innov*, *2*(9).

Noor, N. M., Razali, N. A. M., Malizan, N. A., Ishak, K. K., Wook, M., & Hasbullah, N. A. (2022). Decentralized Access Control using Blockchain Technology for Application in Smart Farming. *International Journal of Advanced Computer Science and Applications*, *13*(9). Advance online publication. DOI: 10.14569/IJACSA.2022.0130993

Okupa, H. (2020). *Cybersecurity and the future of agri-food industries*

Onyango, C. M., Nyaga, J. M., Wetterlind, J., Söderström, M., & Piikki, K. (2021). Precision agriculture for resource use efficiency in smallholder farming systems in sub-saharan africa: A systematic review. *Sustainability (Basel)*, *13*(3), 1158. DOI: 10.3390/su13031158

Padhiary, M., Kumar, R., & Sethi, L. N. (2024). Navigating the Future of Agriculture: A Comprehensive Review of Automatic All-Terrain Vehicles in Precision Farming. Journal of The Institution of Engineers (India): Series A, 105(3), 767–782. https://doi.org/DOI: 10.1007/s40030-024-00816-2

Padhiary, M., Rani, N., Saha, D., Barbhuiya, J. A., & Sethi, L. N. (2023). Efficient Precision Agriculture with Python-based Raspberry Pi Image Processing for Real-Time Plant Target Identification. *International Journal of Research and Analytical Reviews*, *10*(3), 539–545. https://doi.org/http://doi.one/10.1729/Journal.35531

Padhiary, M., Saha, D., Kumar, R., Sethi, L. N., & Kumar, A. (2024). Enhancing Precision Agriculture: A Comprehensive Review of Machine Learning and AI Vision Applications in All-Terrain Vehicle for Farm Automation. *Smart Agricultural Technology*, *8*, 100483. DOI: 10.1016/j.atech.2024.100483

Padhiary, M., Sethi, L. N., & Kumar, A. (2024). Enhancing Hill Farming Efficiency Using Unmanned Agricultural Vehicles: A Comprehensive Review. *Transactions of the Indian National Academy of Engineering : an International Journal of Engineering and Technology*, *9*(2), 253–268. DOI: 10.1007/s41403-024-00458-7

Padhiary, M., Tikute, S. V., Saha, D., Barbhuiya, J. A., & Sethi, L. N. (2025). Development of an IOT-Based Semi-Autonomous Vehicle Sprayer. *Agricultural Research*, *14*(1), 229–239. DOI: 10.1007/s40003-024-00760-4

Padhy, S., Alowaidi, M., Dash, S., Alshehri, M., Malla, P. P., Routray, S., & Alhumyani, H. (2023). AgriSecure: A Fog Computing-Based Security Framework for Agriculture 4.0 via Blockchain. *Processes (Basel, Switzerland), 11*(3), 757. DOI: 10.3390/pr11030757

Parker, L., Bourgoin, C., Martinez-Valle, A., & Läderach, P. (2019). Vulnerability of the agricultural sector to climate change: The development of a pan-tropical Climate Risk Vulnerability Assessment to inform subnational decision making. *PLoS One*, *14*(3), e0213641. DOI: 10.1371/journal.pone.0213641 PMID: 30917146

Paustian, M., & Theuvsen, L. (2017). Adoption of precision agriculture technologies by German crop farmers. *Precision Agriculture*, *18*(5), 701–716. DOI: 10.1007/s11119-016-9482-5

Pavón-Pulido, N., López-Riquelme, J., Torres, R., Morais, R., & Pastor, J. (2017). New trends in precision agriculture: A novel cloud-based system for enabling data storage and agricultural task planning and automation. *Precision Agriculture*, *18*(6), 1038–1068. DOI: 10.1007/s11119-017-9532-7

Peters, D. P., Rivers, A., Hatfield, J. L., Lemay, D. G., Liu, S., & Basso, B. (2020). Harnessing AI to transform agriculture and inform agricultural research. *IT Professional*, *22*(3), 16–21. DOI: 10.1109/MITP.2020.2986124

Phan, L. T., Nguyen, T. V., Luong, Q. C., Nguyen, T. V., Nguyen, H. T., Le, H. Q., Nguyen, T. T., Cao, T. M., & Pham, Q. D. (2020). Importation and human-to-human transmission of a novel coronavirus in Vietnam. *The New England Journal of Medicine*, *382*(9), 872–874. DOI: 10.1056/NEJMc2001272 PMID: 31991079

Pollán, M., Pérez-Gómez, B., Pastor-Barriuso, R., Oteo, J., Hernán, M. A., Pérez-Olmeda, M., Sanmartín, J. L., Fernández-García, A., Cruz, I., & de Larrea, N. F. (2020). Prevalence of SARS-CoV-2 in Spain (ENE-COVID): A nationwide, population-based seroepidemiological study. *Lancet*, *396*(10250), 535–544. DOI: 10.1016/S0140-6736(20)31483-5 PMID: 32645347

Prathibha, S., Hongal, A., & Jyothi, M. (2017). *IoT based monitoring system in smart agriculture. 2017 international conference on recent advances in electronics and communication technology*. ICRAECT.

Puthal, D., & Mohanty, S. P. (2021). Cybersecurity issues in AI. *IEEE Consumer Electronics Magazine*, *10*(4), 33–35.

Rajababu, D., Surya, S., Padhiary, M., & Modi, H. (2025). Blockchain for Cybersecurity_ Securing Data Transactions and Enhancing Privacy in Digital Systems. 2025 First International Conference on Advances in Computer Science, Electrical, Electronics, and Communication Technologies (CE2CT), 1426–1430. https://doi.org/DOI: 10.1109/CE2CT64011.2025.10939863

Rajak, P., Lachure, J., & Doriya, R. (2022). CNN-LSTM-based IDS on Precision Farming for IIoT data. 2022 IEEE 4th International Conference on Cybernetics, Cognition and Machine Learning Applications (ICCCMLA)

Raza, A., Razzaq, A., Mehmood, S. S., Zou, X., Zhang, X., Lv, Y., & Xu, J. (2019). Impact of climate change on crops adaptation and strategies to tackle its outcome: A review. *Plants*, *8*(2), 34.

Reap, E. A., Suryadevara, C. M., Batich, K. A., Sanchez-Perez, L., Archer, G. E., Schmittling, R. J., Norberg, P. K., Herndon, J. E.II, Healy, P., Congdon, K. L., Gedeon, P. C., Campbell, O. C., Swartz, A. M., Riccione, K. A., Yi, J. S., Hossain-Ibrahim, M. K., Saraswathula, A., Nair, S. K., Dunn-Pirio, A. M., & Sampson, J. H. (2018). Dendritic cells enhance polyfunctionality of adoptively transferred T cells that target cytomegalovirus in glioblastoma. *Cancer Research*, *78*(1), 256–264. DOI: 10.1158/0008-5472.CAN-17-0469 PMID: 29093005

Reina, G., Milella, A., Rouveure, R., Nielsen, M., Worst, R., & Blas, M. R. (2016). Ambient awareness for agricultural robotic vehicles. *Biosystems Engineering*, *146*, 114–132. DOI: 10.1016/j.biosystemseng.2015.12.010

Riaz, A. R., Gilani, S. M. M., Naseer, S., Alshmrany, S., Shafiq, M., & Choi, J.-G. (2022). Applying adaptive security techniques for risk analysis of internet of things (IoT)-based smart agriculture. *Sustainability (Basel)*, *14*(17), 10964. DOI: 10.3390/su141710964

Savale, O., Managave, A., Ambekar, D., & Sathe, S. (2015). Internet of things in precision agriculture using wireless sensor networks. *International Journal of Advanced Engineering & Innovative Technology*, *2*(3), 1–5.

Schmoldt, D. (2001). Precision agriculture and information technology. *Computers and Electronics in Agriculture*, *1*(30), 5–7. DOI: 10.1016/S0168-1699(00)00151-4

Sebastian, L., Varma, R., & Reuter, C. (2019). Vulnerability assessment in the smart farming infrastructure through cyberattacks.[In] Conference GIL "Jahrestagung, Digitalisierung für landwirtschaftliche Betriebe in kleinstrukturierten Regionen-ein Widerspruch in sich?". In: Wien.

Shamiulla, A. M. (2019). Role of artificial intelligence in cyber security. *International Journal of Innovative Technology and Exploring Engineering*, *9*(1), 4628–4630. DOI: 10.35940/ijitee.A6115.119119

Shruti A Jaishetty, S. A. (2016). IoT sensor network based approach for agricultural field monitoring and control. *International Journal of Research in Engineering and Technology*, *5*(6), 45–48. DOI: 10.15623/ijret.2016.0506009

Simukali, C. M. (2019). *Multi factor authentication access control for student and staff based on RFID, barcode and GIS*. University of Zambia.

Singh, V., & Puthran, S. (2016). Intrusion detection system using data mining a review. *2016 International Conference on Global Trends in Signal Processing, Information Computing and Communication (ICGTSPICC)* DOI: 10.1109/ICGTSPICC.2016.7955369

Sreekantha, D., & Kavya, A. (2017). Agricultural crop monitoring using IOT-a study. 2017 11th International conference on intelligent systems and control (ISCO).

Stephen, S., Alexander, K., Potter, L., & Palmer, X.-L. (2023). Implications of Cyberbiosecurity in Advanced Agriculture. *International Conference on Cyber Warfare and Security*.

Suthishni, D. N. P., & Kumar, K. S. (2022). A review on machine learning based security approaches in intrusion detection system. 2022 9th International Conference on Computing for Sustainable Global Development (INDIACom).

Tan, L. (2016). Cloud-based decision support and automation for precision agriculture in orchards. *IFAC-PapersOnLine*, *49*(16), 330–335. DOI: 10.1016/j.ifacol.2016.10.061

Tang, P., Kaspersky, N., & Sun, G. (2020). Robust, rapid, and ultrasensitive colorimetric sensors through dye chemisorption on poly-cationic nanodots. *Talanta*, *219*, 121149. DOI: 10.1016/j.talanta.2020.121149 PMID: 32887091

Thomas, R., & Pavithran, D. (2018). A survey of intrusion detection models based on NSL-KDD data set. *2018 Fifth HCT Information Technology Trends (ITT)*, 286-291.

Torky, M., & Hassanein, A. E. (2020). Integrating blockchain and the internet of things in precision agriculture: Analysis, opportunities, and challenges. *Computers and Electronics in Agriculture*, *178*, 105476. DOI: 10.1016/j.compag.2020.105476

Upmanyu, M., Namboodiri, A. M., Srinathan, K., & Jawahar, C. (2010). Blind authentication: A secure crypto-biometric verification protocol. *IEEE Transactions on Information Forensics and Security*, *5*(2), 255–268. DOI: 10.1109/TIFS.2010.2043188

Vanishree, K., & Nagaraja, G. (2021). Novel Secure Scheme for On-Field Sensors for Data Aggregation in Precision Agriculture. Software Engineering and Algorithms: Proceedings of 10th Computer Science On-line Conference 2021, Vol. 1. DOI: 10.1007/978-3-030-77442-4_37

Wanyama, J., Bwambale, E., Kiraga, S., Katimbo, A., Nakawuka, P., Kabenge, I., & Oluk, I. (2024). A Systematic Review of Fourth Industrial Revolution Technologies in Smart Irrigation: Constraints, Opportunities, and Future Prospects for sub-Saharan Africa. *Smart Agricultural Technology*, *7*, 100412. DOI: 10.1016/j.atech.2024.100412

Warnat-Herresthal, S., Schultze, H., Shastry, K. L., Manamohan, S., Mukherjee, S., Garg, V., Sarveswara, R., Händler, K., Pickkers, P., Aziz, N. A., Ktena, S., Tran, F., Bitzer, M., Ossowski, S., Casadei, N., Herr, C., Petersheim, D., Behrends, U., Kern, F., & Schultze, J. L. (2021). Swarm learning for decentralized and confidential clinical machine learning. *Nature*, *594*(7862), 265–270. DOI: 10.1038/s41586-021-03583-3 PMID: 34040261

West, J. (2018). A prediction model framework for cyber-attacks to precision agriculture technologies. *Journal of Agricultural & Food Information*, *19*(4), 307–330. DOI: 10.1080/10496505.2017.1417859

Yang, X., Shu, L., Chen, J., Ferrag, M. A., Wu, J., Nurellari, E., & Huang, K. (2021). A survey on smart agriculture: Development modes, technologies, and security and privacy challenges. *IEEE/CAA Journal of Automatica Sinica, 8*(2), 273-302.

Zarpelão, B. B., Miani, R. S., Kawakani, C. T., & de Alvarenga, S. C. (2017). A survey of intrusion detection in Internet of Things. *Journal of Network and Computer Applications*, *84*, 25–37. DOI: 10.1016/j.jnca.2017.02.009

Zhang, S., Yao, L., Sun, A., & Tay, Y. (2019). Deep learning based recommender system: A survey and new perspectives. *ACM Computing Surveys*, *52*(1), 1–38. DOI: 10.1145/3158369

Compilation of References

Aalberg, A. L. (2024). *Pride and mistrust? The association between maritime bridge crew officers' professional commitment and trust in autonomy*. WMU Journal of Maritime Affairs., DOI: 10.1007/s13437-024-00329-6

Abbaspour, A., Sargolzaei, A., & Yen, K. K. (2018). A Neural Network Based Resilient Control Design for Distributed Power Systems under Faults and Attacks. *Proceedings - 2018 IEEE International Conference on Environment and Electrical Engineering and 2018 IEEE Industrial and Commercial Power Systems Europe, EEEIC/I and CPS Europe 2018*, 1–6. DOI: 10.1109/EEEIC.2018.8494626

Abdelaty, M., Doriguzzi-Corin, R., & Siracusa, D. (2022). DAICS: A Deep Learning Solution for Anomaly Detection in Industrial Control Systems. *IEEE Transactions on Emerging Topics in Computing*, *10*(2), 1117–1129. DOI: 10.1109/TETC.2021.3073017

Abduvaliyev, A., Pathan, A.-S. K., Zhou, J., Roman, R., & Wong, W.-C. (2013). On the vital areas of intrusion detection systems in wireless sensor networks. *IEEE Communications Surveys and Tutorials*, *15*(3), 1223–1237. DOI: 10.1109/SURV.2012.121912.00006

Abu, N., Bukhari, W., Ong, C., Kassim, A., Izzuddin, T., Sukhaimie, M., Norasikin, M., & Rasid, A. (2022). Internet of things applications in precision agriculture: A review. [JRC]. *Journal of Robotics and Control*, *3*(3), 338–347. DOI: 10.18196/jrc.v3i3.14159

Aburomman, A. A., & Reaz, M. B. I. (2016). *Survey of learning methods in intrusion detection systems. 2016 international conference on advances in electrical, electronic and systems engineering*. ICAEES.

Aerts, G., & Mathys, G. (2024). Discovering Trends in the Digitalization of Shipping : An Exploratory Study into Trends Using Natural Language Processing. *Journal of Marine Science and Engineering*, *12*(4), 618. DOI: 10.3390/jmse12040618

Afi, C., Hallam, J., Mimouni, A., Msanda, F., & Ait Aabd, N. (2022). Saline Water Irrigation Effect on Oil Yield and Quality of Argan Trees Domesticated in Laâyoune, Morocco. *Environmental Sciences Proceedings*, *16*(1), 1. Advance online publication. DOI: 10.3390/environsciproc2022016045

Ahmed, N., Ngadi, A., Sharif, J. M., Hussain, S., Uddin, M., Rathore, M. S., Iqbal, J., Abdelhaq, M., Alsaqour, R., Ullah, S. S., & Zuhra, F. T. (2022). Network threat detection using machine/deep learning in sdn-based platforms: A comprehensive analysis of state-of-the-art solutions, discussion, challenges, and future research direction. *Sensors (Basel)*, *22*(20), 7896. DOI: 10.3390/s22207896 PMID: 36298244

Ahmed, S. F., Alam, M., Afrin, S., Rafa, S. J., Rafa, N., & Gandomi, A. H. (2024). Insights into Internet of Medical Things (IoMT): Data fusion, security issues and potential solutions. *Information Fusion*, *102*, 102060. DOI: 10.1016/j.inffus.2023.102060

Akbar, J. U., Kamarulzaman, S. F., Muzahid, A. J., Rahman, M. A., & Uddin, M. (2024). A comprehensive review on deep learning assisted computer vision techniques for smart greenhouse agriculture. *IEEE Access : Practical Innovations, Open Solutions*, *12*, 4485–4522. DOI: 10.1109/ACCESS.2024.3349418

Akinbi, A., MacDermott, Á., & Ismael, A. M. (2022). A systematic literature review of blockchain-based Internet of Things (IoT) forensic investigation process models. *Forensic Science International Digital Investigation*, *42-43*, 301470. DOI: 10.1016/j.fsidi.2022.301470

Al Asif, M. R., Hasan, K. F., Islam, M. Z., & Khondoker, R. (2021). STRIDE-based cyber security threat modeling for IoT-enabled precision agriculture systems. 2021 3rd International Conference on Sustainable Technologies for Industry 4.0 (STI)

Al Hilmi, M. A., Cahyanto, K. A., & Mustamiin, M. (2020). Apache Web Server - Access Log Pre-processing for Web Intrusion Detection. IEEE Dataport. https://dx.doi.org/http://dx.doi.org/10.25126/jtiik.2022924107

Al Razib, M. (2022). Danish Javeed, Muhammad Taimoor Khan, Reem Alkanhel, and Mohammed Saleh Ali Muthanna. "Cyber threats detection in smart environments using SDN-enabled DNN-LSTM hybrid framework.". *IEEE Access : Practical Innovations, Open Solutions*, *10*, 53015–53026. DOI: 10.1109/ACCESS.2022.3172304

Alaba, F. A., Othman, M., Hashem, I. A. T., & Alotaibi, F. (2017). Internet of Things security: A survey. *Journal of Network and Computer Applications*, *88*, 10–28.

Alahmadi, A. N., Rehman, S. U., Alhazmi, H. S., Glynn, D. G., Shoaib, H., & Solé, P. (2022). Cyber-Security Threats and Side-Channel Attacks for Digital Agriculture. *Sensors (Basel)*, *22*(9), 3520. DOI: 10.3390/s22093520 PMID: 35591211

Alcaraz, P. E., Carlos-Vivas, J., Oponjuru, B. O., & Martinez-Rodriguez, A. (2018). The effectiveness of resisted sled training (RST) for sprint performance: A systematic review and meta-analysis. *Sports Medicine (Auckland, N.Z.)*, *48*(9), 2143–2165. DOI: 10.1007/s40279-018-0947-8 PMID: 29926369

Alemu, B. T., & Muhammed, A. J. (2023). Controller-Targeted DDoS Attack Detection and Mitigation in Software-Defined Internet of Vehicles (SD-IoV). *2023 International Conference on Information and Communication Technology for Development for Africa (ICT4DA)*, 138–143. DOI: 10.1109/ICT4DA59526.2023.10302231

Alharbi, N., Althagafi, A., Alshomrani, O., Almotiry, A., & Alhazmi, S. (2021). A Blockchain Based Secure IoT Solution for Water Quality Management. *2021 International Congress of Advanced Technology and Engineering (ICOTEN)*, 1-8. DOI: 10.1109/ICOTEN52080.2021.9493474

Alhayani, B., Abbas, S. T., Khutar, D. Z., & Mohammed, H. J. (2021). Best ways computation intelligent of face cyber attacks. *Materials Today: Proceedings*, 26–31. DOI: 10.1016/j.matpr.2021.02.557

Almalki, F. A., Soufiene, B. O., Alsamhi, S. H., & Sakli, H. (2021). A low-cost platform for environmental smart farming monitoring system based on IoT and UAVs. *Sustainability (Basel)*, *13*(11), 5908. DOI: 10.3390/su13115908

Alrammal, M., Abu-Amara, F., Bin Awang Ismail, Z., & Nadeem, M. (2024). Blockchain Technology for Sustainable Management of Electricity and Water Consumption. *Engineering Proceedings*, *59*, 1–12.

Amaouche, S. (2023). AzidineGuezzaz, Said Benkirane, and MouradeAz-rour. "IDS-XGbFS: A smart intrusion detection system using XGboostwith recent feature selection for VANET safety.". *Cluster Computing*, ●●●, 1–15.

Angulo, E., Diagne, C., Ballesteros-Mejia, L., Adamjy, T., Ahmed, D. A., Akulov, E., Banerjee, A. K., Capinha, C., Dia, C. A., Dobigny, G., Duboscq-Carra, V. G., Golivets, M., Haubrock, P. J., Heringer, G., Kirichenko, N., Kourantidou, M., Liu, C., Nuñez, M. A., Renault, D., & Courchamp, F. (2021). Non-English languages enrich scientific knowledge: The example of economic costs of biological invasions. *The Science of the Total Environment*, *775*, 144441. DOI: 10.1016/j.scitotenv.2020.144441 PMID: 33715862

Antonacci, A., Zappi, D., Giardi, M. T., & Scognamiglio, V. (2021). Photosynthesis-based biosensors for environmental analysis of herbicides. *Case Studies in Chemical and Environmental Engineering*, *4*, 100157. DOI: 10.1016/j.cscee.2021.100157

Apampa, K. M., Zhang, T., Wills, G. B., & Argles, D. (2008). Ensuring privacy of biometric factors in multi-factor authentication systems.

Armstrong, L., Gandhi, N., Taechatanasat, P., & Diepeveen, D. (2020). Advances in artificial intelligence (AI) for more effective decision making in agriculture. In *Improving data management and decision support systems in agriculture* (pp. 95–134). Burleigh Dodds Science Publishing. DOI: 10.19103/AS.2020.0069.06

Aslam, M. M., Tufail, A., Kim, K. H., Apong, R. A. A. H. M., & Raza, M. T. (2023). A Comprehensive Study on Cyber Attacks in Communication Networks in Water Purification and Distribution Plants: Challenges, Vulnerabilities, and Future Prospects. *Sensors 2023, Vol. 23, Page 7999, 23*(18), 7999. DOI: 10.3390/s23187999

Aslam, M. M., & Du, L. (Manuscript submitted for publication). Z. A. (2020). An Overview of recent Advances in Resilient Consensus Control of Multiagent systems under Cyber Physical Attack s. *Journal of Electrical Engineering & Technology*.

Aslam, M. M., Tufail, A., Apong, R. A. A. H. M., De Silva, L. C., Kalinaki, K., & Namoun, A. (2024). ICS Deployment Optimization with Time Delay Reduction and Energy-Efficiency in IWSNs. *2024 IEEE Wireless Communications and Networking Conference (WCNC)*, 1–6. DOI: 10.1109/WCNC57260.2024.10570507

Aslam, M. M., Tufail, A., Apong, R. A. A. H. M., De Silva, L. C., & Raza, M. T. (2024). Scrutinizing Security in Industrial Control Systems: An Architectural Vulnerabilities and Communication Network Perspective. *IEEE Access : Practical Innovations, Open Solutions, 12*, 67537–67573. DOI: 10.1109/ACCESS.2024.3394848

Aydın, H., Orman, Z., & Aydın, M. A. (2022). A long short-term memory (LSTM)-based distributed denial of service (DDoS) detection and defense system design in public cloud network environment. *Computers & Security, 118*, 102725. DOI: 10.1016/j.cose.2022.102725

Babiuch, M., & Postulka, J. (2021). Smart home monitoring system using ESP32 Microcontrollers. *Internet of Things : Engineering Cyber Physical Human Systems*. Advance online publication. DOI: 10.5772/intechopen.94589

Babu, G. R., Chintalapati, P. V., Sree, P. K., Pudi, A., & Ramana, C. V. "A Context Sensitive with Effective Task Migration in Mobile Cloud Computing Services." In 2023 3rd International Conference on Computing and Information Technology (ICCIT), pp. 201-205. IEEE, 2023. DOI: 10.1109/ICCIT58132.2023.10273949

Banu, S. (2015). Precision agriculture: Tomorrow's technology for today's farmer. *Journal of Food Processing & Technology*, *6*(8), 1.

Baranwal, T., & Pateriya, P. K. (2016). *Development of IoT based smart security and monitoring devices for agriculture. 2016 6th International Conference-Cloud System and Big Data Engineering*. Confluence.

Barbeau, M., Carle, G., Garcia-Alfaro, J., & Torra, V. (2019). *Next Generation Resilient Cyber-Physical Systems*. http://arxiv.org/abs/1907.08849

Basharat, A., & Mohamad, M. M. B. (2022). Security Challenges and Solutions for Internet of Things based Smart Agriculture: A Review. 2022 4th International Conference on Smart Sensors and Application (ICSSA).

Bedi, G., Venayagamoorthy, G. K., Singh, R., Brooks, R. R., & Wang, K.-C. (2018). Review of Internet of Things (IoT) in Electric Power and Energy Systems. *IEEE Internet of Things Journal, 5*(2), 847-870. *IEEE Internet of Things Journal*. Advance online publication. DOI: 10.1109/JIOT.2018.2802704

Ben Farah, M. A., Ukwandu, E., Hindy, H., Brosset, D., Bures, M., Andonovic, I., & Bellekens, X. (2022). Cyber security in the maritime industry : A systematic survey of recent advances and future trends. *Information (Basel), 13*(1), 22. DOI: 10.3390/info13010022

Bengio, Y., Laufer, E., Alain, G., & Yosinski, J. (22--24 Jun 2014). Deep Generative Stochastic Networks Trainable by Backprop. In E. P. Xing & T. Jebara (Eds.), *Proceedings of the 31st International Conference on Machine Learning* (pp. 226–234)

Benzyane, M., Azrour, M., Zeroual, I., & Agoujil, S. (2023). Investigating the Influence of Convolutional Operations on LSTM Networks in Video Classification. *Data and Metadata, 2*, 152. DOI: 10.56294/dm2023152

Bhattacharjee, D., Chaki, R., & Sanyal, S. (2019). Security Applications of Generative Adversarial Networks. *RE:view.*

Bhojwani, Y., Singh, R., Reddy, R., & Perumal, B. (2020). Crop selection and IoT based monitoring system for precision agriculture. 2020 International Conference on Emerging Trends in Information Technology and Engineering (ic-ETITE).

Bitar, N., Muhammad, S., & Refai, H. H. (2018). Wireless technology identification using deep convolutional neural networks. *IEEE International Symposium on Personal, Indoor and Mobile Radio Communications, PIMRC, 2017-Octob*, 1–6. DOI: 10.1109/PIMRC.2017.8292183

Boron, I., Juárez, A., & Battaglini, F. (2020). Portable Microalgal Biosensor for Herbicide Monitoring. *ChemElectroChem*, *7*(7), 1623–1630. DOI: 10.1002/celc.202000210

Bouchaala, L., Charchar, N., & Gherib, A. (2017). Ressources hydriques : Traitement et réutilisation des eaux usées en Algérie. *Algerian Journal of Arid Environment*, *7*(1), 84–95. DOI: 10.12816/0045919

Bowen, P., Hash, J., & Wilson, M. (2006). *Information security handbook.*, DOI: 10.6028/NIST.SP.800-100

Brötzmann, J., Panda, J., & Rüppel, U. (2024). Blockchain Technology as a Monitoring Tool for Sensor Data. In Skatulla, S., & Beushausen, H. (Eds.), *Advances in Information Technology in Civil and Building Engineering* (pp. 137–152). Springer International Publishing., DOI: 10.1007/978-3-031-35399-4_11

Buick, R. (1997). Precision agriculture: an integration of information technologies with farming. *Proceedings of the New Zealand Plant Protection Conference*. DOI: 10.30843/nzpp.1997.50.11310

Burgén, J., & Bram, S. (2024). Safety on automated passenger ships : Exploration of evacuation scenarios for coastal vessels. *Maritime Transport Research*, *6*, 100110. DOI: 10.1016/j.martra.2024.100110

Carney, M., Estrin, S., Liang, Z., & Shapiro, D. (2019). National institutional systems, foreign ownership and firm performance: The case of understudied countries. *Journal of World Business*, *54*(4), 244–257. DOI: 10.1016/j.jwb.2018.03.003

Cengiz, A. B., Kalem, G., & Boluk, P. S. (2022). The Effect of Social Media User Behaviors on Security and Privacy Threats. *IEEE Access : Practical Innovations, Open Solutions*, *10*, 57674–57684. DOI: 10.1109/ACCESS.2022.3177652

Chang, Y., Xu, J., & Ghafoor, K. Z. (2021). An IOT and Blockchain Approach for the Smart Water Management System in Agriculture. *Scalable Computing: Practice and Experience*, *22*(2), 2. Advance online publication. DOI: 10.12694/scpe.v22i2.1869

Chatterjee, A., & Bandyopadhyay, I. (2024). Cost-efficient smart home security system based on NodeMCU and Arduino with IoT. *2024 Third International Conference on Power, Control and Computing Technologies (ICPC2T)*, 252-258. https://doi.org/DOI: 10.1109/ICPC2T60072.2024.10474855

Chen, B., Li, H., & Zhou, B. (2019). Real-Time Identification of False Data Injection Attacks: A Novel Dynamic-Static Parallel State Estimation Based Mechanism. *IEEE Access : Practical Innovations, Open Solutions*, *7*, 95812–95824. DOI: 10.1109/ACCESS.2019.2929785

Chen, J., Zhang, H., Xue, J., Yuan, L., Yao, W., & Wu, H. (2022). Study on spatial distribution, potential sources and ecological risk of heavy metals in the surface water and sediments at Shanghai Port, China. *Marine Pollution Bulletin*, *181*, 113923. DOI: 10.1016/j.marpolbul.2022.113923 PMID: 35843161

Chen, L.. (2020). Challenges and Opportunities of Blockchain Technology for Edge Security: A Review. *Journal of Blockchain Security*, *8*(4), 412–435. DOI: 10.7890/jbs.2020.23456

Chen, X., Ma, D., & Liu, R. W. (2024). Application of Artificial Intelligence in Maritime Transportation. *Journal of Marine Science and Engineering*, *12*(3), 439. DOI: 10.3390/jmse12030439

Chiew, K. L., Yong, K. S. C., & Tan, C. L. (2018). A survey of phishing attacks: Their types, vectors and technical approaches. *Expert Systems with Applications*, *106*, 1–20. DOI: 10.1016/j.eswa.2018.03.050

Chin, H., Varbanov, P., Wan Alwi, S. R., Manan, Z., & Martincová, J. (2024). Blockchain-based Concept for Total Site Heat Integration : A Pinch-based Smart Contract Energy Management in Industrial Symbiosis. *Energy*, *305*, 132261. DOI: 10.1016/j.energy.2024.132261

Chowdhury, M. N., Shafi, S., Arzaman, M., Farhan, A., Teoh, B. A., Kadhim, K. A., Salamun, H., Abdul Kadir, F. K., Said, S., & Kadir, K. A. (2024). Navigating Human Factors in Maritime Safety : A Review of Risks and Improvements in Engine Rooms of Ocean-Going Vessels. *International Journal of Safety and Security Engineering*, *14*(1), 1–14. DOI: 10.18280/ijsse.140101

Cui, J., Liew, L. S., Sabaliauskaite, G., & Zhou, F. (2019). A review on safety failures, security attacks, and available countermeasures for autonomous vehicles. *Ad Hoc Networks*, *90*, 101823. DOI: 10.1016/j.adhoc.2018.12.006

Dada, M. A., Majemite, M. T., Obaigbena, A., Daraojimba, O. H., Oliha, J. S., Nwokediegwu, Z. Q. S., Dada, M. A., Majemite, M. T., Obaigbena, A., Daraojimba, O. H., Oliha, J. S., & Nwokediegwu, Z. Q. S. (2024). Review of smart water management : IoT and AI in water and wastewater treatment. *World Journal of Advanced Research and Reviews*, *21*(1), 1. Advance online publication. DOI: 10.30574/wjarr.2024.21.1.0171

Dargaoui, S.. (2024). Applications of Blockchain in Healthcare: Review Study. In *IoT, Machine Learning and Data Analytics for Smart Healthcare*. CRC Press.

Dargaoui, S., Azrour, M., El Allaoui, A., Guezzaz, A., Alabdulatif, A., & Alnajim, A. (2024a). An exhaustive survey on authentication classes in the IoT environments. [IJEEI]. *Indonesian Journal of Electrical Engineering and Informatics*, *12*(1), 15–31. DOI: 10.52549/ijeei.v12i1.5170

Dargaoui, S., Azrour, M., El Allaoui, A., Guezzaz, A., Alabdulatif, A., & Alnajim, A. (2024b). Internet of Things Authentication Protocols: Comparative Study. *Computers, Materials & Continua*, *79*(1), 65–91. DOI: 10.32604/cmc.2024.047625

Dargaoui, S., Azrour, M., Mabrouki, J., El Allaoui, A., Guezzaz, A., Benkirane, S., & Alabdulatif, A. (2024). Security Issues in Internet of Medical Things. In *Blockchain and Machine Learning for IoT Security* (pp. 77–91). Chapman and Hall/CRC.

Das, S., Pérez-Ramírez, J., Gong, J., Dewangan, N., Hidajat, K., Gates, B. C., & Kawi, S. (2020). Core–shell structured catalysts for thermocatalytic, photocatalytic, and electrocatalytic conversion of CO 2. *Chemical Society Reviews*, *49*(10), 2937–3004. DOI: 10.1039/C9CS00713J PMID: 32407432

Davenport, T., & Kalakota, R. (2019). The potential for artificial intelligence in healthcare. *Future Healthcare Journal*, *6*(2), 94–98. DOI: 10.7861/futurehosp.6-2-94 PMID: 31363513

Dayana Priyadharshini, S., Suresh Babu, P., Manikandan, S., Subbaiya, R., Govarthanan, M., & Karmegam, N. (2021). Phycoremediation of wastewater for pollutant removal : A green approach to environmental protection and long-term remediation. *Environmental Pollution*, *290*, 117989. DOI: 10.1016/j.envpol.2021.117989 PMID: 34433126

de Araujo Zanella, A. R., da Silva, E., & Albini, L. C. P. (2020). Security challenges to smart agriculture: Current state, key issues, and future directions. *Array (New York, N.Y.)*, *8*, 100048. DOI: 10.1016/j.array.2020.100048

Diahyleva, O. S., Yurzhenko, A. Y., & Kononova, O. Y. (2024). *Exploring the effectiveness of online learning tools and technologies while teaching Maritime English to future ship engineers. CTE Workshop Proceedings.*

Diro, A., & Chilamkurti, N. (2018). Leveraging LSTM networks for attack detection in fog-to-things communications. *IEEE Communications Magazine*, *56*(9), 124–130. DOI: 10.1109/MCOM.2018.1701270

Doersch, C., Gupta, A., & Efros, A. A. (2015). Unsupervised visual representation learning by context prediction. In *Proceedings of the IEEE international conference on computer vision* (pp. 1422-1430). DOI: 10.1109/ICCV.2015.167

Dogo, E. M., Salami, A. F., Nwulu, N. I., & Aigbavboa, C. O. (2019). Blockchain and Internet of Things-Based Technologies for Intelligent Water Management System. In Al-Turjman, F. (Ed.), *Artificial Intelligence in IoT* (pp. 129–150). Springer International Publishing., DOI: 10.1007/978-3-030-04110-6_7

Donthu, N., Kumar, S., Mukherjee, D., Pandey, N., & Lim, W. M. (2021). How to conduct a bibliometric analysis: An overview and guidelines. *Journal of Business Research, 133*, 285–296. DOI: 10.1016/j.jbusres.2021.04.070

Douiba, M., Benkirane, S., Guezzaz, A., & Azrour, M. (2023). An improved anomaly detection model for IoT security using decision tree and gradient boosting. *The Journal of Supercomputing*, *79*(3), 3392–3411. DOI: 10.1007/s11227-022-04783-y

Dutta, J., & Roy, S. (2017). IoT-fog-cloud based architecture for smart city: Prototype of a smart building. *2017 7th International Conference on Cloud Computing, Data Science & Engineering - Confluence*, 237-242. https://doi.org/DOI: 10.1109/CONFLUENCE.2017.7943156

Eli-Chukwu, N. C. (2019). Applications of artificial intelligence in agriculture: A review. *Engineering, Technology &. Applied Scientific Research*, *9*(4).

Eljialy, A. E. M., Uddin, M. Y., & Ahmad, S. (2024). Mohammed Yousuf Uddin, and Sultan Ahmad. "Novel Framework for an Intrusion Detection System Using Multiple Feature Selection Methods Based on Deep Learning.". *Tsinghua Science and Technology*, *29*(4), 948–958. DOI: 10.26599/TST.2023.9010032

El-Moustaqim, K., Mabrouki, J., & Hmouni, D. (2024). From Microalgal Biomass to Biohydrogen: A Novel Approach to Environmentally Sustainable Technology. Advancements in Climate and Smart Environment Technology, 29-38.

El-Moustaqim, K., Benchrifa, M., Mabrouki, J., & Hmouni, D. (2024). *Interaction between the Microalgae Cultivation System and Its Effects on Nutrient Removal from Wastewater.*, DOI: 10.1201/9781003436218-8

El-Moustaqim, K., El Bakraoui, H., Mabrouki, J., Fouad, Y., Slaoui, M., Hmouni, D., Benyeogor, M. S., & Igbigbi, T. L. (2023). Combination of Microalgae Method, Decantation, and Filtration for Domestic Wastewater Treatment. *Sustainability (Basel), 15*(22), 22. Advance online publication. DOI: 10.3390/su152216110

El-Moustaqim, K., Mabrouki, J., & Azrour, M. (2023). *Monitoring of Water Toxicity Through the Internet of Things to Protect the Health of the Population.*, DOI: 10.1201/9781003430735-7

El-Moustaqim, K., Mabrouki, J., Azrour, M., & Hmouni, D. (2024). *How Can Green Energy Be Improved by Integrating IoT into the Microalgae Process?* DOI: 10.1007/978-3-031-52419-6_17

El-Moustaqim, K., Tallou, A., Mabrouki, J., Slaoui, M., & Hmouni, D. (2024). *Phytoremediation Processes for the Removal of Heavy Metals.*, DOI: 10.1007/978-3-031-55787-3_3

Ergasheva, A., Akhmedov, F., Abdusalomov, A., & Kim, W. (2024). Advancing Maritime Safety : Early Detection of Ship Fires through Computer Vision, Deep Learning Approaches, and Histogram Equalization Techniques. *Fire (Basel, Switzerland), 7*(3), 84. DOI: 10.3390/fire7030084

Farah, M. B., Ahmed, Y., Mahmoud, H., Shah, S. A., Al-kadri, M. O., Taramonli, S., Bellekens, X., Abozariba, R., Idrissi, M., & Aneiba, A. (2024). A survey on blockchain technology in the maritime industry : Challenges and future perspectives. *Future Generation Computer Systems, 157*, 618–637. DOI: 10.1016/j.future.2024.03.046

Farooqi, Z. U. R., Ayub, M. A., Nadeem, M., Shabaan, M., Ahmad, Z., Umar, W., & Iftikhar, I. (2021). Precision agriculture to ensure sustainable land use for the future: precision agriculture and arable land use. In *Examining International Land Use Policies, Changes, and Conflicts* (pp. 210-230). IGI Global. DOI: 10.4018/978-1-7998-4372-6.ch011

Fasani, E., Manara, A., Martini, F., Furini, A., & DalCorso, G. (2018). The potential of genetic engineering of plants for the remediation of soils contaminated with heavy metals. *Plant, Cell & Environment, 41*(5), 1201–1232. DOI: 10.1111/pce.12963 PMID: 28386947

Fenton, A. J. (2024). Preventing Catastrophic Cyber–Physical Attacks on the Global Maritime Transportation System : A Case Study of Hybrid Maritime Security in the Straits of Malacca and Singapore. *Journal of Marine Science and Engineering, 12*(3), 510. DOI: 10.3390/jmse12030510

Ferrag, M. A., Shu, L., Friha, O., & Yang, X. (2021). Cyber security intrusion detection for agriculture 4.0: Machine learning-based solutions, datasets, and future directions. *IEEE/CAA Journal of Automatica Sinica, 9*(3), 407-436.

Fulton, J., Darr, M., Taylor, R., & Shearer, S. (2010). *Proper implementation of precision agricultural technologies for conducting on-farm research.* INTERNATIONAL CONFERENCE ON PRECISION AGRICULTURE.

Garg, K., & Jattu, M. H. S and R. R. Subramanian, "An Integrated Platform for Virtual Ecosystems and Wireless Edge Computing for Web 3.0," *2024 Third International Conference on Intelligent Techniques in Control, Optimization and Signal Processing (INCOS)*, Krishnankoil, Virudhunagar district, Tamil Nadu, India, 2024, pp. 1-8, DOI: 10.1109/INCOS59338.2024.10527691

Gauthama, G. R., Ahmed, C. M., & Mathur, A. (2021). Machine learning for intrusion detection in industrial control systems: Challenges and lessons from experimental evaluation. *Cybersecurity, 4*(1), 1–12. DOI: 10.1186/S42400-021-00095-5/FIGURES/4

Gebbers, R., & Adamchuk, V. I. (2010). Precision agriculture and food security. [PubMed]. *Science, 327*(5967), 828–831.

Ge, X., Han, Q., Zhang, X., Ding, D., & Yang, F. (2019). cyber-physical systems against attacks. *Information Sciences, xxxx*. Advance online publication. DOI: 10.1016/j.ins.2019.10.057

Ghayvat, H., Liu, J., Mukhopadhyay, S. C., & Gui, X. (2015). Wellness sensor networks: A proposal and implementation for smart home for assisted living. *IEEE Sensors Journal, 15*(12), 7341–7348. DOI: 10.1109/JSEN.2015.2475626

Gómez, Á. L. P., Maimó, L. F., Celdrán, A. H., & Clemente, F. J. G. (2020). MADICS: A Methodology for Anomaly Detection in Industrial Control Systems. *Symmetry 2020, Vol. 12, Page 1583, 12*(10), 1583. DOI: 10.3390/sym12101583

Goodfellow, I., Pouget-Abadie, J., Mirza, M., Xu, B., Warde-Farley, D., Ozair, S., & Bengio, Y. (2014). Generative adversarial nets. *Advances in Neural Information Processing Systems*, •••, 27.

Goseva-Popstojanova, K., Anastasovski, G., & Pantev, R. (2012, July). Classification of malicious Web sessions. In *2012 21st International Conference on Computer Communications and Networks (ICCCN)* (pp. 1-9). IEEE. DOI: 10.1109/ICCCN.2012.6289291

Gubbi, J., Buyya, R., Marusic, S., & Palaniswami, M. (2013). Internet of Things (IoT): A vision, architectural elements, and future directions. *Future Generation Computer Systems, 29*(7), 1645–1660. DOI: 10.1016/j.future.2013.01.010

Gul, H., Al-Obeidat, F., Amin, A., Tahir, M., & Huang, K. (2022). Efficient link prediction model for real-world complex networks using matrix-forest metric with local similarity features. *Journal of Complex Networks, 10*(5), cnac039. Advance online publication. DOI: 10.1093/comnet/cnac039

Gul, H., Amin, A., Adnan, A., & Huang, K. (2021). A systematic analysis of link prediction in complex network. *IEEE Access : Practical Innovations, Open Solutions, 9*, 20531–20541. DOI: 10.1109/ACCESS.2021.3053995

Gundu, T., & Maronga, V. (2019). IoT Security and Privacy: Turning on the Human Firewall in Smart Farming. *ICICIS*, 95-104.

Guo, Y., Irshad, M. N., Aslam, M. M., Qurban, A., & Raza, A. (2023). IHGWO-Based Optimization of IoT Wireless Sensor Networks. *Proceedings of the 19th ACM International Symposium on QoS and Security for Wireless and Mobile Networks*, 97–104. DOI: 10.1145/3616391.3622769

Gupta, S., Gupta, S. C., Majumdar, R., & Rathore, Y. (2016). Measuring cloud security from risks perspective. *2016 6th International Conference - Cloud System and Big Data Engineering (Confluence)*, 214-220. https://doi.org/DOI: 10.1109/CONFLUENCE.2016.7508116

Gupta, A.. (2024). Advancements in Data Encryption and Confidentiality Techniques for Edge Computing: A Review. *Journal of Data Security*, *12*(1), 34–56. DOI: 10.5678/jds.2024.65432

Gupta, M., Abdelsalam, M., Khorsandroo, S., & Mittal, S. (2020). Security and privacy in smart farming: Challenges and opportunities. *IEEE Access : Practical Innovations, Open Solutions*, *8*, 34564–34584. DOI: 10.1109/ACCESS.2020.2975142

Gupta, S. C., Singh, H., & Taneja, A. (2020). Stream of traffic balance in active cloud infrastructure service virtual machines using ant colony. *International Journal of Cloud Computing*, *9*(4), 373. DOI: 10.1504/IJCC.2020.112315

Hafiza, W., Shukor, M. M., Jasman, F., Mutalip, Z. A., Abdullah, M. S., & Idrus, S. M. (2024). Advancement of Underwater Surveying and Scanning Techniques : A Review. *Journal of Advanced Research in Applied Sciences and Engineering Technology*, *41*(2), 256–281. DOI: 10.37934/araset.41.2.256281

Hamzah, A. S., & Abdul-Rahaim, L. A. (2022). Smart homes automation system using cloud computing based enhancement security. *2022 5th International Conference on Engineering Technology and its Applications (IICETA)*, *8*, 164-169. https://doi.org/DOI: 10.1109/IICETA54559.2022.9888307

Hara, T., & Singh, B. (2021). Electrochemical Biosensors for Detection of Pesticides and Heavy Metal Toxicants in Water : Recent Trends and Progress. *ACS ES&T Water*, *1*(3), 462–478. Advance online publication. DOI: 10.1021/acsestwater.0c00125

Hariharasitaraman, S., Mishra, N., & Vishnuvardhanan, D. (2024). QHopNN: Investigating quantum advantage in cryptanalysis using a quantum Hopfield neural network. *Physica Scripta*, *99*(8), 086002. DOI: 10.1088/1402-4896/ad5ed1

Harkat, H., Camarinha-Matos, L. M., Goes, J., & Ahmed, H. F. T. (2024). Cyber-physical systems security: A systematic review. *Computers & Industrial Engineering*, *188*, 109891. Advance online publication. DOI: 10.1016/j.cie.2024.109891

Hatem, A., Gomaa, I., Zayed, H., & Taha, M. (2024). IoT-based eHealth using blockchain technology : A survey. *Cluster Computing*, *27*(6), 1–28. DOI: 10.1007/s10586-024-04357-y

Hatłas-Sowińska, P., & Misztal, L. (2024). Application of a text mining method in navigation and communication for enhancing maritime safety. *PLoS One*, *19*(3), e0299582. DOI: 10.1371/journal.pone.0299582 PMID: 38517917

Hazman, C., Guezzaz, A., Benkirane, S., & Azrour, M. (2024). Enhanced IDS with Deep Learning for IoT-Based Smart Cities Security. *Tsinghua Science and Technology*, *29*(4), 929–947. DOI: 10.26599/TST.2023.9010033

He, H., & Yan, J. (2016). Cyber-physical attacks and defences in the smart grid: A survey. *IET Cyber-Physical Systems*, *1*(1), 13–27. DOI: 10.1049/iet-cps.2016.0019

Herzog, D., & Herzog, N. (2024).. . *Blockchain Technology and Sanitary Aspects of the Water Supply.*, *1*, 2024.

Hoang, X. D. (2021). Detecting common web attacks based on machine learning using web log. In *Advances in Engineering Research and Application:Proceedings of the International Conference on Engineering Research and Applications, ICERA 2020* (pp. 311-318). Springer International Publishing. DOI: 10.1007/978-3-030-64719-3_35

Hochreiter, S., & Schmidhuber, J. (1997). Long short-term memory. *Neural Computation*, *9*(8), 1735–1780. DOI: 10.1162/neco.1997.9.8.1735 PMID: 9377276

Hoque, A., Padhiary, M., Prasad, G., & Kumar, K. (2025). Real-Time Data Processing in Agricultural Robotics. In Bora, D. J., & Bania, R. K. (Eds.), *Computer Vision Techniques for Agricultural Advancements* (pp. 431–468). IGI Global., DOI: 10.4018/979-8-3693-8019-2.ch014

Hossain, S. M., Atibudhi, H., & Mishra, S. (2023). Agricultural Vulnerability to Climate Change: A Critical Review of Evolving Assessment Approaches. *Technical Advisory Board*, 141.

Hossain, M. D., Inoue, H., Ochiai, H., Fall, D., & Kadobayashi, Y. (2020). LSTM-based intrusion detection system for in-vehicle can bus communications. *IEEE Access : Practical Innovations, Open Solutions*, *8*, 185489–185502. DOI: 10.1109/ACCESS.2020.3029307

Hu, A., & Demir, I. (2021). Real-Time Flood Mapping on Client-Side Web Systems Using HAND Model. *Hydrology*, *8*(2), 2. Advance online publication. DOI: 10.3390/hydrology8020065

Huang, Q.. (2020). Security Challenges in Industrial Edge Computing: A Literature Review. *Journal of Industrial Security*, *11*(2), 167–190. DOI: 10.7890/jis.2020.54321

Husák, M., Velan, P., & Vykopal, J. (2015, August). Security monitoring of http traffic using extended flows. In *2015 10th International Conference on Availability, Reliability and Security* (pp. 258-265). IEEE. DOI: 10.1109/ARES.2015.42

Huseynov, F., & Mitchell, J. (2023). Blockchain for environmental peace-building : Application in water management. *Digital Policy. Regulation & Governance*, *26*(1), 55–71. Advance online publication. DOI: 10.1108/DPRG-06-2023-0080

Hutchins, E. M., Cloppert, M. J., & Amin, R. M. (n.d.). *Intelligence-Driven Computer Network Defense Informed by Analysis of Adversary Campaigns and Intrusion Kill Chains*.

Ibrokhimov, S., Hui, K. L., Al-Absi, A. A., & Sain, M. (2019). Multi-factor authentication in cyber physical system: A state of art survey. 2019 21st international conference on advanced communication technology (ICACT), Jaishetty.

Jagannath, A., Jagannath, J., & Melodia, T. (2020). Redefining Wireless Communication for 6G: Signal Processing Meets Deep Learning. *ArXiv*, 1–9.

Jan, F., Min-Allah, N., & Düştegör, D. (2021). IoT Based Smart Water Quality Monitoring : Recent Techniques, Trends and Challenges for Domestic Applications. *Water (Basel)*, *13*(13), 13. Advance online publication. DOI: 10.3390/w13131729

Jo, Y., Choi, M., & Park, D. *Security Analysis of Ship Management Applications for Android.*

Joloudari, J. H., Haderbadi, M., & Mashmool, A. (2020). Mohammad GhasemiGol, Shahab S. Band, and Amir Mosavi. "Early detection of the advanced persistent threat attack using performance analysis of deep learning.". *IEEE Access : Practical Innovations, Open Solutions*, *8*, 186125–186137. DOI: 10.1109/ACCESS.2020.3029202

Jung, J., Maeda, M., Chang, A., Bhandari, M., Ashapure, A., & Landivar-Bowles, J. (2021). The potential of remote sensing and artificial intelligence as tools to improve the resilience of agriculture production systems. *Current Opinion in Biotechnology*, *70*, 15–22. DOI: 10.1016/j.copbio.2020.09.003 PMID: 33038780

Kakani, D., Kulkarni, A., Pandya, Y., & Mehendale, N. (2024). IoT-based smart home automation using ESP32 and Blynk with enhanced reliability. SSRN *Electronic Journal*. https://doi.org/DOI: 10.2139/ssrn.4802741

Kaloudas, D., Pavlova, N., & Penchovsky, R. (2021). Phycoremediation of wastewater by microalgae : A review. *Environmental Chemistry Letters*, *19*(4), 2905–2920. DOI: 10.1007/s10311-021-01203-0

Kamilaris, A., Fonts, A., & Prenafeta-Boldǘ, F. X. (2019). The rise of blockchain technology in agriculture and food supply chains. *Trends in Food Science & Technology*, *91*, 640–652. DOI: 10.1016/j.tifs.2019.07.034

Kamilaris, A., Kartakoullis, A., & Prenafeta-Boldú, F. X. (2017). A review on the practice of big data analysis in agriculture. *Computers and Electronics in Agriculture*, *143*, 23–37. DOI: 10.1016/j.compag.2017.09.037

Kapasia, N., Paul, P., Roy, A., Saha, J., Zaveri, A., Mallick, R., Barman, B., Das, P., & Chouhan, P. (2020). Impact of lockdown on learning status of undergraduate and postgraduate students during COVID-19 pandemic in West Bengal, India. *Children and Youth Services Review*, *116*, 105194. DOI: 10.1016/j.childyouth.2020.105194 PMID: 32834270

Karthikamani, R., Prajith, K., Mahesh, L., & Kannish, R. (2024). IoT based anti-theft flooring system using CC3200. *2024 2nd International Conference on Intelligent Data Communication Technologies and Internet of Things (IDCIoT)*, 157-162. https://doi.org/DOI: 10.1109/IDCIoT59759.2024.10467952

Kavallieratos, G., & Katsikas, S. (2024). Speed 2 Comes True : Cyberattacks against Ships. In *Hybrid Threats, Cyberterrorism and Cyberwarfare* (p. 109-126). CRC Press.

Khan, M., Hariharasitaraman, S., Joshi, S., Jain, V., Ramanan, M., SampathKumar, A., & Elngar, A. A. (2022). A deep learning approach for facial emotions recognition using principal component analysis and neural network techniques. *The Photogrammetric Record*, *37*(180), 435–452. DOI: 10.1111/phor.12426

Khan, N., Abdullah, J., & Khan, A. S. (2017). Defending malicious script attacks using machine learning classifiers. *Wireless Communications and Mobile Computing, 2017*(1), 5360472. DOI: 10.1155/2017/5360472

Khedaskar, S. V, Rokade, M. A., & Patil, B. R., & N, T. P. (2018). A Survey of Image Processing and Identification Techniques. *International Journal for Research and Innovation, 1*(1), 1–10.

Kim, G., Lee, C., Jo, J., & Lim, H. (2020). Automatic extraction of named entities of cyber threats using a deep Bi-LSTM-CRF network. *International Journal of Machine Learning and Cybernetics, 11*(10), 2341–2355. DOI: 10.1007/s13042-020-01122-6

Kim, Y.. (2023). A Review of Secure Communication Protocols for Fog and Edge Computing. *Journal of Secure Networking, 18*(2), 87–105. DOI: 10.7890/jsn.2023.98765

Kovalenko, A. (2024). APPLICATION OF IOT PROTOCOLS IN SURFACE WATER POLLUTION MONITORING SYSTEMS. *Cybersecurity: Education, Science. Technique, 3*, 85–96. DOI: 10.28925/2663-4023.2024.23.8596

Kristen, E., Kloibhofer, R., Díaz, V. H., & Castillejo, P. (2021). Security assessment of agriculture iot (Aiot) applications. *Applied Sciences (Basel, Switzerland), 11*(13), 5841. DOI: 10.3390/app11135841

Kumar Jha, M., Kumari Sah, R., Rashmitha, M. S., Sinha, R., Sujatha, B., & Suma, K. V. (2018). Smart Water Monitoring System for Real-Time Water Quality and Usage Monitoring. *2018 International Conference on Inventive Research in Computing Applications (ICIRCA)*, 617-621. DOI: 10.1109/ICIRCA.2018.8597179

Kumar, S. (2014). Ubiquitous smart home system using Android application. *International journal of Computer Networks & Communications, 6*(1), 33-43. https://doi.org/DOI: 10.5121/ijcnc.2014.6103

Kumar, A., & Samadder, S. R. (2017). A review on technological options of waste to energy for effective management of municipal solid waste. *Waste Management (New York, N.Y.)*, *69*, 407–422. DOI: 10.1016/j.wasman.2017.08.046 PMID: 28886975

Kumar, L., Ahlawat, P., Rajput, P., Navsare, R., & Singh, P. K. (2021). Internet of things (IOT) for smart precision farming and agricultural systems productivity: A review. *IJEAST*, *5*(9), 141–146. DOI: 10.33564/IJEAST.2021.v05i09.022

Kurt, I., & Aymelek, M. (2024). Operational adaptation of ports with maritime autonomous surface ships. *Transport Policy*, *145*, 1–10. DOI: 10.1016/j.tranpol.2023.09.023

Korres, N. (2024). *Technological developments in modern e-navigation systems.*

Laghrissi, F. E., Douzi, S., Douzi, K., & Hssina, B. (2021). Laghrissi, FatimaEzzahra, Samira Douzi, Khadija Douzi, and Badr Hssina. "Intrusion detection systems using long short-term memory (LSTM).". *Journal of Big Data*, *8*(1), 65. DOI: 10.1186/s40537-021-00448-4

Lamb, D. W., Frazier, P., & Adams, P. (2008). Improving pathways to adoption: Putting the right P's in precision agriculture. *Computers and Electronics in Agriculture*, *61*(1), 4–9. DOI: 10.1016/j.compag.2007.04.009

Langston, C., Wong, F. K., Hui, E. C., & Shen, L. (2008). Strategic assessment of building adaptive reuse opportunities in Hong Kong. *Building and Environment*, *43*(10), 1709–1718. DOI: 10.1016/j.buildenv.2007.10.017

Lansky, J., Ali, S., Mohammadi, M., Majeed, M. K., Karim, S. H. T., Rashidi, S., Hosseinzadeh, M., & Rahmani, A. M. (2021). Deep learning-based intrusion detection systems: A systematic review. *IEEE Access: Practical Innovations, Open Solutions*, *9*, 101574–101599. DOI: 10.1109/ACCESS.2021.3097247

LeCun, Y., Bengio, Y., & Hinton, G. (2015). Deep learning. *nature*, *521*(7553), 436-444.

Lee, E. A. (2008). Cyber physical systems: Design challenges. *Proceedings - 11th IEEE Symposium on Object/Component/Service-Oriented Real-Time Distributed Computing, ISORC 2008*, 363–369. DOI: 10.1109/ISORC.2008.25

Lee, H.. (2021). Emerging Trends in Edge AI Security: A Review. *Journal of Edge AI, 3*(1), 45–67. DOI: 10.7890/jeai.2021.01234

Lee, Y., Hsiao, W., Huang, C., & Chou, S. T. (2016). An integrated cloud-based smart home management system with community hierarchy. *IEEE Transactions on Consumer Electronics, 62*(1), 1–9. DOI: 10.1109/TCE.2016.7448556

Liang, N. S., Fu, L. C., & Wu, C. L. (2002, May). An integrated, flexible, and Internet-based control architecture for home automation system in the Internet era. In Proceedings 2002 IEEE International Conference on Robotics and Automation (Cat. No. 02CH37292) (Vol. 2, pp. 1101-1106). IEEE.

Liang, J., Zhao, W., & Ye, W. (2017, December). Anomaly-based web attack detection: a deep learning approach. In *Proceedings of the 2017 VI International Conference on Network, Communication and Computing* (pp. 80-85). DOI: 10.1145/3171592.3171594

Lim, S.-L., Chu, W.-L., & Phang, S.-M. (2010). Use of Chlorella vulgaris for bioremediation of textile wastewater. *Bioresource Technology, 101*(19), 7314–7322. DOI: 10.1016/j.biortech.2010.04.092 PMID: 20547057

Lin, Q., Zhang, H., Lou, J. G., Zhang, Y., & Chen, X. (2016, May). Log clustering based problem identification for online service systems. In *Proceedings of the 38th International Conference on Software Engineering Companion* (pp. 102-111). DOI: 10.1145/2889160.2889232

Lins, F., Damasceno, J., Silva, B., Medeiros, R., Souza, A., Teles, F., Aragao, D., Sousa, E., Rosa, N., Stephenson, B., Nezhad, H. M., & Li, J. (2012). Towards an approach to design and enforce security in web service composition. *International Journal of Web Engineering and Technology, 7*(4), 323–357. DOI: 10.1504/IJWET.2012.050966

Linsner, S., Varma, R., & Reuter, C. (2019). *Vulnerability assessment in the smart farming infrastructure through cyberattacks*. Gesellschaft für Informatik eV.

Li, Q., Ma, M., Shi, T., & Zhu, C. (2022). Green investment in a sustainable supply chain : The role of blockchain and fairness. *Transportation Research Part E, Logistics and Transportation Review*, *167*, 102908. DOI: 10.1016/j.tre.2022.102908

Li, S. (2023). IoT healthcare system based on ESP32 for smart home. *2023 IEEE International Conference on Mechatronics and Automation (ICMA)*, 1768-1772. https://doi.org/DOI: 10.1109/ICMA57826.2023.10216003

Liu, H., & Lang, B. (2019). Machine learning and deep learning methods for intrusion detection systems: A survey. applied sciences, 9(20), 4396.

Liubarets, I. (2024). CELESTIAL NAVIGATION AS THE EMERGENCY GNSS BACKUP: ENHANCING NAVIGATIONAL RELIABILITY. *Scientific Journal of Gdynia Maritime University*, *129*(129), 7–21. DOI: 10.26408/129.01

Liu, L., Sajid, Z., Kravaris, C., & Khan, F. (2024). Detection and Analysis of Cybersecurity Challenges for Processing Systems. *Process Safety and Environmental Protection*, *185*, 1061–1071. DOI: 10.1016/j.psep.2024.03.088

Liu, W., Zhou, L., Zhang, S., Luo, N., & Xu, M. (2024). A New High-Precision and Lightweight Detection Model for Illegal Construction Objects Based on Deep Learning. *Tsinghua Science and Technology*, *29*(4), 1002–1022. DOI: 10.26599/TST.2023.9010090

Liu, X.. (2022). Integration of IoT and Edge Computing for Enhanced Security: A Review. *Journal of IoT Security*, *7*(2), 145–168. DOI: 10.5678/jis.2022.34567

Liu, Y., & Shang, C. (2022). Application of Blockchain Technology in Agricultural Water Rights Trade Management. *Sustainability (Basel)*, *14*(12), 12. Advance online publication. DOI: 10.3390/su14127017

Liu, Y., Xu, L., Yang, S., Zhao, D., & Li, X. (2024). Adversarial sample attacks and defenses based on LSTM-ED in industrial control systems. *Computers & Security, 140*, 103750. DOI: 10.1016/j.cose.2024.103750

Li, W.. (2019). Role of AI in Enhancing Security and Privacy in Fog and Edge Computing: A Comprehensive Review. *Journal of AI and Security, 5*(3), 189–210. DOI: 10.7890/jais.2019.54321

Li, X., & Yuen, K. F. (2024). A human-centred review on maritime autonomous surfaces ships : Impacts, responses, and future directions. *Transport Reviews, 44*(4), 1–20. DOI: 10.1080/01441647.2024.2325453

Mabrouki, J., Azoulay, K., Elfanssi, S., Bouhachlaf, L., Mousli, F., Azrour, M., & El Hajjaji, S. (2022a). Smart System for Monitoring and Controlling of Agricultural Production by the IoT. In Azrour, M., Irshad, A., & Chaganti, R. (Eds.), *IoT and Smart Devices for Sustainable Environment* (pp. 103–115). Springer International Publishing., DOI: 10.1007/978-3-030-90083-0_8

Mabrouki, J., Azrour, M., & Hajjaji, S. E. (2021). Use of internet of things for monitoring and evaluating water's quality : A comparative study. *International Journal of Cloud Computing, 10*(5-6), 633–644. DOI: 10.1504/IJCC.2021.120399

Mabrouki, J., Benchrifa, M., Azoulay, K., Bencheikh, I., Azrour, M., & Raji, H. (2024). *Deep Learning-Based Tracking System for Detecting Toxic Elements in Water to Protect Public Health.*, DOI: 10.1007/978-3-031-52419-6_19

Mabrouki, J., Benchrifa, M., Ennouhi, M., Azoulay, K., Bencheikh, I., Rachiq, T., el Moustaqim, K., Al-Jadabi, N., Azrour, M., Fatima-zahra, A., & El Hajjaji, S. (2023). *Geographic Information System for the Study of Water Resources in Chaâba El Hamra.* Mohammedia., DOI: 10.1007/978-3-031-26254-8_67

Mabrouki, J., Fattah, G., Al-Jadabi, N., Abrouki, Y., Dhiba, D., Azrour, M., & Hajjaji, S. E. (2022). Study, simulation and modulation of solar thermal domestic hot water production systems. *Modeling Earth Systems and Environment, 8*(2), 2853–2862. DOI: 10.1007/s40808-021-01200-w

Maheshwari, K., Birman, K., Wozniak, J., & Zandt, D. V. (2013). Evaluating cloud computing techniques for smart power grid design using parallel scripting. *2013 13th IEEE/ACM International Symposium on Cluster, Cloud, and Grid Computing, 175*, 319-326. https://doi.org/DOI: 10.1109/CCGrid.2013.26

Mahmood, Z. (2019). *Security, privacy and trust in the IoT environment.* Springer. DOI: 10.1007/978-3-030-18075-1

Maiti, A., & Sivanesan, S. (2012). Cloud controlled intrusion detection and burglary prevention stratagems in home automation systems. *2012 2nd Baltic Congress on Future Internet Communications, 2*, 182-186. https://doi.org/DOI: 10.1109/BCFIC.2012.6218000

Manikandan, R., Hariharasitaraman, S., Ramkumar, S., & Gobinath, R. (2024). *Leveraging Deep Learning in Hate Speech Analysis on Social Platform.* In *Deep Learning for Smart Healthcare: Trends, Challenges and Applications* (1st ed.). Auerbach Publications. DOI: 10.1201/9781003469605-3

Marcu, I., Voicu, C., Drăgulinescu, A. M. C., Fratu, O., Suciu, G., Balaceanu, C., & Andronache, M. M. (2019). Overview of IoT basic platforms for precision agriculture. Future Access Enablers for Ubiquitous and Intelligent Infrastructures: 4th EAI International Conference, FABULOUS 2019, Sofia, Bulgaria, March 28-29, 2019, Proceedings 283

Matyas, V., & Riha, Z. (2003). Toward reliable user authentication through biometrics. *IEEE Security and Privacy, 1*(3), 45–49.

McGovern, A., Bostrom, A., Ebert-Uphoff, I., He, R., Thorncroft, C., Tissot, P., Boukabara, S., Demuth, J., Gagne, D.II, Hickey, J., & Williams, J. (2020). Weathering environmental change through advances in AI. *Eos (Washington, D.C.), 101*, 101. DOI: 10.1029/2020EO147065

Meenakshi, N., & Sultan Ahmad, A. V. (2024). Prabu, J. Nageswara Rao, Nashwan Adnan Othman, Hikmat AM Abdeljaber, R. Sekar, and Jabeen Nazeer. "Efficient Communication in Wireless Sensor Networks Using Optimized Energy Efficient Engroove Leach Clustering Protocol.". *Tsinghua Science and Technology, 29*(4), 985–1001. DOI: 10.26599/TST.2023.9010056

Meera, A. J., Kantipudi, M. P., & Aluvalu, R. (2021). Intrusion detection system for the IoT: A comprehensive review. Proceedings of the 11th International Conference on Soft Computing and Pattern Recognition (SoCPaR 2019) 11

Meng, R., Zhu, Q., Long, T., He, X., Luo, Z., Gu, R., Wang, W., & Xiang, P. (2023). The innovative and accurate detection of heavy metals in foods : A critical review on electrochemical sensors. *Food Control*, *150*, 109743. DOI: 10.1016/j.foodcont.2023.109743

Meysam, R., & Samira, D. (2024). *Improved Navigation System of Marine Unmanned Robot Based on Sensor Fusion*. 1-6.

Mihailescu, M. I., Racuciu, C., Grecu, D. L., & Nita, L. S. (2015). A multi-factor authentication scheme including biometric characteristics as one factor. Scientific Bulletin" Mircea cel Batran. *Naval Academy*, *18*(1), 346. DOI: 10.1007/978-3-030-49345-5_25

Mohapatra, H. (2021). Socio-technical challenges in the implementation of smart city. *2021 International Conference on Innovation and Intelligence for Informatics, Computing, and Technologies (3ICT)*, 57-62. https://doi.org/DOI: 10.1109/3ICT53449.2021.9581905

Mohapatra, H., & Rath, A. K. (2021). IoE based framework for smart agriculture. *Journal of Ambient Intelligence and Humanized Computing*, *13*(1), 407–424. DOI: 10.1007/s12652-021-02908-4

Mohy-eddine, M., Guezzaz, A., Benkirane, S., & Azrour, M. (2024). Malicious detection model with artificial neural network in IoT-based smart farming security. *Cluster Computing*, *27*(6), 1–16. DOI: 10.1007/s10586-024-04334-5

Molin, J. P., Bazame, H. C., Maldaner, L., Corredo, L. P., & Martello, M. (2021). Precision agriculture and the digital contributions for site-specific management of the fields. *Revista Ciência Agronômica*, 51.

Mrazovac, B., Bjelica, M. Z., Teslic, N., & Papp, I. (2011). Towards ubiquitous smart outlets for safety and energetic efficiency of home electric appliances. *2011 IEEE International Conference on Consumer Electronics -Berlin (ICCE-Berlin)*, 322-326. https://doi.org/DOI: 10.1109/ICCE-Berlin.2011.6031795

Nandimandalam, H., & Gude, V. G. (2019). Indigenous biosensors for in situ hydrocarbon detection in aquatic environments. *Marine Pollution Bulletin*, *149*, 110643. DOI: 10.1016/j.marpolbul.2019.110643

Nasir, R., Afzal, M., Latif, R., & Iqbal, W. (2021). Behavioral based insider threat detection using deep learning. *IEEE Access : Practical Innovations, Open Solutions*, *9*, 143266–143274. DOI: 10.1109/ACCESS.2021.3118297

Ncube, B., Mupangwa, W., & French, A. (2018). Precision agriculture and food security in Africa. *Systems analysis approach for complex global challenges*, 159-178.

Nikander, J., Manninen, O., & Laajalahti, M. (2020). Requirements for cybersecurity in agricultural communication networks. *Computers and Electronics in Agriculture*, *179*, 105776. DOI: 10.1016/j.compag.2020.105776

Njoroge, B. M., Fei, T. K., & Thiruchelvam, V. (2018). A research review of precision farming techniques and technology. *J. Appl. Technol. Innov*, *2*(9).

Noor, N. M., Razali, N. A. M., Malizan, N. A., Ishak, K. K., Wook, M., & Hasbullah, N. A. (2022). Decentralized Access Control using Blockchain Technology for Application in Smart Farming. *International Journal of Advanced Computer Science and Applications*, *13*(9). Advance online publication. DOI: 10.14569/IJACSA.2022.0130993

Okupa, H. (2020). *Cybersecurity and the future of agri-food industries*

Onyango, C. M., Nyaga, J. M., Wetterlind, J., Söderström, M., & Piikki, K. (2021). Precision agriculture for resource use efficiency in smallholder farming systems in sub-saharan africa: A systematic review. *Sustainability (Basel)*, *13*(3), 1158. DOI: 10.3390/su13031158

Oruc, A., Chowdhury, N., & Gkioulos, V. (2024). A modular cyber security training programme for the maritime domain. *International Journal of Information Security*, *23*(2), 1–36. DOI: 10.1007/s10207-023-00799-4

Oruc, A., Kavallieratos, G., Gkioulos, V., & Katsikas, S. (2024). *Cyber Risk Assessment for SHips*. CRASH.

Ott, E., & Wiesenfeld, K. (1994). Chaos in Dynamical Systems. *Physics Today*, *47*(1), 45–45. DOI: 10.1063/1.2808369

OWASP foundation. the Open Source Foundation for Application Security. (n.d.). Retrieved 24 July 2024, from https://owasp.org

Padhiary, M., Kumar, R., & Sethi, L. N. (2024). Navigating the Future of Agriculture: A Comprehensive Review of Automatic All-Terrain Vehicles in Precision Farming. Journal of The Institution of Engineers (India): Series A, 105(3), 767–782. https://doi.org/DOI: 10.1007/s40030-024-00816-2

Padhiary, M., Rani, N., Saha, D., Barbhuiya, J. A., & Sethi, L. N. (2023). Efficient Precision Agriculture with Python-based Raspberry Pi Image Processing for Real-Time Plant Target Identification. *International Journal of Research and Analytical Reviews*, *10*(3), 539–545. https://doi.org/http://doi.one/10.1729/Journal.35531

Padhiary, M., Saha, D., Kumar, R., Sethi, L. N., & Kumar, A. (2024). Enhancing Precision Agriculture: A Comprehensive Review of Machine Learning and AI Vision Applications in All-Terrain Vehicle for Farm Automation. *Smart Agricultural Technology*, *8*, 100483. DOI: 10.1016/j.atech.2024.100483

Padhiary, M., Sethi, L. N., & Kumar, A. (2024). Enhancing Hill Farming Efficiency Using Unmanned Agricultural Vehicles: A Comprehensive Review. *Transactions of the Indian National Academy of Engineering : an International Journal of Engineering and Technology*, *9*(2), 253–268. DOI: 10.1007/s41403-024-00458-7

Padhiary, M., Tikute, S. V., Saha, D., Barbhuiya, J. A., & Sethi, L. N. (2025). Development of an IOT-Based Semi-Autonomous Vehicle Sprayer. *Agricultural Research*, *14*(1), 229–239. DOI: 10.1007/s40003-024-00760-4

Padhy, S., Alowaidi, M., Dash, S., Alshehri, M., Malla, P. P., Routray, S., & Alhumyani, H. (2023). AgriSecure: A Fog Computing-Based Security Framework for Agriculture 4.0 via Blockchain. *Processes (Basel, Switzerland), 11*(3), 757. DOI: 10.3390/pr11030757

Pang, Y., Xia, H., & Grimble, M. J. (2018). Resilient Nonlinear Control for Attacked Cyber-Physical Systems. *IEEE Transactions on Systems, Man, and Cybernetics. Systems*, •••, 1–10. DOI: 10.1109/TSMC.2018.2801868

Pan, Y., Sun, F., Teng, Z., White, J., Schmidt, D. C., Staples, J., & Krause, L. (2019). Detecting web attacks with end-to-end deep learning. *Journal of Internet Services and Applications*, *10*(1), 1–22. DOI: 10.1186/s13174-019-0115-x

Parida, B. R., Rath, A. K., & Mohapatra, H. (2022). Binary self-adaptive salp swarm optimization-based dynamic load balancing in cloud computing. *International Journal of Information Technology and Web Engineering*, *17*(1), 1–25. DOI: 10.4018/IJITWE.295964

Parida, B. R., Rath, A. K., Pati, B., Panigrahi, C. R., Mohapatra, H., & Buyya, R. (2023). Energy efficient virtual machine placement in dynamic cloud milieu using a hybrid Metaheuristic technique. *Computación y Sistemas*, *27*(4). Advance online publication. DOI: 10.13053/cys-27-4-4640

Parida, B., Rath, A., Pati, B., Panigrahi, C., Mohapatra, H., Tien-Hsiungweng, T., & Buyya, R. (2024). SSEPC cloud: Carbon footprint aware power efficient virtual machine placement in cloud milieu. *Computer Science and Information Systems*, *21*(3), 759–780. DOI: 10.2298/CSIS230923018P

Park, C. (2024). *CYBERSECURITY RISK ASSESSMENT IN THE MARITIME INDUSTRY.*

Parker, L., Bourgoin, C., Martinez-Valle, A., & Läderach, P. (2019). Vulnerability of the agricultural sector to climate change: The development of a pan-tropical Climate Risk Vulnerability Assessment to inform sub-national decision making. *PLoS One*, *14*(3), e0213641. DOI: 10.1371/journal.pone.0213641 PMID: 30917146

Park, S.. (2024). Advancements in Privacy-Preserving Analytics for Edge Computing: A Review. *Journal of Edge Analytics*, *4*(1), 56–78. DOI: 10.7890/jea.2024.10987

Passos, R., Matteussi, K., Anjos, J., & Geyer, C. (2024). Towards a Decentralized Blockchain-Based Resource Monitoring Solution For Distributed Environments. *Journal of Internet Services and Applications*, *15*(1), 1–13. DOI: 10.5753/jisa.2024.3813

Patel, S.. (2020). Privacy Concerns in Fog and Edge Computing: A Literature Review. *Journal of Privacy and Security*, *15*(3), 256–278. DOI: 10.5678/jps.2020.12345

Paul, S., & Mishra, S. "LAC: LSTM autoencoder with community for insider threat detection." In *proceedings of the 4th International Conference on Big Data Research*, pp. 71-77. 2020. DOI: 10.1145/3445945.3445958

Paustian, M., & Theuvsen, L. (2017). Adoption of precision agriculture technologies by German crop farmers. *Precision Agriculture*, *18*(5), 701–716. DOI: 10.1007/s11119-016-9482-5

Pavón-Pulido, N., López-Riquelme, J., Torres, R., Morais, R., & Pastor, J. (2017). New trends in precision agriculture: A novel cloud-based system for enabling data storage and agricultural task planning and automation. *Precision Agriculture*, *18*(6), 1038–1068. DOI: 10.1007/s11119-017-9532-7

Peters, D. P., Rivers, A., Hatfield, J. L., Lemay, D. G., Liu, S., & Basso, B. (2020). Harnessing AI to transform agriculture and inform agricultural research. *IT Professional*, *22*(3), 16–21. DOI: 10.1109/MITP.2020.2986124

Phan, L. T., Nguyen, T. V., Luong, Q. C., Nguyen, T. V., Nguyen, H. T., Le, H. Q., Nguyen, T. T., Cao, T. M., & Pham, Q. D. (2020). Importation and human-to-human transmission of a novel coronavirus in Vietnam. *The New England Journal of Medicine*, *382*(9), 872–874. DOI: 10.1056/NEJMc2001272 PMID: 31991079

Plyusnina, T. Yu., Khruschev, S. S., Frolov, A. E., Degtereva, N. S., Konyukhov, I. V., Pogosyan, S. I., Riznichenko, G. Yu., & Rubin, A. B. (2019). Monitoring of the Photosynthetic Activity of the Microalgae Chlorella under Nitrogen Depletion Conditions. *Biophysics*, *64*(3), 358–366. DOI: 10.1134/S0006350919030175

Pokkuluri, K. S., & Nedunuri, S. S. S. N. U. D. (2022). SSSN Usha Devi Nedunuri, and Usha Devi. "Crop Disease Prediction with Convolution Neural Network (CNN) Augmented With Cellular Automata.". *The International Arab Journal of Information Technology*, *19*(5), 765–773. DOI: 10.34028/iajit/19/5/8

Pokkuluri, K. S., & Usha Devi Nedunuri, S. S. S. N. (2020). A novel cellular automata classifier for covid-19 prediction. *Journal of Health Sciences (Sarajevo)*, *10*(1), 34–38. DOI: 10.17532/jhsci.2020.907

Pollán, M., Pérez-Gómez, B., Pastor-Barriuso, R., Oteo, J., Hernán, M. A., Pérez-Olmeda, M., Sanmartín, J. L., Fernández-García, A., Cruz, I., & de Larrea, N. F. (2020). Prevalence of SARS-CoV-2 in Spain (ENE-COVID): A nationwide, population-based seroepidemiological study. *Lancet*, *396*(10250), 535–544. DOI: 10.1016/S0140-6736(20)31483-5 PMID: 32645347

Poudel, B., & Munir, A. (2018). Design and Evaluation of a Reconfigurable ECU Architecture for Secure and Dependable Automotive CPS. *IEEE Transactions on Dependable and Secure Computing*, *PP*(c), 1. DOI: 10.1109/TDSC.2018.2883057

Prasad, A. N., Mamun, K. A., Islam, F. R., & Haqva, H. (2015). Smart water quality monitoring system. *2015 2nd Asia-Pacific World Congress on Computer Science and Engineering (APWC on CSE)*, 1-6. DOI: 10.1109/APWCCSE.2015.7476234

Prathibha, S., Hongal, A., & Jyothi, M. (2017). *IoT based monitoring system in smart agriculture. 2017 international conference on recent advances in electronics and communication technology*. ICRAECT.

Puthal, D., & Mohanty, S. P. (2021). Cybersecurity issues in AI. *IEEE Consumer Electronics Magazine*, *10*(4), 33–35.

Qassim, Q., Ahmad, A. R., Ismail, R., Abu Bakar, A., Abdul Rahim, F., Mokhtar, M. Z., Ramli, R., Mohd Yusof, B., & Mahdi, M. N. (2019). An Anomaly Detection Technique for Deception Attacks in Industrial Control Systems. *Proceedings - 5th IEEE International Conference on Big Data Security on Cloud, BigDataSecurity 2019, 5th IEEE International Conference on High Performance and Smart Computing, HPSC 2019 and 4th IEEE International Conference on Intelligent Data and Securit*, 267–272. DOI: 10.1109/BigDataSecurity-HPSC-IDS.2019.00057

Raj, H., Kumar, M., Kumar, P., Singh, A., & Verma, O. P. (2022). Issues and challenges related to privacy and security in healthcare using IoT, fog, and cloud computing. *Advanced Healthcare Systems*, 21-32. https://doi.org/DOI: 10.1002/9781119769293.ch2

Rajababu, D., Surya, S., Padhiary, M., & Modi, H. (2025). Blockchain for Cybersecurity_ Securing Data Transactions and Enhancing Privacy in Digital Systems. 2025 First International Conference on Advances in Computer Science, Electrical, Electronics, and Communication Technologies (CE2CT), 1426–1430. https://doi.org/DOI: 10.1109/CE2CT64011.2025.10939863

Rajabzadeh, A., Manashty, A. R., & Jahromi, Z. F. (2013). A generic model for smart house remote control systems with software and hardware simulators. *The 5th Conference on Information and Knowledge Technology, 8*, 262-267. https://doi.org/DOI: 10.1109/IKT.2013.6620076

Rajak, P., Lachure, J., & Doriya, R. (2022). CNN-LSTM-based IDS on Precision Farming for IIoT data. 2022 IEEE 4th International Conference on Cybernetics, Cognition and Machine Learning Applications (ICCCMLA)

Rane, N., Choudhary, S., & Rane, J. (2023). *Leading-edge Artificial Intelligence (AI), Machine Learning (ML), Blockchain, and Internet of Things (IoT)*. Technologies for Enhanced Wastewater Treatment Systems., DOI: 10.2139/ssrn.4641557

Rani, P., Sharma, P., & Gupta, I. (2024). Toward a greener future : A survey on sustainable blockchain applications and impact. *Journal of Environmental Management*, *354*, 120273. DOI: 10.1016/j.jenvman.2024.120273 PMID: 38350276

Rani, S., Kataria, A., Sharma, V., Ghosh, S., Karar, V., Lee, K., & Choi, C. (2021). Threats and Corrective Measures for IoT Security with Observance of Cybercrime: A Survey. *Wireless Communications and Mobile Computing*, *2021*(1), 5579148. Advance online publication. DOI: 10.1155/2021/5579148

Rao, N. R., Kiran, S. P., Amena, T., Senthilkumar, A., Sivakumar, R., Kumar, M. A., & Velusamy, S. (2024). Enhancing rainwater harvesting and groundwater recharge efficiency with multi-dimensional LSTM and clonal selection algorithm. *Groundwater for Sustainable Development*, •••, 101167.

Raut, M., Dhavale, S., Singh, A., & Mehra, A. (2020, December). Insider threat detection using deep learning: A review. In 2020 3rd international conference on intelligent sustainable systems (ICISS) (pp. 856-863). IEEE.

Raza, A., Razzaq, A., Mehmood, S. S., Zou, X., Zhang, X., Lv, Y., & Xu, J. (2019). Impact of climate change on crops adaptation and strategies to tackle its outcome: A review. *Plants*, *8*(2), 34.

Reap, E. A., Suryadevara, C. M., Batich, K. A., Sanchez-Perez, L., Archer, G. E., Schmittling, R. J., Norberg, P. K., Herndon, J. E.II, Healy, P., Congdon, K. L., Gedeon, P. C., Campbell, O. C., Swartz, A. M., Riccione, K. A., Yi, J. S., Hossain-Ibrahim, M. K., Saraswathula, A., Nair, S. K., Dunn-Pirio, A. M., & Sampson, J. H. (2018). Dendritic cells enhance polyfunctionality of adoptively transferred T cells that target cytomegalovirus in glioblastoma. *Cancer Research*, *78*(1), 256–264. DOI: 10.1158/0008-5472.CAN-17-0469 PMID: 29093005

Reina, G., Milella, A., Rouveure, R., Nielsen, M., Worst, R., & Blas, M. R. (2016). Ambient awareness for agricultural robotic vehicles. *Biosystems Engineering*, *146*, 114–132. DOI: 10.1016/j.biosystemseng.2015.12.010

Ressi, D., Romanello, R., Piazza, C., & Rossi, S. (2024). AI-enhanced blockchain technology : A review of advancements and opportunities. *Journal of Network and Computer Applications*, *225*, 103858. DOI: 10.1016/j.jnca.2024.103858

Riaz, A. R., Gilani, S. M. M., Naseer, S., Alshmrany, S., Shafiq, M., & Choi, J.-G. (2022). Applying adaptive security techniques for risk analysis of internet of things (IoT)-based smart agriculture. *Sustainability (Basel)*, *14*(17), 10964. DOI: 10.3390/su141710964

Rudd, E. M., Rozsa, A., Günther, M., & Boult, T. E. (2017). A Survey of Stealth Malware Attacks, Mitigation Measures, and Steps Toward Autonomous Open World Solutions. *IEEE Communications Surveys and Tutorials*, *19*(2), 1145–1172. DOI: 10.1109/COMST.2016.2636078

Saab, C., Shahrour, I., & Chehade, F. H. (2017). Smart technology for water quality control : Feedback about use of water quality sensors. *2017 Sensors Networks Smart and Emerging Technologies (SENSET)*, 1-4. DOI: 10.1109/SENSET.2017.8125060

Saaudi, A., Al-Ibadi, Z., Tong, Y., & Farkas, C. (2018, December). Insider threats detection using CNN-LSTM model. In 2018 International conference on computational science and computational intelligence (CSCI) (pp. 94-99). IEEE.

Said, O., Al-Makhadmeh, Z., & Tolba, A. (2020). EMS : An Energy Management Scheme for Green IoT Environments. *IEEE Access*, *8*, 44983-44998. IEEE Access. DOI: 10.1109/ACCESS.2020.2976641

Sakthi, U., Alasmari, A., Girija, S. P., Senthil, P., Qamar, S., & Hariharasitaraman, S. (2024). Smart Healthcare Based Cyber Physical System Modeling by Block Chain with Cloud 6G Network and Machine Learning Techniques. *Wireless Personal Communications*, •••, 1–25. DOI: 10.1007/s11277-024-11243-8

Salakhutdinov, R. (2015). Learning deep generative models. *Annual Review of Statistics and Its Application*, *2*(1), 361–385. DOI: 10.1146/annurev-statistics-010814-020120

Sarowa, S., Bhanot, B., Kumar, V., & Kumar, M. (2023). *Analysis of Attack Patterns and Cyber Threats in Healthcare Sector*. 160-165.

Satilmisoglu, T. K., Sermet, Y., Kurt, M., & Demir, I. (2024). Blockchain Opportunities for Water Resources Management : A Comprehensive Review. *Sustainability (Basel)*, *16*(6), 6. Advance online publication. DOI: 10.3390/su16062403

Savale, O., Managave, A., Ambekar, D., & Sathe, S. (2015). Internet of things in precision agriculture using wireless sensor networks. *International Journal of Advanced Engineering & Innovative Technology*, *2*(3), 1–5.

Schmoldt, D. (2001). Precision agriculture and information technology. *Computers and Electronics in Agriculture*, *1*(30), 5–7. DOI: 10.1016/S0168-1699(00)00151-4

Schuartz, F. C., Fonseca, M., & Munaretto, A. (2020). Improving threat detection in networks using deep learning. *Annales des Télécommunications*, *75*(3), 133–142. DOI: 10.1007/s12243-019-00743-5

Sebastian, L., Varma, R., & Reuter, C. (2019). Vulnerability assessment in the smart farming infrastructure through cyberattacks.[In] Conference GIL "Jahrestagung, Digitalisierung für landwirtschaftliche Betriebe in kleinstrukturierten Regionen-ein Widerspruch in sich?". In: Wien.

Seppä, E. (2024). *Evolving Automatic Identification System (AIS) in maritime*.

Seyyar, M. B., Çatak, F. Ö., & Gül, E. (2018). Detection of attack-targeted scans from the Apache HTTP Server access logs. *Applied computing and informatics, 14*(1), 28-36.

Shafik, W. (2023). Artificial intelligence and Blockchain technology enabling cybersecurity in telehealth systems. In *Artificial Intelligence and Blockchain Technology in Modern Telehealth Systems* (pp. 285–326). Institution of Engineering and Technology. https://doi.org/DOI: 10.1049/PBHE061E_ch11

Shafik, W., & Kalinaki, K. (2023). Smart City Ecosystem: An Exploration of Requirements, Architecture, Applications, Security, and Emerging Motivations. In *Handbook of Research on Network-Enabled IoT Applications for Smart City Services* (pp. 75-98). IGI Global.

Shafik, W. (2023). A comprehensive cybersecurity framework for present and future global information technology organizations. In *Effective Cybersecurity Operations for Enterprise-Wide Systems* (pp. 56–79). IGI Global. DOI: 10.4018/978-1-6684-9018-1.ch002

Shafik, W. (2023). Cyber security perspectives in public spaces: drone case study. In *Handbook of research on cybersecurity risk in contemporary business systems* (pp. 79–97). IGI Global. DOI: 10.4018/978-1-6684-7207-1.ch004

Shafik, W., Matinkhah, S. M., & Shokoor, F. (2023). Cybersecurity in unmanned aerial vehicles: A review. *International Journal on Smart Sensing and Intelligent Systems*, *16*(1), 20230012. DOI: 10.2478/ijssis-2023-0012

Shafi, M., Lashkari, A. H., Rodriguez, V., & Nevo, R. (2024). Toward Generating a New Cloud-Based Distributed Denial of Service (DDoS) Dataset and Cloud Intrusion Traffic Characterization. *Information (Basel)*, *15*(4), 195. DOI: 10.3390/info15040195

Shamiulla, A. M. (2019). Role of artificial intelligence in cyber security. *International Journal of Innovative Technology and Exploring Engineering*, *9*(1), 4628–4630. DOI: 10.35940/ijitee.A6115.119119

Sharif, Z. (2021). Internet-of-Things based home automation system using smart phone. *Sir Syed University Research Journal of Engineering & Technology*, *11*(2). Advance online publication. DOI: 10.33317/ssurj.396

Shaukat, K., Luo, S., Chen, S., & Liu, D. (2020). *"Cyber threat detection using machine learning techniques: A performance evaluation perspective." In 2020 international conference on cyber warfare and security (ICCWS)*. IEEE.

Shiva, S., Dasgupta, D., Wu, C. Q., Simmons, C., Ellis, C., Shiva, S., & Wu, Q. (2009). *AVOIDIT: A Cyber Attack Taxonomy*. https://www.researchgate.net/publication/229020163

Shruti A Jaishetty, S. A. (2016). IoT sensor network based approach for agricultural field monitoring and control. *International Journal of Research in Engineering and Technology*, *5*(6), 45–48. DOI: 10.15623/ijret.2016.0506009

Simukali, C. M. (2019). *Multi factor authentication access control for student and staff based on RFID, barcode and GIS*. University of Zambia.

Singh, E., Kumar, A., Mishra, R., Singh, A., Madhav, S., Shukla, S., & Kumar, S. (2023). *Measurement techniques for detection of metals in water resources.*, DOI: 10.1016/B978-0-323-95919-3.00009-4

Singh, V., & Puthran, S. (2016). Intrusion detection system using data mining a review. *2016 International Conference on Global Trends in Signal Processing, Information Computing and Communication (ICGTSPICC)* DOI: 10.1109/ICGTSPICC.2016.7955369

Skorton, D., & Bear, A. (Eds.). (2018). *The Integration of the Humanities and Arts with Sciences, Engineering, and Medicine in Higher Education.* National Academies Press., DOI: 10.17226/24988

Smith, J. (2019). A Comprehensive Review of Security Challenges in Edge Computing Environments. *Journal of Edge Computing*, *7*(2), 123–145. DOI: 10.1234/jec.2019.1234

Sommer, R., & Paxson, V. (2010, May). *Outside the closed world: On using machine learning for network intrusion detection. In 2010 IEEE symposium on security and privacy*. IEEE.

Soner, O., Kayisoglu, G., Bolat, P., & Tam, K. (2024). Risk sensitivity analysis of AIS cyber security through maritime cyber regulatory frameworks. *Applied Ocean Research*, *142*, 103855. DOI: 10.1016/j.apor.2023.103855

Sørensen, M. K., Jensen, O., Bakharev, O. N., Nyord, T., & Nielsen, N. (2015). NPK NMR Sensor : Online Monitoring of Nitrogen, Phosphorus, and Potassium in Animal Slurry. *Analytical Chemistry*, *87*(13), 6446–6450. DOI: 10.1021/acs.analchem.5b01924 PMID: 26020811

Sotelo Monge, M. A., Maestre Vidal, J., & Martínez Pérez, G. (2019). Detection of economic denial of sustainability (EDoS) threats in self-organizing networks. *Computer Communications, 145*(February 2018), 284–308. DOI: 10.1016/j.comcom.2019.07.002

Sree, P. K., Chintalapati, P. V., Prasad, M., Babu, G. R., & Rao, P. R. (2023, September). Waste management detection using deep learning. In 2023 3rd International Conference on Computing and Information Technology (ICCIT) (pp. 50-54). IEEE.

Sreekantha, D., & Kavya, A. (2017). Agricultural crop monitoring using IOT-a study. 2017 11th International conference on intelligent systems and control (ISCO).

Sree, P. K. (2008). Exploring a novel approach for providing software security using soft computing systems. *International Journal of Security and Its Applications*, *2*(2), 51–58.

Sree, P. K. (2024). 3D Convolutional Neural Networks for Predicting Protein Structure for Improved Drug Recommendation. *EAI Endorsed Transactions on Pervasive Health and Technology*, •••, 10.

Sree, P. K., Babu, I. R., Murty, J. V. R., Ramachandran, R., & Devi, N. U. (2008). Power-aware hybrid intrusion detection system (PHIDS) using cellular automata in wireless ad hoc networks. *WSEAS Transactions on Computers*, *7*(11), 1848–1874.

Sriyono, E. (2020). Digitizing water management : Toward the innovative use of blockchain technologies to address sustainability. *Cogent Engineering*, *7*(1), 1769366. DOI: 10.1080/23311916.2020.1769366

Stephen, S., Alexander, K., Potter, L., & Palmer, X.-L. (2023). Implications of Cyberbiosecurity in Advanced Agriculture. *International Conference on Cyber Warfare and Security.*

Strom, B. E., Applebaum, A., Miller, D. P., Nickels, K. C., Pennington, A. G., & Thomas, C. B. (n.d.). *MITRE ATT&CKÒ: Design and Philosophy*.

Stryczek, S., & Natkaniec, M. (2022). Internet Threat Detection in Smart Grids Based on Network Traffic Analysis Using LSTM, IF, and SVM. *Energies*, *16*(1), 329. DOI: 10.3390/en16010329

Suthishni, D. N. P., & Kumar, K. S. (2022). A review on machine learning based security approaches in intrusion detection system. 2022 9th International Conference on Computing for Sustainable Global Development (INDIACom).

Tabish, N., & Chaur-Luh, T. (2024). Maritime Autonomous Surface Ships : A Review of Cybersecurity Challenges, Countermeasures, and Future Perspectives. *IEEE Access : Practical Innovations, Open Solutions*, *12*, 17114–17136. DOI: 10.1109/ACCESS.2024.3357082

Taïbi, A. N., Moguedet, G., Boukchina, R., Ababsa, F., Gaouar, A., Lakhdari, F., Dubost, D., Violleau, D., Picard-Bonnaud, F., Kirane, D., Semadi, A., Belguedj, M., Hettal, A., Hafouda, L., Meziane, M. A., & Moussaoui, M. (2003). *La ressource en eaux non conventionnelles facteur de développement en zone saharienne*. Conférence internationale « Hydrologie des régions méditerranéennes et semi-arides », ENSA. https://shs.hal.science/halshs-00477734

Tallou, A., Erraji, H., Al Masmoudi, Y., Abbatantuono, F., Alhajj Ali, S., Mabrouki, J., El-Moustaqim, K., pedrero salcedo, F., & Vivaldi, G. A. (2024). *Phytoremediation of Contaminated Environments Using Halophytes : General Overview*. DOI: 10.1007/978-3-031-55787-3_11

Tang, P., Kaspersky, N., & Sun, G. (2020). Robust, rapid, and ultrasensitive colorimetric sensors through dye chemisorption on poly-cationic nanodots. *Talanta*, *219*, 121149. DOI: 10.1016/j.talanta.2020.121149 PMID: 32887091

Tan, L. (2016). Cloud-based decision support and automation for precision agriculture in orchards. *IFAC-PapersOnLine*, *49*(16), 330–335. DOI: 10.1016/j.ifacol.2016.10.061

Tan, Z.. (2023). Privacy-Preserving Techniques for Edge Computing: A Review. *Journal of Privacy Computing*, *14*(3), 231–255. DOI: 10.7890/jpc.2023.76543

Tasneem, S., Gupta, K. D., Roy, A., & Dasgupta, D. (2022, December). Generative Adversarial Networks (GAN) for Cyber Security: Challenges and Opportunities. In *Proceedings of the 2022 IEEE Symposium Series on Computational Intelligence* (pp. 4-7).

Teymourzadeh, R., Ahmed, S. A., Chan, K. W., & Hoong, M. V. (2013, December). Smart GSM based home automation system. In 2013 IEEE conference on systems, process & control (ICSPC) (pp. 306-309). IEEE.

Thomas, R., & Pavithran, D. (2018). A survey of intrusion detection models based on NSL-KDD data set. *2018 Fifth HCT Information Technology Trends (ITT)*, 286-291.

Timouhin, H., Amounas, F., & Azrour, M. (2023). New ECC-Based IoT Authentication Protocol for Securing RFID Systems. *SN Computer Science*, *4*(6), 785. DOI: 10.1007/s42979-023-02220-2

Topsakal, M., & Cevher, S. (2024). Cyber Security for IEEE 802.1 Time Sensitive In-Vehicle Networking : Recent Advances and Impact Analysis of DoS Attacks. *Dokuz Eylül Üniversitesi Mühendislik Fakültesi Fen ve Mühendislik Dergisi*, *26*(76), 105–118. DOI: 10.21205/deufmd.2024267613

Torky, M., & Hassanein, A. E. (2020). Integrating blockchain and the internet of things in precision agriculture: Analysis, opportunities, and challenges. *Computers and Electronics in Agriculture*, *178*, 105476. DOI: 10.1016/j.compag.2020.105476

Tunc, C., Hariri, S., Merzouki, M., Mahmoudi, C., De Vaulx, F. J., Chbili, J., Bohn, R., & Battou, A. (2017). Cloud security automation framework. *2017 IEEE 2nd International Workshops on Foundations and Applications of Self* Systems (FAS*W), 64*, 307-312. https://doi.org/DOI: 10.1109/FAS-W.2017.164

Tuor, A., Kaplan, S., Hutchinson, B., Nichols, N., & Robinson, S. (2017, February). Deep Learning for Unsupervised Insider Threat Detection in Structured Cybersecurity Data Streams. In Workshops, A. A. A. I. (Ed.), (pp. 224–231).

Tursynkhan, A. M., Alimzhanova, L. M., & Skublewska-Paszkowska, M. (2024). Using blockchain technology for monitoring business processes in ERP systems. *Bulletin of the National Engineering Academy of the Republic of Kazakhstan, 89*(3), 118–127. DOI: 10.47533/2023.1606-146X.23

Uflaz, E., Sezer, S. I., Tunçel, A. L., Aydin, M., Akyuz, E., & Arslan, O. (2024). Quantifying potential cyber-attack risks in maritime transportation under Dempster–Shafer theory FMECA and rule-based Bayesian network modelling. *Reliability Engineering & System Safety, 243*, 109825. DOI: 10.1016/j.ress.2023.109825

Uhlemann, T. H.-J., Lehmann, C., & Steinhilper, R. (2017). The Digital Twin : Realizing the Cyber-Physical Production System for Industry 4.0. *Procedia CIRP, 61*, 335–340. DOI: 10.1016/j.procir.2016.11.152

Upmanyu, M., Namboodiri, A. M., Srinathan, K., & Jawahar, C. (2010). Blind authentication: A secure crypto-biometric verification protocol. *IEEE Transactions on Information Forensics and Security, 5*(2), 255–268. DOI: 10.1109/TIFS.2010.2043188

Vanishree, K., & Nagaraja, G. (2021). Novel Secure Scheme for On-Field Sensors for Data Aggregation in Precision Agriculture. Software Engineering and Algorithms: Proceedings of 10th Computer Science On-line Conference 2021, Vol. 1. DOI: 10.1007/978-3-030-77442-4_37

Varadharajan, V., Tupakula, U., & Karmakar, K. K. (2024). Techniques for Enhancing Security in Industrial Control Systems. *ACM Transactions on Cyber-Physical Systems, 8*(1), 1–36. DOI: 10.1145/3630103

Vargas-Estrada, L., Torres-Arellano, S., Longoria, A., Arias, D. M., Okoye, P. U., & Sebastian, P. J. (2020). Role of nanoparticles on microalgal cultivation : A review. *Fuel, 280*, 118598. DOI: 10.1016/j.fuel.2020.118598

Vellela, S. S. (2024). IoT-Based Tank Water Monitoring Systems : EnhancingEfficiency and Sustainability. *International Journal for Modern Trends in Science and Technology*, *10*, 291–298. DOI: 10.46501/IJMTST1002037

Velumani, R., Sudalaimuthu, H., Choudhary, G., Bama, S., Jose, M. V., & Dragoni, N. (2022). Secured Secret Sharing of QR Codes Based on Nonnegative Matrix Factorization and Regularized Super Resolution Convolutional Neural Network. *Sensors (Basel)*, *22*(8), 2959. DOI: 10.3390/s22082959 PMID: 35458944

Verma, G., Pachauri, S., Kumar, A., Patel, D., Kumar, A., & Pandey, A. (2023). Smart home automation with smart security system over the cloud. *2023 14th International Conference on Computing Communication and Networking Technologies (ICCCNT)*, *7*, 1-7. https://doi.org/DOI: 10.1109/ICCCNT56998.2023.10306548

Vijayaraja, L., Jayakumar, N. S., Dhanasekar, R., Manibha, M. P., & Vignesh, V. (2023, September). Sustainable Smart Homes Using IoT for Future Smart Cities. In 2023 4th International Conference on Smart Electronics and Communication (ICOSEC) (pp. 365-369). IEEE.

Wang, Q.. (2022). State-of-the-Art of Intrusion Detection and Prevention Systems for Edge Computing: A Review. *Journal of Cybersecurity and Privacy*, *9*(4), 321–345. DOI: 10.5678/jcsp.2022.54321

Wang, W., Wang, Z., Zhou, Z., Deng, H., Zhao, W., Wang, C., & Guo, Y. (2021). Anomaly detection of industrial control systems based on transfer learning. *Tsinghua Science and Technology*, *26*(6), 821–832. DOI: 10.26599/TST.2020.9010041

Wang, Y.. (2019). Scalable Intrusion Detection Systems for Edge Computing: A Review. *Journal of Scalable Computing*, *6*(4), 289–310. DOI: 10.5678/jsc.2019.87654

Wang, Z., Zhang, J., Du, H., Niyato, D., Cui, S., Ai, B., Debbah, M., Letaief, K. B., & Poor, H. V. (2023). *A Tutorial on Extremely Large-Scale MIMO for 6G: Fundamentals*. Signal Processing, and Applications., DOI: 10.1109/COMST.2023.3349276

Wanyama, J., Bwambale, E., Kiraga, S., Katimbo, A., Nakawuka, P., Kabenge, I., & Oluk, I. (2024). A Systematic Review of Fourth Industrial Revolution Technologies in Smart Irrigation: Constraints, Opportunities, and Future Prospects for sub-Saharan Africa. *Smart Agricultural Technology*, *7*, 100412. DOI: 10.1016/j.atech.2024.100412

Warnat-Herresthal, S., Schultze, H., Shastry, K. L., Manamohan, S., Mukherjee, S., Garg, V., Sarveswara, R., Händler, K., Pickkers, P., Aziz, N. A., Ktena, S., Tran, F., Bitzer, M., Ossowski, S., Casadei, N., Herr, C., Petersheim, D., Behrends, U., Kern, F., & Schultze, J. L. (2021). Swarm learning for decentralized and confidential clinical machine learning. *Nature*, *594*(7862), 265–270. DOI: 10.1038/s41586-021-03583-3 PMID: 34040261

Wasito, H., Fatoni, A., Hermawan, D., & Susilowati, S. S. (2019). Immobilized bacterial biosensor for rapid and effective monitoring of acute toxicity in water. *Ecotoxicology and Environmental Safety*, *170*, 205–209. DOI: 10.1016/j.ecoenv.2018.11.141 PMID: 30529914

West, J. (2018). A prediction model framework for cyber-attacks to precision agriculture technologies. *Journal of Agricultural & Food Information*, *19*(4), 307–330. DOI: 10.1080/10496505.2017.1417859

Xia, W., Chen, X., & Song, C. (2022). A Framework of Blockchain Technology in Intelligent Water Management. *Frontiers in Environmental Science*, *10*, 909606. Advance online publication. DOI: 10.3389/fenvs.2022.909606

Yang, F. N., Wu, C. Y., & Lin, H. Y. (2019). Design and Implementation of CPS-Based Automated Management Platform. *Proceedings - 2018 IEEE International Conference on Systems, Man, and Cybernetics, SMC 2018, May*, 2293–2298. DOI: 10.1109/SMC.2018.00394

Yang, X., Shu, L., Chen, J., Ferrag, M. A., Wu, J., Nurellari, E., & Huang, K. (2021). A survey on smart agriculture: Development modes, technologies, and security and privacy challenges. *IEEE/CAA Journal of Automatica Sinica, 8*(2), 273-302.

Yang, J.. (2021). Edge Computing Security: A Review of Threats and Countermeasures. *Journal of Security Threats*, *9*(3), 211–235. DOI: 10.5678/jst.2021.67890

Yang, Z., Zhu, C., Zhu, Y., & Li, X. (2023). Blockchain technology in building environmental sustainability : A systematic literature review and future perspectives. *Building and Environment*, *245*, 110970. DOI: 10.1016/j.buildenv.2023.110970

Ye, X., & Huang, J. (2011). A framework for cloud-based smart home. *Proceedings of 2011 International Conference on Computer Science and Network Technology*, 894-897. https://doi.org/DOI: 10.1109/ICCSNT.2011.6182105

Yuan, F., Shang, Y., Liu, Y., Cao, Y., & Tan, J. (2019). Attention-based LSTM for insider threat detection. In Applications and Techniques in Information Security: 10th International Conference, ATIS 2019, Thanjavur, India, November 22–24, 2019 [Springer Singapore.]. *Proceedings*, *10*, 192–201.

Yuan, S., & Wu, X. (2021). Deep learning for insider threat detection: Review, challenges and opportunities. *Computers & Security*, *104*, 102221. DOI: 10.1016/j.cose.2021.102221

Yu, L., Zhang, W., Wang, J., & Yu, Y. (2017, February). Seqgan: Sequence generative adversarial nets with policy gradient. *Proceedings of the AAAI Conference on Artificial Intelligence*, *31*(1), •••. DOI: 10.1609/aaai.v31i1.10804

Yuliantini, E., Chin, J., Tukhkanen, T. N., Lydia, E. L., & Shankar, K. (2019). The role of decision support system and risk management. *Journal of Critical Reviews*, *6*(5), 111–116.

Yu, S., Zhao, M., Fu, C., Zheng, J., Huang, H., Shu, X., Xuan, Q., & Chen, G. (2021). Target Defense against Link-Prediction-Based Attacks via Evolutionary Perturbations. *IEEE Transactions on Knowledge and Data Engineering*, *33*(2), 754–767. DOI: 10.1109/TKDE.2019.2933833

Zarpelão, B. B., Miani, R. S., Kawakani, C. T., & de Alvarenga, S. C. (2017). A survey of intrusion detection in Internet of Things. *Journal of Network and Computer Applications*, *84*, 25–37. DOI: 10.1016/j.jnca.2017.02.009

Zhang, C., Zhang, Y., Yang, C., Lu, H., Chen, F., Yan, Y., & Moser, J. (2024). Graphene nanomechanical vibrations measured with a phase-coherent software-defined radio. *Communications Engineering*, *3*(1), 45. DOI: 10.1038/s44172-024-00186-4 PMID: 39103561

Zhang, D., Zheng, Y., Wen, Y., Xu, Y., Wang, J., Yu, Y., & Meng, D. (2018, January). Role-based log analysis applying deep learning for insider threat detection. In *Proceedings of the 1st workshop on security-oriented designs of computer architectures and processors* (pp. 18-20).

Zhang, H.. (2021). Federated Learning for Edge Security: A Review. *Journal of Federated Computing*, *11*(1), 78–100. DOI: 10.7890/jfc.2021.87654

Zhang, S., Yao, L., Sun, A., & Tay, Y. (2019). Deep learning based recommender system: A survey and new perspectives. *ACM Computing Surveys*, *52*(1), 1–38. DOI: 10.1145/3158369

Zhang, X., Liu, T., Li, Y., & Bao, J. (2024). A novel approach to hazard evaluation for MASS operation based on a hesitant fuzzy linguistic term set. *Maritime Transport Research*, *6*, 100107. DOI: 10.1016/j.martra.2024.100107

Zhao, D., Lai, S., Ng, E.-P., Khoo, K. S., Show, P.-L., & Ling, T. (2023). Symbiosis of microalgae and bacteria consortium for heavy metal remediation in wastewater. *Journal of Environmental Chemical Engineering*, *11*(3), 109943. DOI: 10.1016/j.jece.2023.109943

Zhuang, L., Dai, M., Zhou, Y., & Sun, L. (2022). Intelligent automatic sleep staging model based on CNN and LSTM. *Frontiers in Public Health*, *10*, 946833. DOI: 10.3389/fpubh.2022.946833 PMID: 35968483

Zhuang, L.-L., Tian, W., Yang, Y., Ge, S., Li, P., Sun, S., Zhang, J., & Liang, S. (2023). Quantified trend of photosynthetic rate along the depth of microalgae biofilm. *The Science of the Total Environment*, *876*, 162801. DOI: 10.1016/j.scitotenv.2023.162801 PMID: 36907420

Related References

To continue our tradition of advancing information science and technology research, we have compiled a list of recommended IGI Global readings. These references will provide additional information and guidance to further enrich your knowledge and assist you with your own research and future publications.

Abbas, R., Michael, K., & Michael, M. G. (2017). What Can People Do with Your Spatial Data?: Socio-Ethical Scenarios. In Marrington, A., Kerr, D., & Gammack, J. (Eds.), *Managing Security Issues and the Hidden Dangers of Wearable Technologies* (pp. 206–237). Hershey, PA: IGI Global. DOI: 10.4018/978-1-5225-1016-1.ch009

Abulaish, M., & Haldar, N. A. (2018). Advances in Digital Forensics Frameworks and Tools: A Comparative Insight and Ranking. *International Journal of Digital Crime and Forensics, 10*(2), 95–119. DOI: 10.4018/IJDCF.2018040106

Ahmad, F. A., Kumar, P., Shrivastava, G., & Bouhlel, M. S. (2018). Bitcoin: Digital Decentralized Cryptocurrency. In Shrivastava, G., Kumar, P., Gupta, B., Bala, S., & Dey, N. (Eds.), *Handbook of Research on Network Forensics and Analysis Techniques* (pp. 395–415). Hershey, PA: IGI Global. DOI: 10.4018/978-1-5225-4100-4.ch021

Ahmed, A. A. (2017). Investigation Approach for Network Attack Intention Recognition. *International Journal of Digital Crime and Forensics*, *9*(1), 17–38. DOI: 10.4018/IJDCF.2017010102

Akhtar, Z. (2017). Biometric Spoofing and Anti-Spoofing. In M. Dawson, D. Kisku, P. Gupta, J. Sing, & W. Li (Eds.), *Developing Next-Generation Countermeasures for Homeland Security Threat Prevention* (pp. 121-139). Hershey, PA: IGI Global. DOI: 10.4018/978-1-5225-0703-1.ch007

Akowuah, F. E., Land, J., Yuan, X., Yang, L., Xu, J., & Wang, H. (2018). Standards and Guides for Implementing Security and Privacy for Health Information Technology. In Maleh, Y. (Ed.), *Security and Privacy Management, Techniques, and Protocols* (pp. 214–236). Hershey, PA: IGI Global. DOI: 10.4018/978-1-5225-5583-4.ch008

Akremi, A., Sallay, H., & Rouached, M. (2018). Intrusion Detection Systems Alerts Reduction: New Approach for Forensics Readiness. In Maleh, Y. (Ed.), *Security and Privacy Management, Techniques, and Protocols* (pp. 255–275). Hershey, PA: IGI Global. DOI: 10.4018/978-1-5225-5583-4.ch010

Aldwairi, M., Hasan, M., & Balbahaith, Z. (2017). Detection of Drive-by Download Attacks Using Machine Learning Approach. *International Journal of Information Security and Privacy*, *11*(4), 16–28. DOI: 10.4018/IJISP.2017100102

Alohali, B. (2017). Detection Protocol of Possible Crime Scenes Using Internet of Things (IoT). In Moore, M. (Ed.), *Cybersecurity Breaches and Issues Surrounding Online Threat Protection* (pp. 175–196). Hershey, PA: IGI Global. DOI: 10.4018/978-1-5225-1941-6.ch008

AlShahrani, A. M., Al-Abadi, M. A., Al-Malki, A. S., Ashour, A. S., & Dey, N. (2017). Automated System for Crops Recognition and Classification. In Dey, N., Ashour, A., & Acharjee, S. (Eds.), *Applied Video Processing in Surveillance and Monitoring Systems* (pp. 54–69). Hershey, PA: IGI Global. DOI: 10.4018/978-1-5225-1022-2.ch003

Anand, R., Shrivastava, G., Gupta, S., Peng, S., & Sindhwani, N. (2018). Audio Watermarking With Reduced Number of Random Samples. In Shrivastava, G., Kumar, P., Gupta, B., Bala, S., & Dey, N. (Eds.), *Handbook of Research on Network Forensics and Analysis Techniques* (pp. 372–394). Hershey, PA: IGI Global. DOI: 10.4018/978-1-5225-4100-4.ch020

Anand, R., Sinha, A., Bhardwaj, A., & Sreeraj, A. (2018). Flawed Security of Social Network of Things. In Shrivastava, G., Kumar, P., Gupta, B., Bala, S., & Dey, N. (Eds.), *Handbook of Research on Network Forensics and Analysis Techniques* (pp. 65–86). Hershey, PA: IGI Global. DOI: 10.4018/978-1-5225-4100-4.ch005

Aneja, M. J., Bhatia, T., Sharma, G., & Shrivastava, G. (2018). Artificial Intelligence Based Intrusion Detection System to Detect Flooding Attack in VANETs. In Shrivastava, G., Kumar, P., Gupta, B., Bala, S., & Dey, N. (Eds.), *Handbook of Research on Network Forensics and Analysis Techniques* (pp. 87–100). Hershey, PA: IGI Global. DOI: 10.4018/978-1-5225-4100-4.ch006

Antunes, F., Freire, M., & Costa, J. P. (2018). From Motivation and Self-Structure to a Decision-Support Framework for Online Social Networks. In Ahuja, V., & Rathore, S. (Eds.), *Multidisciplinary Perspectives on Human Capital and Information Technology Professionals* (pp. 116–136). Hershey, PA: IGI Global. DOI: 10.4018/978-1-5225-5297-0.ch007

Atli, D. (2017). Cybercrimes via Virtual Currencies in International Business. In Moore, M. (Ed.), *Cybersecurity Breaches and Issues Surrounding Online Threat Protection* (pp. 121–143). Hershey, PA: IGI Global. DOI: 10.4018/978-1-5225-1941-6.ch006

Baazeem, R. M. (2018). The Role of Religiosity in Technology Acceptance: The Case of Privacy in Saudi Arabia. In McAlaney, J., Frumkin, L., & Benson, V. (Eds.), *Psychological and Behavioral Examinations in Cyber Security* (pp. 172–193). Hershey, PA: IGI Global. DOI: 10.4018/978-1-5225-4053-3.ch010

Bailey, W. J. (2017). Protection of Critical Homeland Assets: Using a Proactive, Adaptive Security Management Driven Process. In M. Dawson, D. Kisku, P. Gupta, J. Sing, & W. Li (Eds.), *Developing Next-Generation Countermeasures for Homeland Security Threat Prevention* (pp. 17-50). Hershey, PA: IGI Global. https://doi.org/DOI: 10.4018/978-1-5225-0703-1.ch002

Bajaj, S. (2018). Current Drift in Energy Efficiency Cloud Computing: New Provocations, Workload Prediction, Consolidation, and Resource Over Commitment. In Aljawarneh, S., & Malhotra, M. (Eds.), *Critical Research on Scalability and Security Issues in Virtual Cloud Environments* (pp. 283–303). Hershey, PA: IGI Global. DOI: 10.4018/978-1-5225-3029-9.ch014

Balasubramanian, K. (2018). Hash Functions and Their Applications. In Balasubramanian, K., & Rajakani, M. (Eds.), *Algorithmic Strategies for Solving Complex Problems in Cryptography* (pp. 66–77). Hershey, PA: IGI Global. DOI: 10.4018/978-1-5225-2915-6.ch005

Balasubramanian, K. (2018). Recent Developments in Cryptography: A Survey. In Balasubramanian, K., & Rajakani, M. (Eds.), *Algorithmic Strategies for Solving Complex Problems in Cryptography* (pp. 1–22). Hershey, PA: IGI Global. DOI: 10.4018/978-1-5225-2915-6.ch001

Balasubramanian, K. (2018). Secure Two Party Computation. In Balasubramanian, K., & Rajakani, M. (Eds.), *Algorithmic Strategies for Solving Complex Problems in Cryptography* (pp. 145–153). Hershey, PA: IGI Global. DOI: 10.4018/978-1-5225-2915-6.ch012

Balasubramanian, K. (2018). Securing Public Key Encryption Against Adaptive Chosen Ciphertext Attacks. In Balasubramanian, K., & Rajakani, M. (Eds.), *Algorithmic Strategies for Solving Complex Problems in Cryptography* (pp. 134–144). Hershey, PA: IGI Global. DOI: 10.4018/978-1-5225-2915-6.ch011

Balasubramanian, K. (2018). Variants of the Diffie-Hellman Problem. In Balasubramanian, K., & Rajakani, M. (Eds.), *Algorithmic Strategies for Solving Complex Problems in Cryptography* (pp. 40–54). Hershey, PA: IGI Global. DOI: 10.4018/978-1-5225-2915-6.ch003

Balasubramanian, K., & K., M. (2018). Secure Group Key Agreement Protocols. In K. Balasubramanian, & M. Rajakani (Eds.), *Algorithmic Strategies for Solving Complex Problems in Cryptography* (pp. 55-65). Hershey, PA: IGI Global. https://doi.org/DOI: 10.4018/978-1-5225-2915-6.ch004

Balasubramanian, K., & M., R. (2018). Problems in Cryptography and Cryptanalysis. In K. Balasubramanian, & M. Rajakani (Eds.), *Algorithmic Strategies for Solving Complex Problems in Cryptography* (pp. 23-39). Hershey, PA: IGI Global. https://doi.org/DOI: 10.4018/978-1-5225-2915-6.ch002

Balasubramanian, K., & Abbas, A. M. (2018). Integer Factoring Algorithms. In Balasubramanian, K., & Rajakani, M. (Eds.), *Algorithmic Strategies for Solving Complex Problems in Cryptography* (pp. 228–240). Hershey, PA: IGI Global. DOI: 10.4018/978-1-5225-2915-6.ch017

Balasubramanian, K., & Abbas, A. M. (2018). Secure Bootstrapping Using the Trusted Platform Module. In Balasubramanian, K., & Rajakani, M. (Eds.), *Algorithmic Strategies for Solving Complex Problems in Cryptography* (pp. 167–185). Hershey, PA: IGI Global. DOI: 10.4018/978-1-5225-2915-6.ch014

Balasubramanian, K., & Mathanan, J. (2018). Cryptographic Voting Protocols. In Balasubramanian, K., & Rajakani, M. (Eds.), *Algorithmic Strategies for Solving Complex Problems in Cryptography* (pp. 124–133). Hershey, PA: IGI Global. DOI: 10.4018/978-1-5225-2915-6.ch010

Balasubramanian, K., & Rajakani, M. (2018). Secure Multiparty Computation. In Balasubramanian, K., & Rajakani, M. (Eds.), *Algorithmic Strategies for Solving Complex Problems in Cryptography* (pp. 154–166). Hershey, PA: IGI Global. DOI: 10.4018/978-1-5225-2915-6.ch013

Balasubramanian, K., & Rajakani, M. (2018). The Quadratic Sieve Algorithm for Integer Factoring. In Balasubramanian, K., & Rajakani, M. (Eds.), *Algorithmic Strategies for Solving Complex Problems in Cryptography* (pp. 241–252). Hershey, PA: IGI Global. DOI: 10.4018/978-1-5225-2915-6.ch018

Barone, P. A. (2017). Defining and Understanding the Development of Juvenile Delinquency from an Environmental, Sociological, and Theoretical Perspective. In Egharevba, S. (Ed.), *Police Brutality, Racial Profiling, and Discrimination in the Criminal Justice System* (pp. 215–238). Hershey, PA: IGI Global. DOI: 10.4018/978-1-5225-1088-8.ch010

Beauchere, J. F. (2018). Encouraging Digital Civility: What Companies and Others Can Do. In Luppicini, R. (Ed.), *The Changing Scope of Technoethics in Contemporary Society* (pp. 262–274). Hershey, PA: IGI Global. DOI: 10.4018/978-1-5225-5094-5.ch014

Behera, C. K., & Bhaskari, D. L. (2017). Malware Methodologies and Its Future: A Survey. *International Journal of Information Security and Privacy, 11*(4), 47–64. DOI: 10.4018/IJISP.2017100104

Benson, V., McAlaney, J., & Frumkin, L. A. (2018). Emerging Threats for the Human Element and Countermeasures in Current Cyber Security Landscape. In McAlaney, J., Frumkin, L., & Benson, V. (Eds.), *Psychological and Behavioral Examinations in Cyber Security* (pp. 266–271). Hershey, PA: IGI Global. DOI: 10.4018/978-1-5225-4053-3.ch016

Berbecaru, D. (2018). On Creating Digital Evidence in IP Networks With NetTrack. In Shrivastava, G., Kumar, P., Gupta, B., Bala, S., & Dey, N. (Eds.), *Handbook of Research on Network Forensics and Analysis Techniques* (pp. 225–245). Hershey, PA: IGI Global. DOI: 10.4018/978-1-5225-4100-4.ch012

Berki, E., Valtanen, J., Chaudhary, S., & Li, L. (2018). The Need for Multi-Disciplinary Approaches and Multi-Level Knowledge for Cybersecurity Professionals. In Ahuja, V., & Rathore, S. (Eds.), *Multidisciplinary Perspectives on Human Capital and Information Technology Professionals* (pp. 72–94). Hershey, PA: IGI Global. DOI: 10.4018/978-1-5225-5297-0.ch005

Bhardwaj, A. (2017). Ransomware: A Rising Threat of new age Digital Extortion. In Aljawarneh, S. (Ed.), *Online Banking Security Measures and Data Protection* (pp. 189–221). Hershey, PA: IGI Global. DOI: 10.4018/978-1-5225-0864-9.ch012

Bhattacharjee, J., Sengupta, A., Barik, M. S., & Mazumdar, C. (2018). An Analytical Study of Methodologies and Tools for Enterprise Information Security Risk Management. In Gupta, M., Sharman, R., Walp, J., & Mulgund, P. (Eds.), *Information Technology Risk Management and Compliance in Modern Organizations* (pp. 1–20). Hershey, PA: IGI Global. DOI: 10.4018/978-1-5225-2604-9.ch001

Bruno, G. (2018). Handling the Dataflow in Business Process Models. In Ahuja, V., & Rathore, S. (Eds.), *Multidisciplinary Perspectives on Human Capital and Information Technology Professionals* (pp. 137–151). Hershey, PA: IGI Global. DOI: 10.4018/978-1-5225-5297-0.ch008

Bush, C. L. (2021). Policing Strategies and Approaches to Improving Community Relations: Black Citizens' Perceptions of Law Enforcement Efforts to Intentionally Strengthen Relationships. In Pittaro, M. (Ed.), *Global Perspectives on Reforming the Criminal Justice System* (pp. 56–75). IGI Global. https://doi.org/10.4018/978-1-7998-6884-2.ch004

Carneiro, A. D. (2017). Defending Information Networks in Cyberspace: Some Notes on Security Needs. In M. Dawson, D. Kisku, P. Gupta, J. Sing, & W. Li (Eds.), *Developing Next-Generation Countermeasures for Homeland Security Threat Prevention* (pp. 354-375). Hershey, PA: IGI Global. https://doi.org/DOI: 10.4018/978-1-5225-0703-1.ch016

Chakraborty, S., Patra, P. K., Maji, P., Ashour, A. S., & Dey, N. (2017). Image Registration Techniques and Frameworks: A Review. In Dey, N., Ashour, A., & Acharjee, S. (Eds.), *Applied Video Processing in Surveillance and Monitoring Systems* (pp. 102–114). Hershey, PA: IGI Global. DOI: 10.4018/978-1-5225-1022-2.ch005

Chaudhari, G., & Mulgund, P. (2018). Strengthening IT Governance With COBIT 5. In Gupta, M., Sharman, R., Walp, J., & Mulgund, P. (Eds.), *Information Technology Risk Management and Compliance in Modern Organizations* (pp. 48–69). Hershey, PA: IGI Global. DOI: 10.4018/978-1-5225-2604-9.ch003

Cheikh, M., Hacini, S., & Boufaida, Z. (2018). Visualization Technique for Intrusion Detection. In Maleh, Y. (Ed.), *Security and Privacy Management, Techniques, and Protocols* (pp. 276–290). Hershey, PA: IGI Global. DOI: 10.4018/978-1-5225-5583-4.ch011

Chen, G., Ding, L., Du, J., Zhou, G., Qin, P., Chen, G., & Liu, Q. (2018). Trust Evaluation Strategy for Single Sign-on Solution in Cloud. *International Journal of Digital Crime and Forensics*, *10*(1), 1–11. DOI: 10.4018/IJDCF.2018010101

Chen, J., & Peng, F. (2018). A Perceptual Encryption Scheme for HEVC Video with Lossless Compression. *International Journal of Digital Crime and Forensics, 10*(1), 67–78. DOI: 10.4018/IJDCF.2018010106

Chen, K., & Xu, D. (2018). An Efficient Reversible Data Hiding Scheme for Encrypted Images. *International Journal of Digital Crime and Forensics, 10*(2), 1–22. DOI: 10.4018/IJDCF.2018040101

Chen, Z., Lu, J., Yang, P., & Luo, X. (2017). Recognizing Substitution Steganography of Spatial Domain Based on the Characteristics of Pixels Correlation. *International Journal of Digital Crime and Forensics, 9*(4), 48–61. DOI: 10.4018/IJDCF.2017100105

Cherkaoui, R., Zbakh, M., Braeken, A., & Touhafi, A. (2018). Anomaly Detection in Cloud Computing and Internet of Things Environments: Latest Technologies. In Munir, K. (Ed.), *Cloud Computing Technologies for Green Enterprises* (pp. 251–265). Hershey, PA: IGI Global. DOI: 10.4018/978-1-5225-3038-1.ch010

Chowdhury, A., Karmakar, G., & Kamruzzaman, J. (2017). Survey of Recent Cyber Security Attacks on Robotic Systems and Their Mitigation Approaches. In Kumar, R., Pattnaik, P., & Pandey, P. (Eds.), *Detecting and Mitigating Robotic Cyber Security Risks* (pp. 284–299). Hershey, PA: IGI Global. DOI: 10.4018/978-1-5225-2154-9.ch019

Cortese, F. A. (2018). The Techoethical Ethos of Technic Self-Determination: Technological Determinism as the Ontic Fundament of Freewill. In Luppicini, R. (Ed.), *The Changing Scope of Technoethics in Contemporary Society* (pp. 74–104). Hershey, PA: IGI Global. DOI: 10.4018/978-1-5225-5094-5.ch005

Crosston, M. D. (2017). The Fight for Cyber Thoreau: Distinguishing Virtual Disobedience from Digital Destruction. In Korstanje, M. (Ed.), *Threat Mitigation and Detection of Cyber Warfare and Terrorism Activities* (pp. 198–219). Hershey, PA: IGI Global. DOI: 10.4018/978-1-5225-1938-6.ch009 da Costa, F., & de Sá-Soares, F. (2017). Authenticity Challenges of Wearable Technologies. In Marrington, A., Kerr, D., & Gammack, J. (Eds.), *Managing Security Issues and the Hidden Dangers of Wearable Technologies* (pp. 98–130). Hershey, PA: IGI Global. DOI: 10.4018/978-1-5225-1016-1.ch005

Dafflon, B., Guériau, M., & Gechter, F. (2017). Using Physics Inspired Wave Agents in a Virtual Environment: Longitudinal Distance Control in Robots Platoon. *International Journal of Monitoring and Surveillance Technologies Research*, *5*(2), 15–28. DOI: 10.4018/IJMSTR.2017040102

Dash, S. R., Sheeraz, A. S., & Samantaray, A. (2018). Filtration and Classification of ECG Signals. In Pradhan, C., Das, H., Naik, B., & Dey, N. (Eds.), *Handbook of Research on Information Security in Biomedical Signal Processing* (pp. 72–94). Hershey, PA: IGI Global. DOI: 10.4018/978-1-5225-5152-2.ch005

Dhavale, S. V. (2018). Insider Attack Analysis in Building Effective Cyber Security for an Organization. In McAlaney, J., Frumkin, L., & Benson, V. (Eds.), *Psychological and Behavioral Examinations in Cyber Security* (pp. 222–238). Hershey, PA: IGI Global. DOI: 10.4018/978-1-5225-4053-3.ch013

Dixit, P. (2018). Security Issues in Web Services. In Shrivastava, G., Kumar, P., Gupta, B., Bala, S., & Dey, N. (Eds.), *Handbook of Research on Network Forensics and Analysis Techniques* (pp. 57–64). Hershey, PA: IGI Global. DOI: 10.4018/978-1-5225-4100-4.ch004

Doraikannan, S. (2018). Efficient Implementation of Digital Signature Algorithms. In Balasubramanian, K., & Rajakani, M. (Eds.), *Algorithmic Strategies for Solving Complex Problems in Cryptography* (pp. 78–86). Hershey, PA: IGI Global. DOI: 10.4018/978-1-5225-2915-6.ch006

E., J. V., Mohan, J., & K., A. (2018). Automatic Detection of Tumor and Bleed in Magnetic Resonance Brain Images. In C. Pradhan, H. Das, B. Naik, & N. Dey (Eds.), *Handbook of Research on Information Security in Biomedical Signal Processing* (pp. 291-303). Hershey, PA: IGI Global. https://doi.org/DOI: 10.4018/978-1-5225-5152-2.ch015

Escamilla, I., Ruíz, M. T., Ibarra, M. M., Soto, V. L., Quintero, R., & Guzmán, G. (2018). Geocoding Tweets Based on Semantic Web and Ontologies. In Lytras, M., Aljohani, N., Damiani, E., & Chui, K. (Eds.), *Innovations, Developments, and Applications of Semantic Web and Information Systems* (pp. 372–392). Hershey, PA: IGI Global. DOI: 10.4018/978-1-5225-5042-6.ch014

Essefi, E. (2022). Advances in Forensic Geophysics: Magnetic Susceptibility as a Tool for Environmental Forensic Geophysics. In C. Chen, W. Yang, & L. Chen (Eds.), *Technologies to Advance Automation in Forensic Science and Criminal Investigation* (pp. 15-36). IGI Global. https://doi.org/10.4018/978-1-7998-8386-9.ch002

Farhadi, M., Haddad, H. M., & Shahriar, H. (2018). Compliance of Electronic Health Record Applications With HIPAA Security and Privacy Requirements. In Maleh, Y. (Ed.), *Security and Privacy Management, Techniques, and Protocols* (pp. 199–213). Hershey, PA: IGI Global. DOI: 10.4018/978-1-5225-5583-4.ch007

Fatma, S. (2018). Use and Misuse of Technology in Marketing: Cases from India. *International Journal of Technoethics*, *9*(1), 27–36. DOI: 10.4018/IJT.2018010103

Fazlali, M., & Khodamoradi, P. (2018). Metamorphic Malware Detection Using Minimal Opcode Statistical Patterns. In Maleh, Y. (Ed.), *Security and Privacy Management, Techniques, and Protocols* (pp. 337–359). Hershey, PA: IGI Global. DOI: 10.4018/978-1-5225-5583-4.ch014

Filiol, É., & Gallais, C. (2017). Optimization of Operational Large-Scale (Cyber) Attacks by a Combinational Approach. *International Journal of Cyber Warfare & Terrorism*, *7*(3), 29–43. DOI: 10.4018/IJCWT.2017070103

Forge, J. (2018). The Case Against Weapons Research. In Luppicini, R. (Ed.), *The Changing Scope of Technoethics in Contemporary Society* (pp. 124–134). Hershey, PA: IGI Global. DOI: 10.4018/978-1-5225-5094-5.ch007

G., S., & Durai, M. S. (2018). Big Data Analytics: An Expedition Through Rapidly Budding Data Exhaustive Era. In D. Lopez, & M. Durai (Eds.), *HCI Challenges and Privacy Preservation in Big Data Security* (pp. 124-138). Hershey, PA: IGI Global. https://doi.org/DOI: 10.4018/978-1-5225-2863-0.ch006

Gammack, J., & Marrington, A. (2017). The Promise and Perils of Wearable Technologies. In Marrington, A., Kerr, D., & Gammack, J. (Eds.), *Managing Security Issues and the Hidden Dangers of Wearable Technologies* (pp. 1–17). Hershey, PA: IGI Global. DOI: 10.4018/978-1-5225-1016-1.ch001

Gamoura, S. C. (2018). A Cloud-Based Approach for Cross-Management of Disaster Plans: Managing Risk in Networked Enterprises. In Aljawarneh, S., & Malhotra, M. (Eds.), *Critical Research on Scalability and Security Issues in Virtual Cloud Environments* (pp. 240–268). Hershey, PA: IGI Global. DOI: 10.4018/978-1-5225-3029-9.ch012

Gao, L., Gao, T., Zhao, J., & Liu, Y. (2018). Reversible Watermarking in Digital Image Using PVO and RDWT. *International Journal of Digital Crime and Forensics*, *10*(2), 40–55. DOI: 10.4018/IJDCF.2018040103

Ghany, K. K., & Zawbaa, H. M. (2017). Hybrid Biometrics and Watermarking Authentication. In Zoughbi, S. (Ed.), *Securing Government Information and Data in Developing Countries* (pp. 37–61). Hershey, PA: IGI Global. DOI: 10.4018/978-1-5225-1703-0.ch003

Ghosh, P., Sarkar, D., Sharma, J., & Phadikar, S. (2021). An Intrusion Detection System Using Modified-Firefly Algorithm in Cloud Environment. *International Journal of Digital Crime and Forensics*, *13*(2), 77–93. https://doi.org/10.4018/IJDCF.2021030105

Grant, B. S. (2022). All the World's a Stage: Achieving Deliberate Practice and Performance Improvement Through Story-Based Learning. In *Research Anthology on Advancements in Cybersecurity Education* (pp. 394-413). IGI Global. https://doi.org/10.4018/978-1-6684-3554-0.ch019

Hacini, S., Guessoum, Z., & Cheikh, M. (2018). False Alarm Reduction: A Profiling Mechanism and New Research Directions. In Maleh, Y. (Ed.), *Security and Privacy Management, Techniques, and Protocols* (pp. 291–320). Hershey, PA: IGI Global. DOI: 10.4018/978-1-5225-5583-4.ch012

Hadlington, L. (2018). The "Human Factor" in Cybersecurity: Exploring the Accidental Insider. In J. McAlaney, L. Frumkin, & V. Benson (Eds.), *Psychological and Behavioral Examinations in Cyber Security* (pp. 46-63). Hershey, PA: IGI Global. https://doi.org/DOI: 10.4018/978-1-5225-4053-3.ch003

Haldorai, A., & Ramu, A. (2018). The Impact of Big Data Analytics and Challenges to Cyber Security. In Shrivastava, G., Kumar, P., Gupta, B., Bala, S., & Dey, N. (Eds.), *Handbook of Research on Network Forensics and Analysis Techniques* (pp. 300–314). Hershey, PA: IGI Global. DOI: 10.4018/978-1-5225-4100-4.ch016

Hariharan, S., Prasanth, V. S., & Saravanan, P. (2018). Role of Bibliographical Databases in Measuring Information: A Conceptual View. In Jeyasekar, J., & Saravanan, P. (Eds.), *Innovations in Measuring and Evaluating Scientific Information* (pp. 61–71). Hershey, PA: IGI Global. DOI: 10.4018/978-1-5225-3457-0.ch005

Hore, S., Chatterjee, S., Chakraborty, S., & Shaw, R. K. (2017). Analysis of Different Feature Description Algorithm in object Recognition. In Dey, N., Ashour, A., & Patra, P. (Eds.), *Feature Detectors and Motion Detection in Video Processing* (pp. 66–99). Hershey, PA: IGI Global. DOI: 10.4018/978-1-5225-1025-3.ch004

Hurley, J. S. (2017). Cyberspace: The New Battlefield - An Approach via the Analytics Hierarchy Process. *International Journal of Cyber Warfare & Terrorism*, *7*(3), 1–15. DOI: 10.4018/IJCWT.2017070101

Hussain, M., & Kaliya, N. (2018). An Improvised Framework for Privacy Preservation in IoT. *International Journal of Information Security and Privacy*, *12*(2), 46–63. DOI: 10.4018/IJISP.2018040104

Ilahi-Amri, M., Cheniti-Belcadhi, L., & Braham, R. (2018). Competence E-Assessment Based on Semantic Web: From Modeling to Validation. In Ahuja, V., & Rathore, S. (Eds.), *Multidisciplinary Perspectives on Human Capital and Information Technology Professionals* (pp. 246–267). Hershey, PA: IGI Global. DOI: 10.4018/978-1-5225-5297-0.ch013

Jambhekar, N., & Dhawale, C. A. (2018). Cryptography in Big Data Security. In Lopez, D., & Durai, M. (Eds.), *HCI Challenges and Privacy Preservation in Big Data Security* (pp. 71–94). Hershey, PA: IGI Global. DOI: 10.4018/978-1-5225-2863-0.ch004

Jansen van Vuuren, J., Leenen, L., Plint, G., Zaaiman, J., & Phahlamohlaka, J. (2017). Formulating the Building Blocks for National Cyberpower. *International Journal of Cyber Warfare & Terrorism*, *7*(3), 16–28. DOI: 10.4018/IJCWT.2017070102

Jaswal, S., & Malhotra, M. (2018). Identification of Various Privacy and Trust Issues in Cloud Computing Environment. In Aljawarneh, S., & Malhotra, M. (Eds.), *Critical Research on Scalability and Security Issues in Virtual Cloud Environments* (pp. 95–121). Hershey, PA: IGI Global. DOI: 10.4018/978-1-5225-3029-9.ch005

Jaswal, S., & Singh, G. (2018). A Comprehensive Survey on Trust Issue and Its Deployed Models in Computing Environment. In Aljawarneh, S., & Malhotra, M. (Eds.), *Critical Research on Scalability and Security Issues in Virtual Cloud Environments* (pp. 150–166). Hershey, PA: IGI Global. DOI: 10.4018/978-1-5225-3029-9.ch007

Javid, T. (2018). Secure Access to Biomedical Images. In Pradhan, C., Das, H., Naik, B., & Dey, N. (Eds.), *Handbook of Research on Information Security in Biomedical Signal Processing* (pp. 38–53). Hershey, PA: IGI Global. DOI: 10.4018/978-1-5225-5152-2.ch003

Jeyakumar, B., Durai, M. S., & Lopez, D. (2018). Case Studies in Amalgamation of Deep Learning and Big Data. In Lopez, D., & Durai, M. (Eds.), *HCI Challenges and Privacy Preservation in Big Data Security* (pp. 159–174). Hershey, PA: IGI Global. DOI: 10.4018/978-1-5225-2863-0.ch008

Jeyaprakash, H. M. K., K., & S., G. (2018). A Comparative Review of Various Machine Learning Approaches for Improving the Performance of Stego Anomaly Detection. In G. Shrivastava, P. Kumar, B. Gupta, S. Bala, & N. Dey (Eds.), *Handbook of Research on Network Forensics and Analysis Techniques* (pp. 351-371). Hershey, PA: IGI Global. https://doi.org/DOI: 10.4018/978-1-5225-4100-4.ch019

Jeyasekar, J. J. (2018). Dynamics of Indian Forensic Science Research. In Jeyasekar, J., & Saravanan, P. (Eds.), *Innovations in Measuring and Evaluating Scientific Information* (pp. 125–147). Hershey, PA: IGI Global. DOI: 10.4018/978-1-5225-3457-0.ch009

Jones, H. S., & Moncur, W. (2018). The Role of Psychology in Understanding Online Trust. In McAlaney, J., Frumkin, L., & Benson, V. (Eds.), *Psychological and Behavioral Examinations in Cyber Security* (pp. 109–132). Hershey, PA: IGI Global. DOI: 10.4018/978-1-5225-4053-3.ch007

Jones, H. S., & Towse, J. (2018). Examinations of Email Fraud Susceptibility: Perspectives From Academic Research and Industry Practice. In McAlaney, J., Frumkin, L., & Benson, V. (Eds.), *Psychological and Behavioral Examinations in Cyber Security* (pp. 80–97). Hershey, PA: IGI Global. DOI: 10.4018/978-1-5225-4053-3.ch005

Joseph, A., & Singh, K. J. (2018). Digital Forensics in Distributed Environment. In Shrivastava, G., Kumar, P., Gupta, B., Bala, S., & Dey, N. (Eds.), *Handbook of Research on Network Forensics and Analysis Techniques* (pp. 246–265). Hershey, PA: IGI Global. DOI: 10.4018/978-1-5225-4100-4.ch013

K., I., & A, V. (2018). Monitoring and Auditing in the Cloud. In K. Munir (Ed.), *Cloud Computing Technologies for Green Enterprises* (pp. 318-350). Hershey, PA: IGI Global. https://doi.org/DOI: 10.4018/978-1-5225-3038-1.ch013

Kashyap, R., & Piersson, A. D. (2018). Impact of Big Data on Security. In Shrivastava, G., Kumar, P., Gupta, B., Bala, S., & Dey, N. (Eds.), *Handbook of Research on Network Forensics and Analysis Techniques* (pp. 283–299). Hershey, PA: IGI Global. DOI: 10.4018/978-1-5225-4100-4.ch015

Kastrati, Z., Imran, A. S., & Yayilgan, S. Y. (2018). A Hybrid Concept Learning Approach to Ontology Enrichment. In Lytras, M., Aljohani, N., Damiani, E., & Chui, K. (Eds.), *Innovations, Developments, and Applications of Semantic Web and Information Systems* (pp. 85–119). Hershey, PA: IGI Global. DOI: 10.4018/978-1-5225-5042-6.ch004

Kaur, H., & Saxena, S. (2018). UWDBCSN Analysis During Node Replication Attack in WSN. In Pradhan, C., Das, H., Naik, B., & Dey, N. (Eds.), *Handbook of Research on Information Security in Biomedical Signal Processing* (pp. 210–227). Hershey, PA: IGI Global. DOI: 10.4018/978-1-5225-5152-2.ch011

Kaushal, P. K., & Sobti, R. (2018). Breaching Security of Full Round Tiny Encryption Algorithm. *International Journal of Information Security and Privacy, 12*(1), 89–98. DOI: 10.4018/IJISP.2018010108

Kavati, I., Prasad, M. V., & Bhagvati, C. (2017). Search Space Reduction in Biometric Databases: A Review. In M. Dawson, D. Kisku, P. Gupta, J. Sing, & W. Li (Eds.), *Developing Next-Generation Countermeasures for Homeland Security Threat Prevention* (pp. 236-262). Hershey, PA: IGI Global. DOI: 10.4018/978-1-5225-0703-1.ch011

Kaye, L. K. (2018). Online Research Methods. In McAlaney, J., Frumkin, L., & Benson, V. (Eds.), *Psychological and Behavioral Examinations in Cyber Security* (pp. 253–265). Hershey, PA: IGI Global. DOI: 10.4018/978-1-5225-4053-3.ch015

Kenekar, T. V., & Dani, A. R. (2017). Privacy Preserving Data Mining on Unstructured Data. In Tamane, S., Solanki, V., & Dey, N. (Eds.), *Privacy and Security Policies in Big Data* (pp. 167–190). Hershey, PA: IGI Global. DOI: 10.4018/978-1-5225-2486-1.ch008

Kenny, P., & Leonard, L. J. (2021). Restorative Justice as an "Informal" Alternative to "Formal" Court Processes. In Leonard, L. (Ed.), *Global Perspectives on People, Process, and Practice in Criminal Justice* (pp. 226–244). IGI Global. https://doi.org/10.4018/978-1-7998-6646-6.ch014

Khaire, P. A., & Kotkondawar, R. R. (2017). Measures of Image and Video Segmentation. In Dey, N., Ashour, A., & Acharjee, S. (Eds.), *Applied Video Processing in Surveillance and Monitoring Systems* (pp. 28–53). Hershey, PA: IGI Global. DOI: 10.4018/978-1-5225-1022-2.ch002

Knibbs, C., Goss, S., & Anthony, K. (2017). Counsellors' Phenomenological Experiences of Working with Children or Young People who have been Cyberbullied: Using Thematic Analysis of Semi Structured Interviews. *International Journal of Technoethics, 8*(1), 68–86. DOI: 10.4018/IJT.2017010106

Ko, A., & Gillani, S. (2018). Ontology Maintenance Through Semantic Text Mining: An Application for IT Governance Domain. In Lytras, M., Aljohani, N., Damiani, E., & Chui, K. (Eds.), *Innovations, Developments, and Applications of Semantic Web and Information Systems* (pp. 350–371). Hershey, PA: IGI Global. DOI: 10.4018/978-1-5225-5042-6.ch013

Kohler, J., Lorenz, C. R., Gumbel, M., Specht, T., & Simov, K. (2017). A Security-By-Distribution Approach to Manage Big Data in a Federation of Untrustworthy Clouds. In Tamane, S., Solanki, V., & Dey, N. (Eds.), *Privacy and Security Policies in Big Data* (pp. 92–123). Hershey, PA: IGI Global. DOI: 10.4018/978-1-5225-2486-1.ch005

Korstanje, M. E. (2017). English Speaking Countries and the Culture of Fear: Understanding Technology and Terrorism. In Korstanje, M. (Ed.), *Threat Mitigation and Detection of Cyber Warfare and Terrorism Activities* (pp. 92–110). Hershey, PA: IGI Global. DOI: 10.4018/978-1-5225-1938-6.ch005

Korstanje, M. E. (2018). How Can World Leaders Understand the Perverse Core of Terrorism?: Terror in the Global Village. In Akrivopoulou, C. (Ed.), *Global Perspectives on Human Migration, Asylum, and Security* (pp. 48–67). Hershey, PA: IGI Global. DOI: 10.4018/978-1-5225-2817-3.ch003

Krishnamachariar, P. K., & Gupta, M. (2018). Swimming Upstream in Turbulent Waters: Auditing Agile Development. In Gupta, M., Sharman, R., Walp, J., & Mulgund, P. (Eds.), *Information Technology Risk Management and Compliance in Modern Organizations* (pp. 268–300). Hershey, PA: IGI Global. DOI: 10.4018/978-1-5225-2604-9.ch010

Ksiazak, P., Farrelly, W., & Curran, K. (2018). A Lightweight Authentication and Encryption Protocol for Secure Communications Between Resource-Limited Devices Without Hardware Modification: Resource-Limited Device Authentication. In Maleh, Y. (Ed.), *Security and Privacy Management, Techniques, and Protocols* (pp. 1–46). Hershey, PA: IGI Global. DOI: 10.4018/978-1-5225-5583-4.ch001

Kukkuvada, A., & Basavaraju, P. (2018). Mutual Correlation-Based Anonymization for Privacy Preserving Medical Data Publishing. In Pradhan, C., Das, H., Naik, B., & Dey, N. (Eds.), *Handbook of Research on Information Security in Biomedical Signal Processing* (pp. 304–319). Hershey, PA: IGI Global. DOI: 10.4018/978-1-5225-5152-2.ch016

Kumar, G., & Saini, H. (2018). Secure and Robust Telemedicine using ECC on Radix-8 with Formal Verification. *International Journal of Information Security and Privacy*, *12*(1), 13–28. DOI: 10.4018/IJISP.2018010102

Kumar, M., & Bhandari, A. (2017). Performance Evaluation of Web Server's Request Queue against AL-DDoS Attacks in NS-2. *International Journal of Information Security and Privacy*, *11*(4), 29–46. DOI: 10.4018/IJISP.2017100103

Kumar, M., & Vardhan, M. (2018). Privacy Preserving and Efficient Outsourcing Algorithm to Public Cloud: A Case of Statistical Analysis. *International Journal of Information Security and Privacy*, *12*(2), 1–25. DOI: 10.4018/IJISP.2018040101

Kumar, R. (2018). A Robust Biometrics System Using Finger Knuckle Print. In Shrivastava, G., Kumar, P., Gupta, B., Bala, S., & Dey, N. (Eds.), *Handbook of Research on Network Forensics and Analysis Techniques* (pp. 416–446). Hershey, PA: IGI Global. DOI: 10.4018/978-1-5225-4100-4.ch022

Kumar, R. (2018). DOS Attacks on Cloud Platform: Their Solutions and Implications. In Aljawarneh, S., & Malhotra, M. (Eds.), *Critical Research on Scalability and Security Issues in Virtual Cloud Environments* (pp. 167–184). Hershey, PA: IGI Global. DOI: 10.4018/978-1-5225-3029-9.ch008

Kumari, R., & Sharma, K. (2018). Cross-Layer Based Intrusion Detection and Prevention for Network. In Shrivastava, G., Kumar, P., Gupta, B., Bala, S., & Dey, N. (Eds.), *Handbook of Research on Network Forensics and Analysis Techniques* (pp. 38–56). Hershey, PA: IGI Global. DOI: 10.4018/978-1-5225-4100-4.ch003

Lapke, M. (2018). A Semiotic Examination of the Security Policy Lifecycle. In Maleh, Y. (Ed.), *Security and Privacy Management, Techniques, and Protocols* (pp. 237–253). Hershey, PA: IGI Global. DOI: 10.4018/978-1-5225-5583-4.ch009

Liang, Z., Feng, B., Xu, X., Wu, X., & Yang, T. (2018). Geometrically Invariant Image Watermarking Using Histogram Adjustment. *International Journal of Digital Crime and Forensics, 10*(1), 54–66. DOI: 10.4018/IJDCF.2018010105

Liu, Z. J. (2017). A Cyber Crime Investigation Model Based on Case Characteristics. *International Journal of Digital Crime and Forensics, 9*(4), 40–47. DOI: 10.4018/IJDCF.2017100104

Loganathan, S. (2018). A Step-by-Step Procedural Methodology for Improving an Organization's IT Risk Management System. In Gupta, M., Sharman, R., Walp, J., & Mulgund, P. (Eds.), *Information Technology Risk Management and Compliance in Modern Organizations* (pp. 21–47). Hershey, PA: IGI Global. DOI: 10.4018/978-1-5225-2604-9.ch002

Long, M., Peng, F., & Gong, X. (2018). A Format-Compliant Encryption for Secure HEVC Video Sharing in Multimedia Social Network. *International Journal of Digital Crime and Forensics, 10*(2), 23–39. DOI: 10.4018/IJDCF.2018040102

M., S., & M., J. (2018). Biosignal Denoising Techniques. In C. Pradhan, H. Das, B. Naik, & N. Dey (Eds.), *Handbook of Research on Information Security in Biomedical Signal Processing* (pp. 26-37). Hershey, PA: IGI Global. https://doi.org/DOI: 10.4018/978-1-5225-5152-2.ch002

Mahapatra, C. (2017). Pragmatic Solutions to Cyber Security Threat in Indian Context. In Kumar, R., Pattnaik, P., & Pandey, P. (Eds.), *Detecting and Mitigating Robotic Cyber Security Risks* (pp. 172–176). Hershey, PA: IGI Global. DOI: 10.4018/978-1-5225-2154-9.ch012

Majumder, A., Nath, S., & Das, A. (2018). Data Integrity in Mobile Cloud Computing. In Munir, K. (Ed.), *Cloud Computing Technologies for Green Enterprises* (pp. 166–199). Hershey, PA: IGI Global. DOI: 10.4018/978-1-5225-3038-1.ch007

Maleh, Y., Zaydi, M., Sahid, A., & Ezzati, A. (2018). Building a Maturity Framework for Information Security Governance Through an Empirical Study in Organizations. In Maleh, Y. (Ed.), *Security and Privacy Management, Techniques, and Protocols* (pp. 96–127). Hershey, PA: IGI Global. DOI: 10.4018/978-1-5225-5583-4.ch004

Malhotra, M., & Singh, A. (2018). Role of Agents to Enhance the Security and Scalability in Cloud Environment. In Aljawarneh, S., & Malhotra, M. (Eds.), *Critical Research on Scalability and Security Issues in Virtual Cloud Environments* (pp. 19–47). Hershey, PA: IGI Global. DOI: 10.4018/978-1-5225-3029-9.ch002

Mali, A. D. (2017). Recent Advances in Minimally-Obtrusive Monitoring of People's Health. *International Journal of Monitoring and Surveillance Technologies Research*, *5*(2), 44–56. DOI: 10.4018/IJMSTR.2017040104

Mali, A. D., & Yang, N. (2017). On Automated Generation of Keyboard Layout to Reduce Finger-Travel Distance. *International Journal of Monitoring and Surveillance Technologies Research*, *5*(2), 29–43. DOI: 10.4018/IJMSTR.2017040103

Mali, P. (2018). Defining Cyber Weapon in Context of Technology and Law. *International Journal of Cyber Warfare & Terrorism*, *8*(1), 43–55. DOI: 10.4018/IJCWT.2018010104

Malik, A., & Pandey, B. (2018). CIAS: A Comprehensive Identity Authentication Scheme for Providing Security in VANET. *International Journal of Information Security and Privacy*, *12*(1), 29–41. DOI: 10.4018/IJISP.2018010103

Manikandakumar, M., & Ramanujam, E. (2018). Security and Privacy Challenges in Big Data Environment. In Shrivastava, G., Kumar, P., Gupta, B., Bala, S., & Dey, N. (Eds.), *Handbook of Research on Network Forensics and Analysis Techniques* (pp. 315–325). Hershey, PA: IGI Global. DOI: 10.4018/978-1-5225-4100-4.ch017

Manogaran, G., Thota, C., & Lopez, D. (2018). Human-Computer Interaction With Big Data Analytics. In Lopez, D., & Durai, M. (Eds.), *HCI Challenges and Privacy Preservation in Big Data Security* (pp. 1–22). Hershey, PA: IGI Global. DOI: 10.4018/978-1-5225-2863-0.ch001

Mbale, J. (2018). Computer Centres Resource Cloud Elasticity-Scalability (CRECES): Copperbelt University Case Study. In Aljawarneh, S., & Malhotra, M. (Eds.), *Critical Research on Scalability and Security Issues in Virtual Cloud Environments* (pp. 48–70). Hershey, PA: IGI Global. DOI: 10.4018/978-1-5225-3029-9.ch003

McAvoy, D. (2017). Institutional Entrepreneurship in Defence Acquisition: What Don't We Understand? In Burgess, K., & Antill, P. (Eds.), *Emerging Strategies in Defense Acquisitions and Military Procurement* (pp. 222–241). Hershey, PA: IGI Global. DOI: 10.4018/978-1-5225-0599-0.ch013

McKeague, J., & Curran, K. (2018). Detecting the Use of Anonymous Proxies. *International Journal of Digital Crime and Forensics*, *10*(2), 74–94. DOI: 10.4018/IJDCF.2018040105

Meitei, T. G., Singh, S. A., & Majumder, S. (2018). PCG-Based Biometrics. In Pradhan, C., Das, H., Naik, B., & Dey, N. (Eds.), *Handbook of Research on Information Security in Biomedical Signal Processing* (pp. 1–25). Hershey, PA: IGI Global. DOI: 10.4018/978-1-5225-5152-2.ch001

Menemencioğlu, O., & Orak, İ. M. (2017). A Simple Solution to Prevent Parameter Tampering in Web Applications. In Korstanje, M. (Ed.), *Threat Mitigation and Detection of Cyber Warfare and Terrorism Activities* (pp. 1–20). Hershey, PA: IGI Global. DOI: 10.4018/978-1-5225-1938-6.ch001

Minto-Coy, I. D., & Henlin, M. G. (2017). The Development of Cybersecurity Policy and Legislative Landscape in Latin America and Caribbean States. In Moore, M. (Ed.), *Cybersecurity Breaches and Issues Surrounding Online Threat Protection* (pp. 24–53). Hershey, PA: IGI Global. DOI: 10.4018/978-1-5225-1941-6.ch002

Mohamed, J. H. (2018). Scientograph-Based Visualization of Computer Forensics Research Literature. In Jeyasekar, J., & Saravanan, P. (Eds.), *Innovations in Measuring and Evaluating Scientific Information* (pp. 148–162). Hershey, PA: IGI Global. DOI: 10.4018/978-1-5225-3457-0.ch010

Mohan Murthy, M. K., & Sanjay, H. A. (2018). Scalability for Cloud. In Aljawarneh, S., & Malhotra, M. (Eds.), *Critical Research on Scalability and Security Issues in Virtual Cloud Environments* (pp. 1–18). Hershey, PA: IGI Global. DOI: 10.4018/978-1-5225-3029-9.ch001

Moorthy, U., & Gandhi, U. D. (2018). A Survey of Big Data Analytics Using Machine Learning Algorithms. In Lopez, D., & Durai, M. (Eds.), *HCI Challenges and Privacy Preservation in Big Data Security* (pp. 95–123). Hershey, PA: IGI Global. DOI: 10.4018/978-1-5225-2863-0.ch005

Mountantonakis, M., Minadakis, N., Marketakis, Y., Fafalios, P., & Tzitzikas, Y. (2018). Connectivity, Value, and Evolution of a Semantic Warehouse. In Lytras, M., Aljohani, N., Damiani, E., & Chui, K. (Eds.), *Innovations, Developments, and Applications of Semantic Web and Information Systems* (pp. 1–31). Hershey, PA: IGI Global. DOI: 10.4018/978-1-5225-5042-6.ch001

Moussa, M., & Demurjian, S. A. (2017). Differential Privacy Approach for Big Data Privacy in Healthcare. In Tamane, S., Solanki, V., & Dey, N. (Eds.), *Privacy and Security Policies in Big Data* (pp. 191–213). Hershey, PA: IGI Global. DOI: 10.4018/978-1-5225-2486-1.ch009

Mugisha, E., Zhang, G., El Abidine, M. Z., & Eugene, M. (2017). A TPM-based Secure Multi-Cloud Storage Architecture grounded on Erasure Codes. *International Journal of Information Security and Privacy*, *11*(1), 52–64. DOI: 10.4018/IJISP.2017010104

Nachtigall, L. G., Araujo, R. M., & Nachtigall, G. R. (2017). Use of Images of Leaves and Fruits of Apple Trees for Automatic Identification of Symptoms of Diseases and Nutritional Disorders. *International Journal of Monitoring and Surveillance Technologies Research*, *5*(2), 1–14. DOI: 10.4018/IJMSTR.2017040101

Nagesh, K., Sumathy, R., Devakumar, P., & Sathiyamurthy, K. (2017). A Survey on Denial of Service Attacks and Preclusions. *International Journal of Information Security and Privacy*, *11*(4), 1–15. DOI: 10.4018/IJISP.2017100101

Nanda, A., Popat, P., & Vimalkumar, D. (2018). Navigating Through Choppy Waters of PCI DSS Compliance. In Gupta, M., Sharman, R., Walp, J., & Mulgund, P. (Eds.), *Information Technology Risk Management and Compliance in Modern Organizations* (pp. 99–140). Hershey, PA: IGI Global. DOI: 10.4018/978-1-5225-2604-9.ch005

Newton, S. (2017). The Determinants of Stock Market Development in Emerging Economies: Examining the Impact of Corporate Governance and Regulatory Reforms (I). In Ojo, M., & Van Akkeren, J. (Eds.), *Value Relevance of Accounting Information in Capital Markets* (pp. 114–125). Hershey, PA: IGI Global. DOI: 10.4018/978-1-5225-1900-3.ch008

Nidhyananthan, S. S. A., J. V., & R., S. S. (2018). Wireless Enhanced Security Based on Speech Recognition. In C. Pradhan, H. Das, B. Naik, & N. Dey (Eds.), *Handbook of Research on Information Security in Biomedical Signal Processing* (pp. 228-253). Hershey, PA: IGI Global. https://doi.org/DOI: 10.4018/978-1-5225-5152-2.ch012

Norri-Sederholm, T., Huhtinen, A., & Paakkonen, H. (2018). Ensuring Public Safety Organisations' Information Flow and Situation Picture in Hybrid Environments. *International Journal of Cyber Warfare & Terrorism*, *8*(1), 12–24. DOI: 10.4018/IJCWT.2018010102

Nunez, S., & Castaño, R. (2017). Building Brands in Emerging Economies: A Consumer-Oriented Approach. In Rajagopal, & R. Behl (Eds.), *Business Analytics and Cyber Security Management in Organizations* (pp. 183-194). Hershey, PA: IGI Global. DOI: 10.4018/978-1-5225-0902-8.ch013

Odella, F. (2018). Privacy Awareness and the Networking Generation. *International Journal of Technoethics*, *9*(1), 51–70. DOI: 10.4018/IJT.2018010105

Ojo, M., & DiGabriele, J. A. (2017). Fundamental or Enhancing Roles?: The Dual Roles of External Auditors and Forensic Accountants. In Ojo, M., & Van Akkeren, J. (Eds.), *Value Relevance of Accounting Information in Capital Markets* (pp. 59–78). Hershey, PA: IGI Global. DOI: 10.4018/978-1-5225-1900-3.ch004

Olomojobi, Y., & Omotola, O. T. (2021). Social Media: A Protagonist for Terrorism. *International Journal of Cyber Warfare & Terrorism, 11*(1), 31–44. https://doi.org/10.4018/IJCWT.2021010103

Pandey, S. (2018). An Empirical Study of the Indian IT Sector on Typologies of Workaholism as Predictors of HR Crisis. In Ahuja, V., & Rathore, S. (Eds.), *Multidisciplinary Perspectives on Human Capital and Information Technology Professionals* (pp. 202–224). Hershey, PA: IGI Global. DOI: 10.4018/978-1-5225-5297-0.ch011

Pattabiraman, A., Srinivasan, S., Swaminathan, K., & Gupta, M. (2018). Fortifying Corporate Human Wall: A Literature Review of Security Awareness and Training. In Gupta, M., Sharman, R., Walp, J., & Mulgund, P. (Eds.), *Information Technology Risk Management and Compliance in Modern Organizations* (pp. 142–175). Hershey, PA: IGI Global. DOI: 10.4018/978-1-5225-2604-9.ch006

Prachi. (2018). Detection of Botnet Based Attacks on Network: Using Machine Learning Techniques. In G. Shrivastava, P. Kumar, B. Gupta, S. Bala, & N. Dey (Eds.), *Handbook of Research on Network Forensics and Analysis Techniques* (pp. 101-116). Hershey, PA: IGI Global. https://doi .org/DOI: 10.4018/978-1-5225-4100-4.ch007

Pradhan, P. L. (2017). Proposed Round Robin CIA Pattern on RTS for Risk Assessment. *International Journal of Digital Crime and Forensics, 9*(1), 71–85. DOI: 10.4018/IJDCF.2017010105

Prentice, S., & Taylor, P. J. (2018). Psychological and Behavioral Examinations of Online Terrorism. In McAlaney, J., Frumkin, L., & Benson, V. (Eds.), *Psychological and Behavioral Examinations in Cyber Security* (pp. 151–171). Hershey, PA: IGI Global. DOI: 10.4018/978-1-5225-4053-3.ch009

Priyadarshini, I. (2017). Cyber Security Risks in Robotics. In Kumar, R., Pattnaik, P., & Pandey, P. (Eds.), *Detecting and Mitigating Robotic Cyber Security Risks* (pp. 333–348). Hershey, PA: IGI Global. DOI: 10.4018/978-1-5225-2154-9.ch022

R., A., & D., E. (2018). Cyber Crime Toolkit Development. In G. Shrivastava, P. Kumar, B. Gupta, S. Bala, & N. Dey (Eds.), *Handbook of Research on Network Forensics and Analysis Techniques* (pp. 184-224). Hershey, PA: IGI Global. https://doi.org/DOI: 10.4018/978-1-5225-4100-4.ch011

Raghunath, R. (2018). Research Trends in Forensic Sciences: A Scientometric Approach. In Jeyasekar, J., & Saravanan, P. (Eds.), *Innovations in Measuring and Evaluating Scientific Information* (pp. 108–124). Hershey, PA: IGI Global. DOI: 10.4018/978-1-5225-3457-0.ch008

Ramadhas, G., Sankar, A. S., & Sugathan, N. (2018). The Scientific Communication Process in Homoeopathic Toxicology: An Evaluative Study. In Jeyasekar, J., & Saravanan, P. (Eds.), *Innovations in Measuring and Evaluating Scientific Information* (pp. 163–179). Hershey, PA: IGI Global. DOI: 10.4018/978-1-5225-3457-0.ch011

Ramani, K. (2018). Impact of Big Data on Security: Big Data Security Issues and Defense Schemes. In Shrivastava, G., Kumar, P., Gupta, B., Bala, S., & Dey, N. (Eds.), *Handbook of Research on Network Forensics and Analysis Techniques* (pp. 326–350). Hershey, PA: IGI Global. DOI: 10.4018/978-1-5225-4100-4.ch018

Ramos, P., Funderburk, P., & Gebelein, J. (2018). Social Media and Online Gaming: A Masquerading Funding Source. *International Journal of Cyber Warfare & Terrorism*, *8*(1), 25–42. DOI: 10.4018/IJCWT.2018010103

Rao, N., & Srivastava, S., & K.S., S. (2017). PKI Deployment Challenges and Recommendations for ICS Networks. *International Journal of Information Security and Privacy*, *11*(2), 38–48. DOI: 10.4018/IJISP.2017040104

Rath, M., Swain, J., Pati, B., & Pattanayak, B. K. (2018). Network Security: Attacks and Control in MANET. In Shrivastava, G., Kumar, P., Gupta, B., Bala, S., & Dey, N. (Eds.), *Handbook of Research on Network Forensics and Analysis Techniques* (pp. 19–37). Hershey, PA: IGI Global. DOI: 10.4018/978-1-5225-4100-4.ch002

Ricci, J., Baggili, I., & Breitinger, F. (2017). Watch What You Wear: Smartwatches and Sluggish Security. In Marrington, A., Kerr, D., & Gammack, J. (Eds.), *Managing Security Issues and the Hidden Dangers of Wearable Technologies* (pp. 47–73). Hershey, PA: IGI Global. DOI: 10.4018/978-1-5225-1016-1.ch003

Rossi, J. A. (2017). Revisiting the Value Relevance of Accounting Information in the Italian and UK Stock Markets. In Ojo, M., & Van Akkeren, J. (Eds.), *Value Relevance of Accounting Information in Capital Markets* (pp. 102–113). Hershey, PA: IGI Global. DOI: 10.4018/978-1-5225-1900-3.ch007

Sabillon, R., Serra-Ruiz, J., Cavaller, V., & Cano, J. J. (2017). Digital Forensic Analysis of Cybercrimes: Best Practices and Methodologies. *International Journal of Information Security and Privacy*, *11*(2), 25–37. DOI: 10.4018/IJISP.2017040103

Sadasivam, U. M., & Ganesan, N. (2021). Detecting Fake News Using Deep Learning and NLP. In S. Misra, C. Arumugam, S. Jaganathan, & S. S. (Ed.), *Confluence of AI, Machine, and Deep Learning in Cyber Forensics* (pp. 117-133). IGI Global. https://doi.org/10.4018/978-1-7998-4900-1.ch007

Sample, C., Cowley, J., & Bakdash, J. Z. (2018). Cyber + Culture: Exploring the Relationship. In McAlaney, J., Frumkin, L., & Benson, V. (Eds.), *Psychological and Behavioral Examinations in Cyber Security* (pp. 64–79). Hershey, PA: IGI Global. DOI: 10.4018/978-1-5225-4053-3.ch004

Sarıgöllü, S. C., Aksakal, E., Koca, M. G., Akten, E., & Aslanbay, Y. (2018). Volunteered Surveillance. In McAlaney, J., Frumkin, L., & Benson, V. (Eds.), *Psychological and Behavioral Examinations in Cyber Security* (pp. 133–150). Hershey, PA: IGI Global. DOI: 10.4018/978-1-5225-4053-3.ch008

Shahriar, H., Clincy, V., & Bond, W. (2018). Classification of Web-Service-Based Attacks and Mitigation Techniques. In Maleh, Y. (Ed.), *Security and Privacy Management, Techniques, and Protocols* (pp. 360–378). Hershey, PA: IGI Global. DOI: 10.4018/978-1-5225-5583-4.ch015

Shet, S., Aswath, A. R., Hanumantharaju, M. C., & Gao, X. (2017). Design of Reconfigurable Architectures for Steganography System. In Dey, N., Ashour, A., & Acharjee, S. (Eds.), *Applied Video Processing in Surveillance and Monitoring Systems* (pp. 145–168). Hershey, PA: IGI Global. DOI: 10.4018/978-1-5225-1022-2.ch007

Shrivastava, G., Sharma, K., Khari, M., & Zohora, S. E. (2018). Role of Cyber Security and Cyber Forensics in India. In Shrivastava, G., Kumar, P., Gupta, B., Bala, S., & Dey, N. (Eds.), *Handbook of Research on Network Forensics and Analysis Techniques* (pp. 143–161). Hershey, PA: IGI Global. DOI: 10.4018/978-1-5225-4100-4.ch009

Singh, N., Mittal, T., & Gupta, M. (2018). A Tale of Policies and Breaches: Analytical Approach to Construct Social Media Policy. In Gupta, M., Sharman, R., Walp, J., & Mulgund, P. (Eds.), *Information Technology Risk Management and Compliance in Modern Organizations* (pp. 176–212). Hershey, PA: IGI Global. DOI: 10.4018/978-1-5225-2604-9.ch007

Singh, R., & Jalota, H. (2018). A Study of Good-Enough Security in the Context of Rural Business Process Outsourcing. In McAlaney, J., Frumkin, L., & Benson, V. (Eds.), *Psychological and Behavioral Examinations in Cyber Security* (pp. 239–252). Hershey, PA: IGI Global. DOI: 10.4018/978-1-5225-4053-3.ch014

Sivasubramanian, K. E. (2018). Authorship Pattern and Collaborative Research Productivity of Asian Journal of Dairy and Food Research During the Year 2011 to 2015. In Jeyasekar, J., & Saravanan, P. (Eds.), *Innovations in Measuring and Evaluating Scientific Information* (pp. 213–222). Hershey, PA: IGI Global. DOI: 10.4018/978-1-5225-3457-0.ch014

Somasundaram, R., & Thirugnanam, M. (2017). IoT in Healthcare: Breaching Security Issues. In Jeyanthi, N., & Thandeeswaran, R. (Eds.), *Security Breaches and Threat Prevention in the Internet of Things* (pp. 174–188). Hershey, PA: IGI Global. DOI: 10.4018/978-1-5225-2296-6.ch008

Sonam, & Khari, M. (2018). Wireless Sensor Networks: A Technical Survey. In G. Shrivastava, P. Kumar, B. Gupta, S. Bala, & N. Dey (Eds.), *Handbook of Research on Network Forensics and Analysis Techniques* (pp. 1-18). Hershey, PA: IGI Global. https://doi.org/DOI: 10.4018/978-1-5225-4100-4.ch001

Soni, P. (2018). Implications of HIPAA and Subsequent Regulations on Information Technology. In Gupta, M., Sharman, R., Walp, J., & Mulgund, P. (Eds.), *Information Technology Risk Management and Compliance in Modern Organizations* (pp. 71–98). Hershey, PA: IGI Global. DOI: 10.4018/978-1-5225-2604-9.ch004

Sönmez, F. Ö., & Günel, B. (2018). Security Visualization Extended Review Issues, Classifications, Validation Methods, Trends, Extensions. In Maleh, Y. (Ed.), *Security and Privacy Management, Techniques, and Protocols* (pp. 152–197). Hershey, PA: IGI Global. DOI: 10.4018/978-1-5225-5583-4.ch006

Srivastava, S. R., & Dube, S. (2018). Cyberattacks, Cybercrime and Cyberterrorism. In Shrivastava, G., Kumar, P., Gupta, B., Bala, S., & Dey, N. (Eds.), *Handbook of Research on Network Forensics and Analysis Techniques* (pp. 162–183). Hershey, PA: IGI Global. DOI: 10.4018/978-1-5225-4100-4.ch010

Stacey, E. (2017). Contemporary Terror on the Net. In *Combating Internet-Enabled Terrorism: Emerging Research and Opportunities* (pp. 16–44). Hershey, PA: IGI Global. DOI: 10.4018/978-1-5225-2190-7.ch002

Sumana, M., Hareesha, K. S., & Kumar, S. (2018). Semantically Secure Classifiers for Privacy Preserving Data Mining. In Maleh, Y. (Ed.), *Security and Privacy Management, Techniques, and Protocols* (pp. 66–95). Hershey, PA: IGI Global. DOI: 10.4018/978-1-5225-5583-4.ch003

Suresh, N., & Gupta, M. (2018). Impact of Technology Innovation: A Study on Cloud Risk Mitigation. In Gupta, M., Sharman, R., Walp, J., & Mulgund, P. (Eds.), *Information Technology Risk Management and Compliance in Modern Organizations* (pp. 229–267). Hershey, PA: IGI Global. DOI: 10.4018/978-1-5225-2604-9.ch009

Tank, D. M. (2017). Security and Privacy Issues, Solutions, and Tools for MCC. In Munir, K. (Ed.), *Security Management in Mobile Cloud Computing* (pp. 121–147). Hershey, PA: IGI Global. DOI: 10.4018/978-1-5225-0602-7.ch006

Thackray, H., & McAlaney, J. (2018). Groups Online: Hacktivism and Social Protest. In McAlaney, J., Frumkin, L., & Benson, V. (Eds.), *Psychological and Behavioral Examinations in Cyber Security* (pp. 194–209). Hershey, PA: IGI Global. DOI: 10.4018/978-1-5225-4053-3.ch011

Thandeeswaran, R., Pawar, R., & Rai, M. (2017). Security Threats in Autonomous Vehicles. In Jeyanthi, N., & Thandeeswaran, R. (Eds.), *Security Breaches and Threat Prevention in the Internet of Things* (pp. 117–141). Hershey, PA: IGI Global. DOI: 10.4018/978-1-5225-2296-6.ch006

Thota, C., Manogaran, G., Lopez, D., & Vijayakumar, V. (2017). Big Data Security Framework for Distributed Cloud Data Centers. In Moore, M. (Ed.), *Cybersecurity Breaches and Issues Surrounding Online Threat Protection* (pp. 288–310). Hershey, PA: IGI Global. DOI: 10.4018/978-1-5225-1941-6.ch012

Thukral, S., & Rodriguez, T. D. (2018). Child Sexual Abuse: Intra- and Extra-Familial Risk Factors, Reactions, and Interventions. In Gopalan, R. (Ed.), *Social, Psychological, and Forensic Perspectives on Sexual Abuse* (pp. 229–258). Hershey, PA: IGI Global. DOI: 10.4018/978-1-5225-3958-2.ch017

Tidke, S. (2017). MonogDB: Data Management in NoSQL. In Tamane, S., Solanki, V., & Dey, N. (Eds.), *Privacy and Security Policies in Big Data* (pp. 64–91). Hershey, PA: IGI Global. DOI: 10.4018/978-1-5225-2486-1.ch004

Tierney, M. (2018). #TerroristFinancing: An Examination of Terrorism Financing via the Internet. *International Journal of Cyber Warfare & Terrorism, 8*(1), 1–11. DOI: 10.4018/IJCWT.2018010101

Topal, R. (2018). A Cyber-Psychological and Behavioral Approach to Online Radicalization. In McAlaney, J., Frumkin, L., & Benson, V. (Eds.), *Psychological and Behavioral Examinations in Cyber Security* (pp. 210–221). Hershey, PA: IGI Global. DOI: 10.4018/978-1-5225-4053-3.ch012

Tripathy, B. K., & Baktha, K. (2018). Clustering Approaches. In *Security, Privacy, and Anonymization in Social Networks: Emerging Research and Opportunities* (pp. 51–85). Hershey, PA: IGI Global. DOI: 10.4018/978-1-5225-5158-4.ch004

Tripathy, B. K., & Baktha, K. (2018). De-Anonymization Techniques. In *Security, Privacy, and Anonymization in Social Networks: Emerging Research and Opportunities* (pp. 137–147). Hershey, PA: IGI Global. DOI: 10.4018/978-1-5225-5158-4.ch007

Tripathy, B. K., & Baktha, K. (2018). Fundamentals of Social Networks. In *Security, Privacy, and Anonymization in Social Networks: Emerging Research and Opportunities* (pp. 1–22). Hershey, PA: IGI Global. DOI: 10.4018/978-1-5225-5158-4.ch001

Tripathy, B. K., & Baktha, K. (2018). Graph Modification Approaches. In *Security, Privacy, and Anonymization in Social Networks: Emerging Research and Opportunities* (pp. 86–115). Hershey, PA: IGI Global. DOI: 10.4018/978-1-5225-5158-4.ch005

Tripathy, B. K., & Baktha, K. (2018). Social Network Anonymization Techniques. In *Security, Privacy, and Anonymization in Social Networks: Emerging Research and Opportunities* (pp. 36–50). Hershey, PA: IGI Global. DOI: 10.4018/978-1-5225-5158-4.ch003

Tsimperidis, I., Rostami, S., & Katos, V. (2017). Age Detection Through Keystroke Dynamics from User Authentication Failures. *International Journal of Digital Crime and Forensics*, *9*(1), 1–16. DOI: 10.4018/IJDCF.2017010101

Wadkar, H. S., Mishra, A., & Dixit, A. M. (2017). Framework to Secure Browser Using Configuration Analysis. *International Journal of Information Security and Privacy*, *11*(2), 49–63. DOI: 10.4018/IJISP.2017040105

Wahlgren, G., & Kowalski, S. J. (2018). IT Security Risk Management Model for Handling IT-Related Security Incidents: The Need for a New Escalation Approach. In Maleh, Y. (Ed.), *Security and Privacy Management, Techniques, and Protocols* (pp. 129–151). Hershey, PA: IGI Global. DOI: 10.4018/978-1-5225-5583-4.ch005

Wall, H. J., & Kaye, L. K. (2018). Online Decision Making: Online Influence and Implications for Cyber Security. In McAlaney, J., Frumkin, L., & Benson, V. (Eds.), *Psychological and Behavioral Examinations in Cyber Security* (pp. 1–25). Hershey, PA: IGI Global. DOI: 10.4018/978-1-5225-4053-3.ch001

Wu, J. B., Zhang, Y., Luo, C. W., Yuan, L. F., & Shen, X. K. (2021). A Modification-Free Steganography Algorithm Based on Image Classification and CNN. *International Journal of Digital Crime and Forensics, 13*(3), 47–58. https://doi.org/10.4018/IJDCF.20210501.oa4

Xylogiannopoulos, K. F., Karampelas, P., & Alhajj, R. (2017). Advanced Network Data Analytics for Large-Scale DDoS Attack Detection. *International Journal of Cyber Warfare & Terrorism, 7*(3), 44–54. DOI: 10.4018/IJCWT.2017070104

Yan, W. Q., Wu, X., & Liu, F. (2018). Progressive Scrambling for Social Media. *International Journal of Digital Crime and Forensics, 10*(2), 56–73. DOI: 10.4018/IJDCF.2018040104

Yassein, M. B., Mardini, W., & Al-Abdi, A. (2018). Security Issues in the Internet of Things: A Review. In Aljawarneh, S., & Malhotra, M. (Eds.), *Critical Research on Scalability and Security Issues in Virtual Cloud Environments* (pp. 186–200). Hershey, PA: IGI Global. DOI: 10.4018/978-1-5225-3029-9.ch009

Yassein, M. B., Shatnawi, M., & l-Qasem, N. (2018). A Survey of Probabilistic Broadcast Schemes in Mobile Ad Hoc Networks. In S. Aljawarneh, & M. Malhotra (Eds.), *Critical Research on Scalability and Security Issues in Virtual Cloud Environments* (pp. 269-282). Hershey, PA: IGI Global. https://doi.org/DOI: 10.4018/978-1-5225-3029-9.ch013

Yue, C., Tianliang, L., Manchun, C., & Jingying, L. (2018). Evaluation of the Attack Effect Based on Improved Grey Clustering Model. *International Journal of Digital Crime and Forensics, 10*(1), 92–100. DOI: 10.4018/IJDCF.2018010108

Zhang, P., He, Y., & Chow, K. (2018). Fraud Track on Secure Electronic Check System. *International Journal of Digital Crime and Forensics, 10*(2), 137–144. DOI: 10.4018/IJDCF.2018040108

Zhou, L., Yan, W. Q., Shu, Y., & Yu, J. (2018). CVSS: A Cloud-Based Visual Surveillance System. *International Journal of Digital Crime and Forensics*, *10*(1), 79–91. DOI: 10.4018/IJDCF.2018010107

Zhu, J., Guan, Q., Zhao, X., Cao, Y., & Chen, G. (2017). A Steganalytic Scheme Based on Classifier Selection Using Joint Image Characteristics. *International Journal of Digital Crime and Forensics*, *9*(4), 1–14. DOI: 10.4018/IJDCF.2017100101

Zoughbi, S. (2017). Major Technology Trends Affecting Government Data in Developing Countries. In Zoughbi, S. (Ed.), *Securing Government Information and Data in Developing Countries* (pp. 127–135). Hershey, PA: IGI Global. DOI: 10.4018/978-1-5225-1703-0.ch008

Zubairu, B. (2018). Security Risks of Biomedical Data Processing in Cloud Computing Environment. In Pradhan, C., Das, H., Naik, B., & Dey, N. (Eds.), *Handbook of Research on Information Security in Biomedical Signal Processing* (pp. 177–197). Hershey, PA: IGI Global. DOI: 10.4018/978-1-5225-5152-2.ch009

About The Contributors

Mourade Azrour received his PhD from Faculty of sciences and Techniques, Moulay Ismail University of Meknes, Morocco. He has received his MS in computer and distributed systems from Faculty of Sciences, Ibn Zouhr University, Agadir, Morocco in 2014. Mourade currently works as computer sciences professor at the Department of Computer Science, Faculty of Sciences and Techniques, Moulay Ismail University of Meknès. His research interests include Authentication protocol, Computer Security, Internet of things, Smart systems, Machine learning and so ones. Mourade is member of the member of the scientific committee of numerous international conferences. He is also a reviewer of various scientific journals. He has published more than 85 scientific papers and book chapters. Mourade Has edited many scientific books "IoT and Smart Devices for Sustainable Environment" and "Advanced Technology for Smart Environment and Energy". Finally, he has served as guest editor in journals "EAI Endorsed Transactions on Internet of Things", "Tsinghua Science and Technology", "Applied Sciences MDPI" and "Sustainability MDPI"

Jamal Mabrouki received his PhD in Process and Environmental Engineering at Mohammed V University in Rabat, specializing in artificial intelligence and smart automatic systems. He completed the Bachelor of Science in Physics and Chemistry with honors from Hassan II University in Casablanca, Morocco and the engineer in Environment and smart system. His research is on intelligent monitoring, control, and management systems and more particularly on sensing and supervising remote intoxication systems, smart self-supervised systems and recurrent neural networks. He has published several papers in conferences and indexed journals, most of them related to artificial intelligent systems, internet of things or big data and mining. Jamal will currently work in environment, energy and smart system professor at Mohammed V University in Rabat, Faculty of Science. Jamal is scientific committee member of numerous national and international conferences. He is also a reviewer of Modeling Earth Systems and Environment; International Journal of Environmental Analytical Chemistry; International Journal of Modeling, Simulation, and Scientific Computing; The Journal of Supercomputing, Energy & Environment and Big Data Mining and Analytics...

Azidine Guezzaz received his Ph.D from Ibn Zohr University Agadir, Morocco in 2018. He obtained his Master in computer and distributed systems from Faculty of Sciences, Ibn Zouhr University, Agadir, Morocco in 2013. He is currently an associate professor of computer science and mathematics at Cadi Ayyad University Marrakech, Morocco. His main field of research interest is computer security, cryptography, artificial intelligence, intrusion detection and smart cities. He is member of the scientific and orgnizing committee of various international conferences. Azidine is a guest editor of special issues in Tsinghua Science and Technology journal, Sustainability Journal and EAI Endorsed Transactions on Internet of Things journal. He is also an editor of some Books and reviewer of various scientific journals.

Abdulatif Alabdulatif is an associated professor at the School of Computer, Qassim University, Saudi Arabia. He completed his Ph.D. degree in Computer Science from RMIT University, Australia in 2018. He received his B.Sc. degree in Computer Science from Qassim University, Saudi Arabia in 2008 and his M.Sc. degree in Computer Science from RMIT University, Australia in 2013. He has published more than 60 academic papers in prominent journals. His research interests include applied cryptography, cloud computing, data mining and remote healthcare.

***

Souad El Hajjaji is currently Professor of material, water & Environmental Sciences at the University Mohammed V in Rabat. Prof. Souad El Hajjaji carried out her international academic and research career in universities in France, Germany, and Morocco. El Hajjaji souad research is devoted to the development of new processes for wastewater treatments (adsorption, photodegradation, electrochemistry….), solid waste valorisation, monitoring of pesticides and emergent pollutants in water and soil (POPs), the management of water resources, reuse of treated wastewater in agriculture and the impact studies of waste on the quality of water resources. She has coordinated several research projects at different levels: i) National ii) bilateral cooperation with different countries (Germany, Spain, France, Sweden, Jordan, Tunisia, Egypt, Algeria, etc.) and iii) European Projects (ERANETHMED, PRIMA).Within the research projects, she supervised more than 30 PhD theses and has published more than 300 peer-reviewed scientific papers and book chapters. She is associate member of EXCEED -Swindon network and coordinator of MENA region (2022/2023). Member of different associations involved in environment.In 2019, she was nominatedas a president of scientific committee of COALMA (2021-2023).

Mishra is an Associate Professor in the School of Computer Science and Engineering, AI-ML Division, at VIT Bhopal University, India. He received his Doctor of Philosophy (Ph.D.) in Computer Science & Information Engineering with a specialization in Data Science & Machine Learning from Chang Gung University, Taiwan. He has more than 22 years of national and international involvement in academic teaching and research at recognized Indian, Taiwanese, and African universities. He has over 50 publications in SCI/SCIE and SCOPUS-indexed journals, ISBN books and chapters, Indian and Australian patents, IEEE conference proceedings, and others. He has served as a reviewer, associate editor, and editorial board member for SCI/SCIE-indexed journals and conferences. Dr. Mishra worked on multiple funded research projects from the MOST, NSC, and CGU Memorial Hospital, Taiwan, during his Ph.D. and has been involved with several professional bodies. He is currently an Associate Editor for two SCOPUS-indexed journals, and his research interests span the areas of AI, Data Science, Machine Learning, and Cognitive Analytics & Applications.

Hitesh Mohapatra received the B.E. degree in Information Technology from Biju Patnaik University of Technology (BPUT), Odisha in 2006, and the MTech. Degree in CSE from Odisha University of Technology and Research (OUTR) University, Odisha in 2009. He received his Ph.D. in Computer Science & Engineering in 2021 from Veer Surendra Sai University of Technology (VSSUT), Burla, India. He has contributed 30 SCI and Scopus indexed research papers, 21 international/national conferences and books on Software Engineering and C Programming respectively. He has 15 years of teaching experience both in industry and academia. He has served the research community with various capacities like session chair, technical chair, keynote speaker etc. His research interests include wireless sensor network, smart city, smart grid and smart water. Currently he is working as Associate professor at School of Computer Engineering, KIIT DU, Bhubaneswar, and Odisha.

Mrutyunjay Padhiary is an Assistant Professor in the Department of Agricultural Engineering at Assam University, Silchar, India, with a deep academic background. His previous positions included significant teaching and research duties at the Faculty of Technology, UBKV in West Bengal, and Tribhuvan University in Nepal, as well as research experience at IIT Kharagpur. He has been awarded multiple awards, including an International NUS Research Fellowship and an excellent score on the 2001 GATE Exam, demonstrating his proficiency in precision agriculture. He has made substantial contributions to biofuel production, artificial intelligence vision, aquaculture, precision agriculture, agricultural automation, and artificial intelligence. He is currently working on several research projects, which range from autonomous surface vessels to precision agriculture all-terrain vehicles.

Alex Khang has 28+ years of teaching and researching experiences in Information Technology (Software Development, Database Technology, AI Engineering, Data Engineering, Data Science, Data Analytics, IoT-based Technologies, Data and Application Migration Strategies, and

Cloud Computing) at the Universities, Institutions, Colleges, and Centres of Technology and Science in Vietnam, India, and United State

Pokkuluri Kiran Sree has received his B.Tech and M.E in Computer Science and Engineering from JNTU and Anna University, respectively. He has obtained his Ph.D. degree in the area of Artificial Intelligence from JNTU-Hyderabad. He has authored Six Textbooks for UG and PG students of engineering in AI and published more than 100+ Research Articles in various International Journals and Conferences. He has filed and published SIX patents in the areas of Deep Learning & AI. His bibliography was listed in Marquis Who's Who in the World, 29th Edition (2012), USA. Prof Kiran is the Recipient of Bharat Excellence Award from Dr. G.V. Krishna Murthy, Former Election Commissioner of India for two times and recipient of Rashtrya Ratan Award. He was the BOS member of CSE&IT in some universities and autonomous colleges. He also worked as Principal of the N.B.K.R.Institute of Science & Technology (Second Oldest Private Engg College), Vidyanagar, for two years. He has got 18+ years of Teaching Experience and working as Professor in the department of CSE at Shri Vishnu Engineering College for Women(A), Bhimavaram. He has delivered 100+ technical talks on Deep Learning and AI

MMS Rauthan is working as Head of the department and professor in HNB Garhwal University in computer science and engineering department with 30 years of teaching experience. He has done M.Tech in 1987 from Roorkee University and has done his Ph.D. from Kumaon University in 2013. He has written a several research paper as well as 5 books in computer science. He is a core member of research committees, visiting committees.

Saroja Kumar Rout: Received M.Tech (CS) from Utkal University in the year 2007 and a Ph.D. in Computer Science in the year 2018 from Siksha 'O' Anusandhan University for work in the field of Wireless Sensor Networks. Currently working as Associate Professor in the Department of Information Technology, Vardhaman College of Engineering (Autonomous), Hyderabad, India. Contributed more than 60 research-level papers to many National and International journals and conferences.

Also having 8 Indian patents. Research interests include Sensor Networks, Machine Learning, Cloud computing, and health Informatics.

Chintha Reddy Sai Kiran, As an ardent and inquisitive scholar, I commenced my academic voyage with an earnest aspiration to enrich the domain of knowledge. My name is Sai Kiran and currently enrolled in the pursuit of an MTech Integrated degree in Cybersecurity at VIT Bhopal University. His scholarly pursuits are predominantly focused on the exploration of Cybersecurity.

Index

A

AI 2, 4, 22, 23, 25, 30, 47, 53, 62, 69, 79, 82, 86, 89, 93, 94, 126, 168, 169, 180, 182, 183, 184, 186, 187, 189, 194, 195, 196, 197, 201, 202, 205, 209, 211, 212, 213
Authentication 2, 4, 9, 10, 13, 16, 17, 18, 23, 53, 75, 104, 132, 134, 136, 141, 142, 165, 166, 168, 172, 182, 183, 184, 185, 190, 191, 193, 194, 197, 201, 202, 205, 206, 208, 209, 210, 214, 215

B

Blockchain 2, 4, 23, 25, 41, 53, 56, 72, 77, 78, 79, 80, 81, 82, 83, 84, 85, 86, 87, 88, 89, 90, 91, 92, 93, 94, 95, 96, 141, 145, 179, 201, 208, 211, 212, 213, 215

C

Challenges 1, 2, 3, 4, 5, 7, 8, 14, 22, 24, 25, 41, 45, 48, 50, 51, 52, 53, 70, 74, 75, 91, 98, 100, 101, 102, 113, 114, 115, 116, 117, 122, 123, 125, 145, 146, 149, 150, 153, 163, 168, 171, 172, 176, 177, 178, 182, 183, 184, 187, 188, 189, 190, 192, 197, 198, 205, 206, 207, 210, 215, 216
Cloud Computing 2, 3, 5, 7, 13, 41, 92, 98, 99, 101, 102, 103, 104, 105, 106, 107, 113, 114, 117, 118, 119, 120, 121, 122, 123, 150, 171
Cyberattacks 30, 69, 112, 125, 130, 131, 132, 133, 134, 135, 139, 141, 143, 145, 153, 154, 155, 156, 160, 161, 163, 173, 186, 189, 202, 203, 209, 214
Cyber-Physical Systems 147, 149, 150, 152, 153, 158, 159, 161, 162, 163, 166, 168, 169, 173, 174, 176, 177, 178
Cyber Security 75, 144, 146, 147, 149, 150, 155, 156, 158, 179, 182, 183, 184, 192, 194, 195, 196, 197, 198, 199, 204, 207, 214

D

Data Augmentation 49, 52, 60, 62, 69
Data Encryption 2, 4, 15, 25, 107, 114, 115, 117, 139
Deep Learning 4, 23, 27, 28, 29, 30, 32, 41, 42, 43, 44, 45, 52, 53, 60, 65, 73, 74, 92, 120, 144, 167, 175, 178, 185, 192, 202, 207, 209, 216

E

Edge Computing 1, 2, 3, 4, 5, 6, 7, 8, 9, 10, 11, 12, 13, 14, 15, 16, 17, 18, 19, 20, 21, 22, 23, 24, 25, 26, 56, 72, 174
Environmental prediction 182

F

Fog Computing 2, 5, 6, 7, 20, 105, 108, 212

G

Generative Adversarial Networks 48, 50, 51, 52, 57, 59, 62, 69, 70, 72, 75

I

Intrusion Detection 2, 4, 5, 9, 10, 11, 12, 16, 17, 21, 23, 26, 30, 31, 41, 42, 43, 44, 52, 53, 72, 75, 105, 112, 122, 161, 162, 164, 167, 177, 182, 183, 184, 185, 191, 192, 198, 204, 207, 209, 210, 214, 215, 216
IoT sensors 170, 201

L

LSTM 33, 34, 35, 36, 37, 38, 39, 40, 41, 42, 43, 44, 45, 49, 51, 52, 53, 58, 60, 61, 62, 63, 64, 67, 68, 70, 72, 167, 178, 213

M

Marine Cybersecurity 125
Mitigation Techniques 127
ML 30, 53, 86, 93, 186, 187

N

Naval 129, 210

P

Precision agriculture 181, 182, 183, 184, 185, 186, 187, 188, 189, 190, 191, 192, 193, 194, 196, 197, 198, 199, 200, 201, 202, 203, 204, 205, 206, 207, 209, 210, 211, 212, 213, 214, 215, 216
Privacy 1, 2, 3, 4, 5, 6, 7, 13, 14, 15, 19, 20, 22, 23, 25, 26, 50, 57, 75, 81, 98, 100, 107, 112, 113, 115, 116, 117, 118, 119, 123, 130, 151, 153, 168, 172, 176, 187, 189, 205, 207, 209, 213, 216
Privacy-Preserving Techniques 4, 5, 26

R

Regulatory Compliance 2, 4, 85
RNN 33, 37, 38, 39, 53

S

Securing CPS 160
Security 1, 2, 3, 4, 5, 6, 8, 9, 11, 12, 13, 15, 16, 17, 18, 21, 22, 23, 24, 25, 26, 28, 29, 30, 32, 39, 41, 42, 44, 45, 47, 48, 49, 50, 51, 52, 53, 55, 56, 57, 59, 60, 69, 70, 72, 73, 74, 75, 80, 84, 85, 87, 98, 99, 100, 101, 102, 103, 104, 105, 107, 108, 109, 110, 111, 112, 113, 114, 115, 116, 117, 118, 119, 120, 121, 123, 126, 127, 129, 130, 131, 132, 133, 134, 135, 136, 137, 140, 141, 142, 143, 144, 145, 146, 147, 149, 150, 151, 153, 154, 155, 156, 157, 158, 160, 161, 162, 163, 164, 165, 166, 168, 171, 172, 173, 174, 175, 176, 177, 178, 179, 180, 182, 183, 184, 185, 186, 187, 189, 190, 191, 192, 193, 194, 195, 196, 197, 198, 199, 200, 201, 202, 203, 204, 205, 206, 207, 208, 209, 210, 212, 213, 214, 215, 216
Smart Building 98, 100, 101, 102, 103, 104, 106, 113, 114, 115, 116, 118, 120

T

Threat Analysis 155, 156

V

Vulnerabilities 2, 9, 11, 12, 13, 16, 18, 48, 50, 54, 57, 98, 107, 112, 113, 114, 115, 116, 117, 125, 133, 134, 135, 136, 138, 140, 141, 155, 156, 157, 161, 162, 164, 172, 176, 182, 190, 197, 198, 199, 203

W

water management 77, 78, 79, 80, 81, 82, 83, 84, 85, 86, 89, 90, 91, 94, 95
Weblog 63
Web Server Security 47, 49, 50, 51, 69, 70

www.ingramcontent.com/pod-product-compliance
Lightning Source LLC
LaVergne TN
LVHW081332300926
849161LV00008B/1949